Knuf

WALTER MALONE
Age Forty Years

SELECTED POEMS

By
WALTER MALONE

PUBLISHERS
JOHN P. MORTON & COMPANY
Incorporated
LOUISVILLE, KENTUCKY

FOREWORD

In loving memory of my brother, the late Judge Walter Malone, this book of selected poems is published. The contents of the volume consists of a large number of unpublished poems together with selections made from his many volumes, including the Epic, Hernando De Soto.

The sketch of his life is written by Frazer Hood, Ph. D. During brother Walter's later years Dr. Hood was one of his most intimate, personal and literary friends.

Ella Malone Watson.

ACKNOWLEDGMENT

Thanks are due the following publishers in giving permission to reprint: To Chas. Scribner's Sons for Solace and Prayer Before Planting Trees; The Four Seas Company for Union of the Seas; The Methodist Quarterly Review for Life and Works of Walter Malone.

CONTENTS

[v]

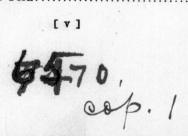

Contents

UNPUBLISHED POEMS

Contents

[vii]

Contents

Contents

IN PRAISE OF MYSELF

I am sick of the lays of love, of the prating of beautiful
   eyes,
Of the ruby lips, of the golden hair, and of cheeks like
   morning skies;
For a day will dawn when the eyes grow dim, and the ringlets of gold are gray,
And Love, like a traitor, when wrinkles come, will silently
   sneak away.

I am weary of lays of Friendship, too, of the truth that
   never turns,
Of the trusting hearts and the helping hands, the faith that
   forever burns;
For when Fate may frown, and when Fortune flies, and
   your golden age is done,
You will find at last, wherever you go, there is left of your
   friends not one.

I am weary alike of Prayer, of beseeching of pitiless skies,
Of the wails for help, of the shrieks for aid as the wretch
   in anguish dies;
For the gods help those who uplift the sword, not those
   who as beggars come,
To the rich they give, from the poor they take, to the weak
   are deaf and dumb.

Whenever you hang on another's arm, the soul of your
   strength is past;
When you give your fate to another's hands, the die of
   your doom is cast;
Whenever you mumble for mercy here, the day of defeat
   draws nigh;
Whenever you weep, whenever you wail, you are left to
   droop and die.

Whenever you win a battle of life, reap riches or gain
    renown,
No hand but your own on the flaming field will place on
    your head the crown.
If the palms you bear, if the bays you wear, if you heap
    and hoard your pelf,
No finger will lift from a friendly arm till first you have
    helped yourself.

I care not what men or women may say when of outside
    aid they tell,
For work others do can never suit you—you only can do
    it well.
And I know this truth, that if win I will, I must win by
    force of might;
What gift I may crave, what reward I seek, I lose if I do
    not fight.

Whatever a friend may do for a friend is only reflected
    light,
From the sun of Self, of splendor the source, and without
    which all is night.
Whenever the fang of a foeman stings, infection never
    takes place
Unless I myself have poisoned myself, nourishing grafted
    disgrace.

So I praise myself for fights I have fought, for the enemies
    underfoot hurled,
And I love myself and I hug myself as I face a hostile
    world;
And I praise myself that I heeded not the hisses and hoots
    and jeers,
And with bulldog grip have clung to my rights through all
    of the friendless years.

Though I blundered oft and I stumbled oft while bleeding
    from thrust on thrust,
I have faced all foes, have endured all blows, have risen
    when hurled to dust.

Though many my faults, and my passions strong, and sins
of Self were to down,
I have forged ahead, and my brow deserves, though never
it wear, a crown.

So I praise myself for the fights I fought against all the
hosts of hell,
Though I knew at last was a greedy grave, and a shroud
and a funeral bell.
I have trod the path which, I know not why, leads on to
the lonely tomb,
And never a man or seraph or saint more boldly has
marched to doom.

I care not what sage or sophist might do, what higher
beings might say,
What counsel of man, what wisdom of God, may have
shown a better way;
Had they fought like me, had they bled like me as they
crept through earth to die,
I would challenge them all to take up my lot and bear it
better than I.

I have asked for aid from the sons of men—they have left
me all alone;
I have prayed the gods for a loaf of bread—they have
always given a stone.
So I clenched my teeth, and doubled my fists, and I fought
to hold my own,
And the mobs of men, when I helped myself, have begged
me accept a throne.

So little I care if they say my words are vanity, pomp or
conceit,
For I know that Self and Self alone, can bring me a mess
of meat.
So the little tin gods of the old-time bards I shove in dust
on the shelf,
And asking no leave of a living soul, I take off my hat to
myself.

Age Six Years

Age Sixteen Years

Age Twenty Years

Age Thirty Years

WALTER MALONE—HIS LIFE AND WORKS

By FRAZER HOOD, Ph. D.

I

The past quarter of a century has witnessed some significant additions to Southern literature. In fiction and in essay, Southern writers have achieved a success which challenges the attention of readers beyond the limits of national boundaries. They have broken the bands of provincialism, which formerly were conspicuous in so many of them, and to-day they write with a vision whose horizon is national in its sweep. In the field of poetry, also, Southern genius has produced creative results; and while this creative activity has invented no new forms of verse, it has breathed into the old forms a dewy freshness and a wholesome sanity.

Among Southern poets, Walter Malone ranks subordinate to none. Indeed, there are reasons—which I shall set forth in this paper—strong enough, it seems to me, to justify the conviction that he deserves the foremost place, not only among Southern poets, but among American poets as well. There is, however, an infirmity of mind, a kind of mental hyperopia, that blurs our perception of a contemporary artist and his art. We never feel quite certain that the image we get upon our mental retina is a true one, and we hesitate to hazard a judgment of values.

European critics, viewing Poe's art, outre mer, got a perspective that the poet's compatriots were unable to get. We are still disputing among ourselves whether Walt Whitman is a poet at all or not, while to foreign critics he bulks large on the Western shores, the most original of the new-world poets. Walter Malone being so near us, it is not to be wondered at that our envisagement of him is far from clear-cut and perspective.

If our analogy between a judgment of values and a sense-perception be permissible, then it is further true that the distance required for a clear focus is directly proportional to the greatness of the achievement. Longfellow and Lowell needed not to be removed in time for our American eyes to see them clearly, but Poe and Whitman did. In the two former pulsed a lesser genius than glowed in the two latter. The beauty that the New England poets felt and perceived was that our familiarity with great poetry had already revealed to us, and their genius was rather that of translating into American idiom what the great masters had uttered in the "grand style."

Walter Malone is one of our American poets whom the critics have reserved for some future attention. It may be that time will bury his memory "deep as the hidden sleep" of those who lie in some forgotten churchyard; but my judgment is that the future holds for him a fadeless crown of amaranth and gold.

II

Walter Malone was born February 10, 1866, in De Soto County, Mississippi, about thirteen miles southeast of Memphis, Tennessee. He was the youngest of a family of twelve children. His father, Dr. Franklin Jefferson Malone, was a man of culture and prominence in Mississippi, serving his State as a member of the Mississippi Constitutional Convention of 1868. In earlier years he had seen service in the Mexican War as an army surgeon. He died in 1873. Thus deprived of a father's care at the age of seven years, Walter did not have those advantages which the older children enjoyed; but his mother, a woman of rare powers, made amends for the loss as only a woman can do. She managed to give her younger children such educational advantages as the local schools afforded. At the age of six years Walter was initiated into the mysteries of formal learning at an "old-field schoolhouse," which stood across the State line in Tennessee, three miles from his home. He continued his attendance here until he was sixteen, trudging the distance from his home every day except when work on the farm required his presence there. During these ten years his young soul unfolded amid the influence of Nature. His spirit was always responsive to the music of birds and water brooks, to the beauty of Southern flowers, and to the grandeur of tree and hill. His early life is reminiscent of Burns who meditated in the opening furrows and caught inspiration for his earlier poems when his young muscles were fatigued from the toil between plow-handles.

When twelve years old he made his first attempt to imprison his fancies and emotions in verse. Always a stern critic of his own work, he later destroyed all these boyish efforts. Between thirteen and fourteen he wrote several articles which were published in the Louisville Courier-Journal. Thus encouraged, he began, at fourteen, seriously to write, and continued with adolescent zeal until he was sixteen, when he published his first volume under the title, "Claribel and Other Poems." This was a book of three hundred pages and contained two long narrative poems and a number of shorter ones. While the poems are crude, revealing the touch of youth, they contain the promise and potency of awakening genius. It was the largest book of verse ever printed by a boy under twenty-one.

In the fall of 1883 he entered the preparatory department of the University of Mississippi, where in due course he became a freshman and graduated in the class of 1887. He was not a student after the old time professors' ideal. He never liked mathematics, and until his last two years was a rather indifferent student, giving more time to the library than to the formal work of the class-room. He became early associated with the college magazine, and during his last year was its editor-in-chief.

In 1885 he published his second volume, "The Outcast and Other Poems." Even a hurried reading will reveal that these poems are less juvenile and show a steadier power. This book brought forth favorable comment from Edmund Clarence Stedman and Oliver Wendell Holmes. John Greenleaf Whittier, writing to the author, said: "The book gives promise, but it is not what it would be were the author ten years older. Why, at thy age, I could not make a respectable rhyme."

After his graduation, Mr. Malone was admitted to the bar at Oxford, Mississippi, and shortly thereafter came to Memphis to engage in the practice of law. He launched himself with a strong initiative into the practice of law, and until 1891 his Muse was neglected. In the next year he published "Narcissus and Other Poems." Two years later came from the press "Songs of Dusk and Dawn." In 1896 followed "Songs of December and June," a little volume of twenty lyrics; and the next year "The Coming of the King," a collection of eight short stories. Such writers as Thomas Bailey Aldrich, Charles Dudley Warner and Edgar Fawcett were high in their praise of this work.

In 1897 he retired from the practice of law and moved to New York, where, for the next three years, he gave himself wholly to literary work. In 1900 he returned to Memphis and published "Songs of North and South," a collection of poems that had appeared in magazines during the previous three years. This volume introduced the author to British readers, receiving generous welcome from Alfred Austin, Israel Zangwill, and English and Scott reviewers. In 1904 he published a complete edition of such of his poems as he considered worthy of perpetuating. In 1906 appeared "Songs of East and West," a book containing twenty-seven poems, many of them being pictures of travel in Europe, California, Florida, Cuba, and Mexico. His most widely known poem, "Opportunity," was published in Munsey's Magazine in 1905.

There is a pretty little incident connected with this poem, which the author told me of, and which very few, even of his intimate friends, know. I relate it because it illustrates not only what I have just said, but also because it gives a side glance of his fondness for children. Briefly, the story is this: One evening while sitting with some friends in a cafe in New York, a little lad of six years came over to the table where the poet sat, and asked: "Is this Mr. Malone?" "Yes," relied the poet. "Well, Mr. Malone," began the boy, "I want to thank you." "Why so, my little man?" "Because, if you had not written 'Opportunity,' I would not be here to-night." The father, coming up, explained how he had become discouraged in life and resolved to commit suicide, but while arranging his affairs, the poet's "Opportunity" fell under his eye, and changed his whole design. A year afterwards, the little lad was born.

Whatever may be the surer judgment of the critics as to the value of this poem, it is a lyric that awakens a response in the common man's breast, and makes him feel stronger for the day's work and superior to the day's faults and failures. In 1905, on petition of practically all the Memphis bar, Mr. Malone was appointed Judge of the Second Circuit Court of Shelby County, and later by election held the office until his death, May 18, 1915.

III

I am writing this on the fourth anniversary of his death, and as I write there comes to my ears the plaintive music of his poem, "To An Unknown Reader":

In years to come, when I have passed away,
    Your careless glance upon this page may fall;
So then, my unknown reader, pause I pray,
    And hearken to my faint and far-off call.

O unknown reader, for your sake I pine;
    Beside you let me cease my wandering.
I love you; let me take your hand in mine
    And tell you stories, laugh or weep or sing.

From death's dark empire shall my soul depart,
   Your smile, your friendship, and your love to win;
Behold!   I come and knock upon your heart:
   For God's sake, reader, rise and let me in!

These lines, so remindful of Beethoven's "Farewell to the Piano," disclose at once a boldness and a childlike unconsciousness not found in a lesser soul.

To those of us who knew him, Mr. Malone was the most modest of men, in whom verily there dwelt no guile nor conceit. But his graces of mind were plenteous, and he had "a memory like the British Museum Library," and its material arranged as orderly. His interests were universal, and whether the discussion, in a company of friends, turned to the merits of champion chess-players or to great events in history, to the name and habitat of some little-known flower or to the latest discoveries in science, he was equally at home, and generally astonished us by the accuracy of his knowledge. He was a keen scholar, a keen artist, and withal a man of modest demeanor, free from those eccentricities and conceits so commonly associated with men of genius. His poetry was the chief concern of his life, and he toiled at uncongenial tasks for the bread that perisheth, only that he might be able to give forth from his soul that which is imperishable. Spinoza, polishing lenses during the day that he might write philosophy at night, presents us with a companion picture. While Judge Malone achieved an enviable eminence in his profession, he never valued this success.

From long familiarity with his poetry, and from a careful study of its qualities, I am convinced that posterity will make amends for the neglect into which contemporary readers and critics have allowed his poetry to fall.

IV

The poetry of Walter Malone is no ordinary verse. The sheer quantity of it compels notice. No poetry can be measured alone in terms of volume; but if the other qualities that go to make great poetry are to be found also, the quantity is a factor that must be given its meed of worth. It is because I find so many evidences of exquisite imagery, so many instances of those characteristics of fine poetry that one must rather feel than describe, I have no timidity in asserting his claim to genius. Lovers of poetry delight in quoting you Browning's fine lines,

That's the wise thrush; he sings each song twice over,
Lest you should think he never could recapture
The first fine careless rapture,

as an example of this indescribable quality of poetic power. In the poetry of our author are many examples of the same power. Describing the strange beauty and melancholy of submarine life, he says:

But never trills or warbling wake those bowers;
No sound uprises in those songless realms;
The petals of those blossoms never thrill
Or tingle with embraces of the bees.

Humming-birds seen in tropical forests are,

bright banditti of the Southern skies
That rifle sylvan hordes of honey dew.

And again, take those lines descriptive of the first feelings of love in the adolescent heart:

Love then was light as the feet of a fawn,
Brilliant of brow as dazzle of dawn,
Jocund as June, unwearied of wing,
Hearing his heart like a goldfinch sing.

And one more example from a Croesus-wealth that makes selection hard:

And that longing for their labor in the freemen's hearts
    shall be
Like the green blood of the springtime, tingling in the turf
    and tree.

(Note the use of "blood" from its common association with color to its truer association with function.)

The range of his poetic vision is as broad as the world itself. He has given us many love lyrics that burn with passion, many that ache with a sorrow that dews the face of a Niobe in tear-drops sharp as acid. There are poems of awakening love; there are poems of youthful love; and songs of wedded bliss enjoyed far into life. Then there are delicate portraits that glow in the bosom of his volumes like cameos fine-cut. Take that most beautiful of them all, the portrait of lovely Isabel when first her beauty burst upon the soul of De Soto:

> Oh, she was lovelier than an April morn,
> With April skies, and April birds and bloom,
> With April songs, and April suns and showers,
> Now laughing and now pouting, now in tears,
> But ever bringing visions of delight.

No one but a poet unconscious of his gift would have hazarded such an adjectival repetition, and none but a master could have achieved such result.

He loved children, and some of his most cunning workmanship is expended in exhibiting boy-life with its wild, care-free days. Here is one of his boys:

> Along the street
> His brown bare feet
> Remind me of a baby faun,
> By fern-fringed pool
> In shadows cool
> Leading a throng of fluting birds at dawn.
>
> No hermit thrush
> Through woodland hush
> Could trill a tune more fresh and free;
> No mocking-bird
> More gladly heard
> Through verdant vine-clad swamps of Tennessee.

Then there are poems of wild fancy that startle us by their very boldness. Take, for instance, that weird conceit suggested by Coleridge's line,

> Woman wailing for her Demon Lover.

The conception is poetic to the core. After a few stanzas describing the overthrow of Satan in heaven and his casting out, the woman who had beheld his defeat speaks:

Here I come to meet thee, Satan, ruined king whom I adore,
Thou, my prince, my lord, my master, and mine idol
    evermore!

Now I see thee come to meet me, and I rush within thine
    arms,
While my bosom bounds with passion for thy wild and
    wondrous charms.

I, the seraph, blest and beauteous, robed in radiant starry
    light,
With my golden locks encircled with the lilies pearly white;

I, that soar on swan-like pinions, blossom-bosomed,
    flower-fair,
I, with eyes like lucid dew-drops, twinkling in the azure air;

I have come to meet thee, Satan, with thy wings of ashen
    gray,
Seared with sins and seared with sorrows that shall never
    pass away!

No excerpt from this poem can do it justice, and one must read it through to get the full force of its stately rhythm and its weird passion.

As an illustration of his calmer mood which reveals his sensitiveness to friendship, the following lines, "To a Friend," may be recalled:

Tormented sorely by the chastening rod,
I muttered to myself, "There is no God!"
But, faithful friend, I found your soul so true,
That God revealed himself in giving you.

Time would fail me to speak of all the themes that attracted his fancy. There are poems dealing with economic conditions; there are descriptive sketches of landscapes in many lands; sunsets burst upon us in his pages with a variety of forms and colors like those the Divine Artist throws upon the evening sky. There are matchless poems on birds and flowers and trees; indeed, no poet has given us more Nature poetry than he. In it all one who reads is astonished at his wealth of simile and metaphor, at the music of his lines and the cooling freshness that delights on every page.

V

It has been remarked by Mr. M. W. Conolly that Judge Malone has given a new note to Southern literature "based upon Southern life, Southern scenes, and Nature as she appears in the South alone. The early writers of America harped on larks and nightingales which they had never heard, and on rosemary and rue which they had never seen . . . . . The mocking-bird was practically the one Southern bird known to literature. . . . Judge Malone has taken the redbird, the bluebird, the woodpecker, the humming-bird, and others, and put them in the place of the feathered songsters of Europe of which we know nothing. He has taken the magnolia, the dogwood, the redbud, the passion flower, the trumpet flower, and others, and made them popular in literature."

While it is true as Alfred Austin said that he finds in the verse of Judge Malone "deference to the best traditions of English poetry," his was no servile imitation of it, and one of the most priceless of these traditions was that a poet was never to try to picture forth anything that he had not first seen and felt in his own experience—a perception of Nature, not the preception of some one else's perception, is demanded by "the best traditions of English poetry."

No one can read the poetry of Walter Malone who has not learned the language and felt the heart-pulse of Nature. He speaks in the vernacular of song-birds, thrills with the melody of water brooks, and palpitates with the passion that the flowers feel when the winds of heaven come a-woo-ing among them. "He came from the soil, and remained a son of it," as a friend expressed it. Nature was to him no

panorama of painted beauty.   She was a mother on whose
breast he could sob out his sorrows, exult in the tonic of
achievement and hope, and to whom he could

> unlock the sleepless brood
> Of fancies from his soul, their lurking place,
> Nor doubt that each would pass ne'er to return
> To one so loved, so watched, and so secure.

He was in something more than a metaphor a child of
Nature, taught to speak her language, cunning to interpret
her moods, and sensitive to feel her great life.   While all
his poetry is by no means Nature poetry, it all is suffused
with her influence.   One could tell, whatever mood the
poet was in, whether revealing the untutored soul of pagan
brave, or exposing the ugly venom in the heart of crafty
Spaniard, or describing the redbird darting zigzag through
the green of forest like a flame—one could note the influence of Nature through it all.

VI

When we come to study his epic poem, Hernando
De Soto, we discover an entirely different attitude toward
Nature.   I think his treatment of Nature here discloses a
conception not to be found anywhere else.   Wordsworth
conceived a preestablished harmony between us and the
natural world so that Humanity and Nature can easily live
and converse together.   Tennyson, with ever-wavering
faith, speaks sometimes as if Nature did not exist at all
apart from our thought: "Her life the eddying life of our
living soul."   Browning conceived Nature as a wild, un-
human, unmoral, unspiritual being who has an elemental
life, but no soul.   She has a certain kind of interest in us,
an interest, however, not sustained.   The powers that play
in Nature, if we happen to be in harmony with them, be-
friend us:

> Their work was done—we might go or stay,
> They relapsed to their ancient mood.

In the De Soto, while Nature appears in her beneficent and benign aspects, often she is "red in tooth and claw." But even here, to Walter Malone, it was not so much a Berserker rage that moves Nature in her destructive force, whether in tornado or miasmas and fevers of a tropical swamp, as it was a godlike resentment at man's shameless intrusion into her sacred sanctuary.

The Oriental bard differs widely from the Western poet in his treatment of Nature. In the poetry of the former, Nature is the great reality, man but an incident. Nature is vast, mysterious, transcendent; man a puny creature, scarcely in the thought of Nature at all, and then only as a despicable, sprawling thing. To the Western poet, Nature is but little more than a background of impalpable cloud and sky to his picture of man. Nature sometimes is the theater boards, upon which man stalks in gigantic strides and plays his part. Sometimes Nature is the Ganymede who bears the goblet to the great Olympian, sometimes the gentle Hebe adorning and enlivening the courts of men. However variant the accent, the dynamic stress is always on man. In the De Soto there is another treatment yet. Man and Nature are related not in subordinance. They are peers. Often there are dubious battles waged between them. Sometimes there is a truce, whose term is conditioned upon the observance by each of the other's rights. "The contest with Nature," says the author, "is one which all must face; it is inevitable; it is one that from the cradle to the coffin ceases not. We may live in peace with our neighbors, or we may contend with them, grow weary of strife, and agree on an armistice. But with Nature we can never negotiate a truce; between us there can be no cessation of hostilities." How strangely out of harmony does this conception seem with his treatment of Nature in his earlier poems. This is the conception presented in his epic poem. A careful study of this apparent disharmony may be resolved, I think. If there is nothing new in his treatment of Nature in his earlier poetry, certainly in his epic there is.

VII

A few words must be said on the quality and literary value of his masterpiece, Hernando De Soto. It was the work of eight years. Five years before it was published I read it in manuscript, and the author then thought it would be published shortly; but so careful an artist was he that he was unwilling to let it go from his hand until he was sure he had exhausted his powers upon it. It is a long poem; its author is one of our generation. These two facts afford sufficient evidence to the minds of many to find an indictment upon. But some of us are willing to overlook the first fault if the interest is sustained, and will be inclined to hear further evidence which may mitigate the severity of the second. Among critics there is a diversity of opinion as to whether the poem has the power to hold one's interest. My early association with its authorship makes me feel incompetent to pass a judgment free from bias. I have resorted to a method in vogue in psychology study. I arranged certain tests. I read it to rather large audiences—one time to a woman's club, another time to several hundred high-school pupils, again to some fifty business and professional men, and finally to a small group of children. From the results obtained, I am convinced, in my own mind, that whatever other literary merits this epic may lack, it is a story with power to catch and hold the interest. The narrative is full of action, and flows with a strong current which does not eddy into distracting episode. The author is master of the story-teller's art. But some have criticised the poem because there is such an abundance of description. To my mind the criticism reveals a misconception of the author's purpose. A more careful reading will show that what is taken as simple description is in reality narrative, wherein not man, but Nature, is in action. Our author says: "In the life of a pioneer like De Soto, the fight against Nature is no mere episode, no passing phase of his mission. It is the beginning, the middle, and the end of all his labors." How else could this fight against

Nature be exhibited but by description? It is a description, however, full of movement, and partakes of the nature of narration.

It has not been my purpose to write critically of the poetry of Judge Malone. Mine has been the humbler task of registering an appreciation of his work with the hope that the reader will be drawn to the poems themselves. The poet is no longer a contemporary, and judgment may be the more safely pronounced. On May 18, 1915, in the city of Memphis, in a room looking out upon the Mississippi, the river he loved so well, the gentle soul of the poet passed into the Great Beyond. It was a fitting season for the passing of a poet of Nature, for in mid-May, West Tennessee is riot of floral color and vocal of bird and bee.

Let us hope that the longing pulsing through the following lines from his pen has had its fruition:

> I long to soar from sod,
>   And tread in glory of celestial grace;
> To live beyond the time my grave is trod,
>   Proving a crown-prince of immortal race;
> To emulate beatitudes of God,
>   To reach his Kingdom and behold His face.

PREFACE TO A BOOK OF POEMS

Forever perished seems the age of gold,
  With all the May-morn glory of the past;
Where now the songs the minstrels sang of old,
  A-thrill with fervor like a trumpet blast?

Ah, in those days Life sipped of morning dew
  Fresh from the bosom of a springtime bud;
Youth's pink-white feet on skylark pinions flew,
  All April's ardor tingling through his blood.

Now is the sordid age of greed and gain:
  Now bloated Mammon rules the market-place;
The Poet, like the Painter, strives in vain,—
  O glorious doom, to share their Art's disgrace!

Ah, we are only struggling pioneers,
  To blaze the path for others yet to be;
Ours is the task to dig through thankless years,
  And found the temples we shall never see.

Some time that golden age again shall come,
  The olden glory shine once more for men.
But that far day shall dawn when we are dumb,
  And who shall mourn us, who shall miss us then?

Far in the future, through the jealous haze,
  We see the golden city reared to Art;
We see its cloud-encircled turrets blaze,
  As splendid as the sunset's burning heart.

That promised land our feet shall never tread,
  Our hands shall never pluck its flowers and fruits;
Our cheeks shall never flush from white to red
  From passion-pealing of its lovers' lutes.

Yet in that purple age I wish one bard
    To say of me these little words of praise:
"He plodded on through sharpened flint and shard,
    Though sordid cares pursued him all his days.

"In darkest hours he wrought with cheerful will:
    He shared the exile of his precious Art;
Though men denied applause, he labored still,
    Nor wrote one line to please the vulgar mart.

"So, like a priest who guards a temple's light,
    He trimmed the lamp whose flame was nearly gone:
He kept his vow to watch it through the night,
    And died beside it at the birth of dawn."

SELECTED POEMS

❧

TOILER AND IDLER

The laborer is the great high-priest of God,
  Creator like the Lord who gave him breath,
The father of all fruits, spouse of the sod,
  The friend of life, and enemy of death.
But he who toils not, bears a shriveled soul,
  Is fit for deserts, or for realms of rocks;
For him no victor's palm, no race, no goal,
  Mate for the sloth, true brother to the ox.

The man who tills the fields breathes wholesome air,
  And sleeps a sleep remorse can not affright;
His peace of mind is stranger to despair,
  His freedom unconfined as morning light.
What though the Summer glares with scorching heat?
  That Winter winds his blood and bone may chill?
His manhood scatters hardships in defeat,
  And every battle makes him stronger still.

The brown bee flits amid the clover there,
  To make him gifts of golden honeycomb;
For him the cherry and the plum and pear,
  The grapevine swinging on his happy home.
For him the daisy dripping with the dew,
  Peach-blooms above and cowslips at his feet;
For him the green grass and skies of blue,
  The scarlet poppies and the golden wheat.

For him are thrushes warbling in delight
  On breezes tripping lightly as a fawn;
For him the swan-like noonday's wings of white,
  The pansy twilight and the primrose dawn.

[1]

For him, Spring like a virgin violet blooms,
   And Summer blossoms like a yellow rose,
Then Autumn like an orange aster looms,
   And Winter comes, a lily of the snows.

The tiller owns no master but his God,
   And earns by right a heritage divine;
A prophet, striking dust with potent rod,
   His plow makes earth gush honey, milk, and wine.
His hillocks are the altars of the Lord,
   His granary like a pious temple stands;
The kingdom of the earth his rich reward,
   The scythe becomes a scepter in his hands.

But he, who, discontented with that lot,
   Tramps through the city, vainly begging work,
Shall find his rosy dreams a wretched blot,
   Facing worse evils than he sought to shirk.
O pity not the tiller of the soil,
   But pity him, the straggler of the street;
O pity not the hardened hands of toil,
   Remembering this poor wanderer's wayworn feet!

At night the keen winds pierce his threadbare coat,
   The rain beats hard down on his dizzy head;
Half-mad, half-starved, he begs a rusty groat,
   When hope and pride from shivering soul have fled.
He sees the street-lamps dripping in the rain,
   The engine hoarsely thundering through the night;
The dragon Town is heedless of his pain,
   And spits upon him in his piteous plight.

He lounges in the city parks, and sees
   Ten thousand like himself, in dirt and rags—
Poor stranded wrecks by seas of miseries,
   Surrendered ships, with tattered, conquered flags!

[2]

Night comes again, and hungry still, he goes
   Half-crazed for lack of sleep, in dull despair,
To freeze to death when fall the Winter snows,
   Or plunge, self-murdered, in the river there.

The idler is a menace unto heaven,
   A misery to himself, a foe to man,
Unsettled, discontented, dumbly driven,
   Drainer of life-blood since the world began.
No burden breaks the back like idleness,
   No toil is half so hard, no strain so great,
No curse of care has half so much distress,
   No armored foe a more portentous threat.

Ashamed of toil, he wooes no fruit from earth,
   He beggars those who look to him for aid,
And spurred by foolish pride, scorns homely worth,
   Longing for camp and court, for reeking blade.
He can not blame one being but himself
   If he should crawl with creatures of the mud;
For he who plows is more than prince of pelf,
   A nobler Knight than any man of blood.

MEMORIAL DAY

Once more we gather under skies of May,
   When lilac blossoms and when violet blows,
And on these grassy graves we twine a spray
   Of Northern lily and of Southern rose.

Once more we hear the bluebird's song afloat,
   The thrush's piping in the dewy dell;
We thrill to hear the Northern robin's note,
   And stand ensnared by Southern mock-bird's spell.

[3]

Once more the winds through odorous orchards blow,
  The creamy hawthorns through the fences twine.
See! all the sunrise splendors are aglow
  Like cataracts of red and golden wine.

We bring a wreath, O martyrs numberless,
  Who perished that your country still might live;
Who fought and bled, the unborn babe to bless,
  That we should still be brothers, and forgive.

But now we come, not as in bygone years,
  When anger poisoned sorrow through and through;
When no one cried, with blended love and tears,
  "Forgive them, for they know not what they do!"

Thank God, those days have now forever passed,
  With all their strife of party, clique and clan;
The Northerner, the Southerner, at last
  Is simply, solely an American.

On Santiago summits we unite
  The grizzled foes of Chickamauga's day;
The hatreds of a Shiloh sink from sight
  Beneath the waters of Manila Bay.

Above your graves exultant anthems swell,
  When Peace and Love have healed the battle's blows;
We thrill with pride to think those fought so well
  With these, so brave to overcome such foes.

Peace unto Grant, the advocate of peace,
  To Stonewall, of the valor-vibrant name;
Peace unto Lee, whose honors shall not cease,
  To Lincoln, of the everlasting fame!
  1899.

FORGOTTEN HEROES

I would sing a song to the unknown heroes, who have
    striven and battled and bled,
To the unknown heroes, existing obscure, who are left
    forgotten when dead,
Who have gone to their graves for you and for me, and
    are sleeping in silent ranks
With never a wreath of laurel, or medal, or badge for a
    nation's thanks.

I would sing a song to the heroes neglected so long by you
    and by me,
In the pestilent tropic marshes, on the blistering ships in
    the tropic sea,
To the yoemen, the stokers, the gunners, with perilous
    duties and beggarly pay,
As we shout for the admirals, generals, captains, who
    bear all the honors away.

There in the stifling holds of the ships, half-naked and
    fainting in fearful heat,
And there in the matted vines, or swordgrass stubble that
    pierces their half-shod feet,
And there in the rattle of rifles, where the cynical bullets
    go snarling by,
For me and for you they swelter, for me and for you they
    reel and they die.

No Congress shall ever reward them, no nation ever be
    filled with their fame,
Though they sweat and they swoon and they perish in
    the pitiless flood or flame;
They are only the unknown heroes, and the mob-world
    neither heeds nor cares,
Though they do and dare for their country more feats than
    a million millionaires.

They pant by the ship's fierce furnace, that you and I may
    rest at ease in the shade,
They rake and they rout the foeman, that you and I may
    laugh at his broken blade,
They laurel the brows of others, though their own triumph
    they never shall see,
They fight and they bleed and they fall forsaken, for the
    sake of you and me.

I would sing a song to the heroes who have met their doom
    on the other side,
Whose plainings are drowned in our paeans, whose pangs
    forgot in our flush of pride;
So then, O dying foemen, to your sinking ships and your
    flaming flags still true,
I have brought you a branch of laurel, and a heartfelt song
    that is all for you.

ABRAHAM LINCOLN

A blend of mirth and sadness, smiles and tears;
A quaint knight-errant of the pioneers;
A homely hero, born of star and sod;
A Peasant-Prince; a Masterpiece of God.

ROBERT E. LEE

As strong to smite as thunderbolts above,
And yet as gentle as a blameless dove.
O star of honor, flower of chivalry,
Our highest hope should be to be like thee.

[6]

FORREST IN MEMPHIS

August 21, 1864.

Forrest has come from the country down
  A-raiding the streets of Memphis town;
He comes post-haste, a-whiz and a-whir,
  With clank of sabre and clink of spur.

Swooping he speeds with his fearless boys
  In a cloud of dust, in a storm of noise,
With their slouching hats and their coats of gray,
  Through the half-wake town at the peep o' day.

Ahead of them all the leader comes
  With hurry of hoofs and din of drums,
Gallant and grand on his nimble mare,
  With his coal-black beard and his iron-gray hair.

Startled from sleep is the Yankee host,
  And every man seeks his appointed post;
The town is a-whirl in its vague alarms,
  There's a shout to wake and a call to arms.

"Forrest is here!" is the sentry's cry,
  As the gray troopers go like a hurricane by;
"Forrest is here!" men shout on the street,
  As they see his mare with her flying feet.

"Forrest is here!" all the newsboys call,
  "Forrest is here!" all the bootblacks bawl,
"Forrest is here!" cries the red cock, "hark!"
  "Forrest is here!" all the watch-dogs bark.

Washburn, aroused from his soft, snug bed,
  Sans trousers, sans boots, sans waistcoat, has fled;
Like a flag of truce, with the winds a-flirt,
  There flaunts in his rear the tail of his shirt.

Forrest rides straight through the hotel door,
 And in Centaur style he paces the floor;
Dismounting, he orders a drink and cigar,
 As in bygone days at the hotel bar.

"Come, give us a drink—some mint if you please,
 My boys, too, are here; give a drink to these;
Though their pockets aren't puffed with dollars and dimes,
 You'll give us a nip for the sake of old times.

"No sugar, no water, stop! there is enough!
 Your health, my old fellow: Don't be in a huff;
And now for a smoke; we must go, you see,
 So now, Mike, my friend, charge it all to me."

Forrest remounts on his restless steed,
 And soon with his boys has started a-speed;
The kettle drums rattle, the bass drums beat,
 The streets are a-din with the tramp of feet.

No matter! he leaves as quick as he came,
 And with hot-haste hoofs the flints are a-flame;
Though the bluecoats rush, they have come too late,
 And Forrest glides safe through the city gate.

And the bluecoat boys they follow him fast,
 But they lose the trace, and return at last;
Too swift and too sly! So none of his foes
 Will follow the path where Forrest goes.

THE RETURN OF DEWEY

A Nation lifts her voice to greet him home
   Who raised her flag where East and West are one,
Where blends the rising with the setting sun.
   For this knight-errant of the ocean foam
Are cheers from cottage and from marble dome.
   From sea to sea is heard the cry, "Well done!
Among our millions, rivals you have none,
   Recalling triumphs sung by Greece and Rome."

His country offers him a laurel bough,
   Returning round the planet's purple rim;
But though she seeks to do him honor now,
   Beside his fame such little gifts grow dim:
He placed a greener wreath upon her brow
   Than any wreath which she can give to him.

From pine-plumed mountains by Wisconsin lake,
   From citrons orchard by Floridian seas;
Where white Alaska's rills and rivers freeze,
   Where Porto Rico's orchard-blooms awake;
From rocks of Maine, where hoary billows break,
   From Georgia swamps, where jasmines scent the breeze;
From Vermont valleys, green Kentucky leas,
   We greet with pride our Nelson and our Blake.

Then make the greetings more resounding still,
   To him whose gaze was onward and above.
For they whose hearts heroic deeds can thrill,
   Have found the White Ideal, like a dove,
And they who honor courage, faith and skill,
   Have crowned themselves in crowning him they love.

AMERICA AND ENGLAND

One of the highest compliments paid to the late Walter Malone is contained in Book 29, Chapter 161 (last page) of Ridpath's History of the World, and this consists of coupling his name not only with those of the greatest present-day poets of England and America, but the author closes this part of his history with a quotation from Walter Malone. The passage is as follows:

"The British writers of the period (at the close of the Nineteenth Century) took up our favorite characters and published panegyrics on Washington and Lincoln and Grant and Lee. Mutual admiration was fanned, and the bards broke out with their rhapsodies. William Watson and Alfred Austin, the new poet laureate, were answered in America by Robert Underwood Johnson, Thomas Bailey Aldrich, and other American poets of first rank, who strove to express the prevailing aspiration of Great Britain and the United States for the closer touch and a more cordial fraternity. Among the expressions of poetic enthusiasm rising into the realm of race affinities and international relations, we may select the following Sonnet by Walter Malone as a fitting conclusion to this brief section of the History of the British Empire:

"Beneath the arctic peaks of silent snow;
Through tropic isles enwreathed with orange blooms;
Where brown Gibraltar like a giant looms;
Where furnaces of red Sahara glow;
In spicy groves, where softest breezes blow;
In tangled Hindu jungles' deepest glooms;
By mummied Pharaohs' immemorial tombs,—
The Saxon legions conquer every foe.

"So Alfred's spear and Nelson's sword shall be
Guards for the flag that Washington unfurled;
With might of Cromwell, Lincoln, Blake and Lee
Our gauntlet at invaders shall be hurled;
Lords of the land and emperors of the sea,
The Eagle and the lion face the world!"

AMERICA AT MANILA

Through mazy moonbeams of the secret night
The ships of Dewy reach Manila Bay.
The tropic sun leaps forth in sudden light,
And lo, the dawn-flushed city far away!
Then fleets and forts like waking giants scowl,
The swift projectiles whizz and burst a-whirl,
The batteries like ferocious lions growl,
A hundred guns their hoarse defiance hurl.

Then thunder answers thunder, shock on shock,
Shell answers shell, blood-curdling shriek on shriek,
Gun answers gun, from shuddering ships a-rock,
And flaming decks with crimson rivers reek.
A storm of steel tears down Spain's haughty crest,
Her glory sinks a-blaze in blood and tears;
The olden East has met the youthful West
Rewriting history of six thousand years.

Men say the age is sordid, yet we find
No Spartans ever breathed from breasts more bold,
No doughtier Norsemen fought with wave and wind,
No true knights lived with hearts of purer gold.
Lo, ancient Asia stands in mute amaze;
Few deeds like this Japan hath ever told;
Memorial China turns with startled gaze;
Arabia sees come true her dreams of old.

Far from the sunrise of their native West,
They wake the world at thunder of their guns—
What glory added to your country's crest,
O proudest of the proudest of her sons!
With regal riches in her kingdom wide,
With untold treasures ever at her call,
Columbia, like Cornelia, points with pride
To you, her jewels, prized above them all.

These valorous vikings leave transcendent names
To live through ages that are yet to come,
Though records perish in the floods and flames,
Though marbles crumble, and though lips grow dumb,
As long as day shall dawn on shores and seas
Where they have won Fame's chaplet, Honor's crown,
So long shall sun of glory shine on these,
True heroes, everlasting in renown.

THE BATTLE

At first a few blasts shake the startled air,
And then a hundred burst in serried flame,
While all the Earth is quaking in its fear
And all the hills are rocking to their base.
The iron balls are rushing, crushing by,
And all is ruin where they quiver past;
They scatter leaves like fierce December winds,
And giant trees come crashing to the ground;
The stones are splintered high upon the hills,
The sod is ploughed, the sky is dim with dust;
The baleful bombs are bursting far and near,
And frightened echoes answer back the sounds.
It seems as if the ancient days of Earth
Have now returned with all their giant brood,
And all the Titans, hurled from lofty heaven,
Are struggling with the Thunderer on his throne.

THE CAPTURED BATTLESHIP

In days long past no happier ship than I
    Flung forth her empire's banner to the breeze;
No bolder bark withstood a stormy sky,
    With fiercer ardor fought the foaming seas.

But then at last a day of evil came
    On which we met the onslaught of the foe.
Oh, who shall tell the story of my shame,
    My desolation, my disgrace, my woe?

My hull was splintered by their bursting shells,
    My tottering turrets down the deck were hurled;
I heard my dying seamen's shrieks and yells,
    As red flames through the black smoke waved and
        whirled.

I saw my gunners fall beside their guns,
    I saw my captain, sword in hand, drop dead;
Shot after shot struck down my splendid sons,
    And splashed my bosom with a frightful red.

Ah, could I then have foundered in the flood,
    And won the glorious death that waits the brave!
Could I have sunk, baptized in precious blood,
    To endless honor in an ocean grave!

But no, they took me to their far-off shore,
    And nailed their haughty standard to my mast;
I served my king, my fatherland, no more;
    I fought the flag I bled for in the past!

So, like a Judas, I must sail the sea,
    A traitor to the master loved so well;
A hated outcast, still I flee and flee,
    Around me ocean—in my heart a hell!

And since that time, when days of peace have come,
    I sometimes meet old comrade-ships I knew;
Ah, how they spurn me as they spurn the scum,
    And pass me, shamed, and shrinking from their view!

Sometimes at dusk I hear my sailors call,
    And see their hands up-beckoning from the deep;
"Oh, come!" they tell me, "show them after all,
    Your faith, your honor, you will die to keep!"

God grant some night an awful storm shall rise,
    And give me chance for vengeance on this foe;
How I should gloat to hear their craven cries,
    As I should pitch to take them all below!

Then I should shout above their last wild yell,
    "I bring them, sons, a sacrifice to you!
They lied who said I did not love you well;
    O darling sailor boys, my soul is true!"

[13]

CUBA FREE

Like Cinderella in her tattered gown,
　　She sits barefooted in the ashes there,
Robbed of her sceptre and her throne and crown,
　　A beggar-child, once fairest of the fair.

Take courage, little orphan!　There shall be
　　A morn of triumph for thy night of woes;
There is a necklace and a ring for thee,
　　A silken garment and a wreath of rose.

Like Juliet in her old ancestral halls,
　　Beset by foemen and their treacherous spies,
She gazes at the grim, forbidding walls,
　　And spends the weary day in sobs and sighs.

Fear not!　For Freedom is thy Romeo,
　　And he shall snatch thee from thy hateful cell,
Though three-score thousand vassals bid him go,
　　And three-score thousand churls stand sentinel.

O captive maiden, though thy castle tower
　　Be girt with fifty battlements of stone,
Though flaming dragons should surround thy bower,
　　Thy lover soon shall win thee for his own.

So thou shalt come forth blushing by his side,
　　From dungeon, iron gate, and granite wall,
His fairy princess and his beauteous bride—
　　For he shall woo and wed thee, spite of all.

A NIGHT IN CUBA

Far out to sea the home-bound seabirds wing,
  Dim in brief twilight of the tropic day;
Then, one by one, lights of the city swing
  A sparkling semicircle round the bay.

Above me, from its broad-leaved sheath of green
  A great banana hangs its purple husk;
Beside me, like a seraph half unseen,
  An odorous oleander haunts the dusk.

The moon seems fallen from her throne on high,
  So clear and close she comes to earthly view,
And in the blue corolla of the sky
  Canopus quivers like a drop of dew.

A-thrill with passion, pierced with bliss and pain,
  A light guitar obeys a lover's hands,
And pours a fervid and heart-broken strain,
  Now sweet, now bitter, from its trembling strands.

O lovelorn youth, your dark-brown liquid eyes
  Need sweet caresses of the dews of sleep:
Your lips were made for laughter, not for sighs;
  Youth comes to gladden, not to make you weep!

Youth's wild young feet were made to dance for joy;
  Youth's sweet wild heart was made to leap with bliss;
O revel in your glory, splendid boy,
  For all the world is craving for your kiss!

In Cuban skies, the palm's imperial crest
  Lifts plumes forever free from winter snows;
No frost shall ever blight the lily's breast,
  Nor dim the glory of the ardent rose.

Remember, while that flower is free from frost,
   That bud forever free from winter blight,
Youth, once escaping, is forever lost,
   His feet have wings more swift than swallows' flight!

MY FIRST BOOK

Poor little volume, awkard, rough and crude,
Now soiled and battered like a tarnished toy!
Yet thou wert once my childhood's pride and joy
Before contemptuous critics might intrude;
And so I treasure still thy verses rude,
As some poor mother loves her first-born boy,
Who comes deformed, her high hopes to destroy,
And fill her breast with sad solicitude.

Still, I was happy in those perished years,
Ere Sin had lured me onward to her snare,
While now my soul is racked with fitful fears,
And Sorrow makes my gloomy heart her lair.
O for thy childish joys, to dry my tears,
Thy childish hopes, to soothe my dark despair!

TO AN UNKNOWN READER

In years to come, when I have passed away,
   Your careless glance upon this page may fall;
So then, my unknown reader, pause, I pray,
   And hearken to my faint and far-off call.

O youth, as graceful as a willow bough,
   As gladsome as a fawn with nimble feet;
O youth, with noble alabaster brow,
   Flushed with your morning splendor, fresh and sweet:—

Dear boy, mine ears shall never know your voice,
   Mine eyes shall never know your princely grace,
And I shall never in your smile rejoice,
   And never, never see your fine frank face.

O maiden, with the starry eyes of brown,
   With golden ringlets, peach-bloom cheeks aglow;
O maiden, wearing love's and beauty's crown,
   As radiant as a sunrise over snow:—

Dear Girl, I never by your side shall tread,
   And never shall I hear your gentle sighs:
I never shall behold your lips of red,
   And never, never see your splendid eyes.

I love you, though our paths shall never meet,
   Though you shall flourish after I have fled,
Though living voices seem to you more sweet
   Than lays of him deserted with the dead.

For you, the birds and blossoms of the day,
   For you, the brilliance of the banquet halls;
For me, the lonesome churchyard, old and gray,
   For me, the prison under charnel walls.

For you, the light, the life, the music, mirth,
   For you love's triumph and love's sweet, sweet pain;
For me, a pillow in the gloomy earth,
   For me, the sobbing of the midnight rain.

Will you neglect me in that far-off day?
   Shall I forgotten and forsaken lie?
Ah, then my heart should bleed, though turned to clay,
   And that would be another death to die.

O unknown reader, for your sake I pine;
   Beside you let me cease my wandering.
I love you; let me take your hand in mine,
   And tell you stories, laugh or weep or sing.

For you I suffered in far-distant days;
　For you I lost man's favor, maiden's hand;
For you my feet forsook their boyhood ways;
　For you I wandered through the stranger's land.

From death's dark empire shall my soul depart,
　Your smile, your friendship, and your love to win;
Behold! I come and knock upon your heart:
　For God's sake, reader, rise and let me in!

THE HUMBLER POETS

The critic wonders why the lowly bards
　Still write and write when no one seems to read,
When fame and fortune still refuse rewards,
　And when the world gives but a wreath of weed.

But still, Sir Critic, they have done their best,
　And more than that not Shakespeare's self has done;
For while God gave ten talents to the rest,
　To these poor poets He has given but one.

And if a lowly singer dries one tear,
　Or soothes one humble human heart in pain,
Be sure his homely verse to God is dear,
　And not one stanza has been sung in vain.

So when they give their humble songs of praise,
　Their simple lines find favor in His sight,
And when He loves to hear their little lays,
　Rebuke not, for His spirit sayeth, "Write!"

They do not come as kings and queens of song,
　Surrounded by the pomp of spears and shields,
But patient peasants, suffering scorn and wrong,
　To labor in His vineyards and his fields.

Theirs not the strain of thrushes' golden throats
  That haunt the soul with dreamings of delight,
Nor peerless mock-birds' palpitating notes,
  That thrill the morning and the noon and night;

But like the robins, with their hopeful trill,
  They bring first tidings of the coming spring,
Or, like brown snow-birds in the winter chill,
  They cheer us when their brothers will not sing.

They come not like the roses, winged with fire,
  In scarfs of scarlet or in gowns of gold,
Nor like the lilies, spotless in attire,
  Whose leaflets like a seraph's plumes unfold;

But, like wild cowslips, fresh from nature's woof,
  That make a poet of a farmer boy,
Or daisies on a dusty city roof,
  That give a poor sick working-woman joy.

Then sing on, humble poet! God will hear,
  And He will praise you for your work well done;
Then, when you see Him, you may find no peer
  Among the throngs that sing around His Throne.

THE POET TO HIS BOOK

I send thee forth upon an unknown sea,
  Where many a bark hath perished long before.
In thee, my ship, I put the heart of me,
  To sail, or sink from sight forevermore.

My treasures all are there like silken bales,
  Ambitions, aspirations, fancies, fears,
And in thy cargo, under snowy sails,
  Are all my joys and smiles and hopes and tears.

[19]

I see thy white breast, like a stately swan,
　Go forth to brave the wild waves of the deep,
When summer skies are rosy with the dawn,
　And all deceitful tempests seem asleep.

God grant thee strength to live through stormy shocks,
　God guide thee ever under Summer skies,
And send thee safely by the reefs and rocks
　To ever-blooming isles of Paradise.

Mayhap thy verse in ages yet to come
　Shall tell my secrets unto alien ears,
When these poor lips have lain for centuries dumb
　And I have mouldered for a thousand years;

When she to whom in vain my love is told
　No longer reigns a Princess young and proud,
When clods have covered all her locks of gold
　And starry eyes are hidden in her shroud.

And then perchance when all our tribes have fled,
　When all the sceptres of the earth are rust,
When all the kingdoms of our day are dead,
　And all our cities crumbled into dust;

When other nations with another tongue
　Have overcome the nations of to-day,
When heroes now unknown are praised and sung,
　And unborn poets hold the world in sway;

When empires of the Australasian seas
　Have stolen Europe's light and Europe's soul,
And when the traveler knows all mysteries
　From Afric jungle to the Northern pole;

When crumbling idols, wreathed with weeds and vines,
　Gaze from the ruined temples of to-day,
When strange, new gods are throned in other shrines,
　And all our earth and heaven have passed away;—

Then may my thoughts in others live again,
    A million bosoms may my transports share,
A million friends may feel my joy and pain,
    A million lovers feel my deep despair;

And gentle maids may give me soulful sighs
    For true love offered that was not returned,
May hearken to my fervent melodies,
    And sob at learning how my bosom burned;

And I will tell to all the sons of men
    How fair the maiden whom I now adore,
And they shall hearken to my story then,
    And learn how I grew sad forevermore;

And they shall know my hours of loneliness,
    My true heart's anguish and unheeded sighs,
And how she slew my hopes of happiness
    With daggers of her splendor-streaming eyes.

TO A POET

He greatly errs who hopes to win the bays
    Without a battle and without a scar,
To walk among the lilies all his ways,
    Or lie in sloth, yet reach and seize a star.

O youth, who knockest at the gate of Fame,
    Long must thy waiting and thy watching be;
Beside that gate, with two-edged sword of flame,
    A Shape stands guarding that shall challenge thee.

Long years shall pass, and find thee waiting still,
    With eyes grown dim, and bonny locks turned gray;
Long years shall pass, and high upon a hill
    The palace that thou seekest far away!

Long years shall pass, and then the shades of night
   Shall rust the golden twilight into brown;
Long years shall pass, and in the fading light
   Far, far away shall shine the promised crown.

Who weds the Muse must others all forsake,
   Who takes her hand must never look behind;
He must not falter, though his heart may break,
   To all allurements deaf and dumb and blind.

To far, far places must thy feet be turned,
   Where strangers only meet thee with a scowl,
When thy brave heart, which once with ardor burned,
   Shall seem to throb beneath a sable cowl.

The love thou longest for may be denied,
   Thy soul without a comrade evermore,
No one to cheer thee, treading at thy side,
   No fair-haired children playing at thy door.

Old friends will say, when other friends have fled,
   "Forsake the hopeless task thy soul hath sworn!
Poor and neglected, thou dost want for bread,
   Thy coat is threadbare and thy cloak is worn."

Like England's Alfred, fleeing in disguise,
   And hotly hunted, planning desperate schemes,
A hag may harry with her shrewish cries
   For letting cakes burn as you dream your dreams.

But yet, like Douglas with the heart of Bruce,
   Keep safe thy treasures, scorning still to fly;
That tempter spurn who would thy soul seduce,
   And fight to win, or with thy Charge to die.

THE DEATH OF POETRY

They tell us that the poet's day is past,
That Song no more shall gush from human heart;
They tell us all the old dreams must depart,
The old ideals by the way be cast.
What babbling folly!   Frailest dreams outlast
The noisiest jargon of the mightiest mart;
Great empires crumble, yet the realm of Art,
Unconquered, glorious, stands forever fast.

When Spring comes not in triumph as of yore,
When Earth's last rose her last sweet leaf hath shed;
When oceans cease to swell, and peaks to soar,
When man and maid no longer woo and wed;
When starry skies proclaim their God no more,—
Not till that day shall Poesie be dead.

SONNET
ON MY TWENTY-FIRST BIRTHDAY
February 10, 1887

The restless years at last have reached this day,
    When youth must leave me, never to return,
When Nature's kindly face grows cold and stern,
    And life seems short, which once stretched far **away**.
No longer shall I rove through fields of May;
    New toils and cares are mine, hard truths to learn,
Which ever faster fall from Sorrow's urn,
    Since life no longer means a childish play.

O Voiceless Future! what fate dost thou hide?
    Hast thou a tale of darkness or of light?
Shall sin and sorrow snare my feet untried,
    And shall I stand or fall before their might?
But lose or win, or weal or woe betide,
    All is forgotten soon in endless night.

[23]

THE READING BOY

Sunk in the cushion of a high arm-chair,
  A volume resting where his knees are crost,
With one hand slowly fumbling through his hair,
  There sits the boy in magic pages lost.

At times he lifts a grave, though youthful face,
  Revealing depths of eyes of liquid brown;
He seems a traveler from some far-off place
  Who flees us as his flitting glance turns down.

O dreamy boy, with fair May-morning brow,
  What realms of wonders lure your restless feet?
In what far kingdom are you treading now?
  What distant ocean bears your wandering fleet?

You sail with Sinbad through enchanted seas,
  Your pockets stuffed with diamonds from his caves;
You and Aladdin gather gems from trees;
  You give your orders to a thousand slaves.

With Crusoe you have rifled rich old wrecks,
  You tame his parrot and you herd his goats;
With Captain Kidd you rake the foeman's decks,
  And smiling, cut freebooting rivals' throats.

Columbus-like, you find another world,
  You help Magellan sail the globe around;
Your flags with Drake and Raleigh float unfurled
  From Dutch Guiana unto Puget Sound.

You sit with Alexander on his throne,
  Yet conquer other worlds beyond his wake;
With Cæsar you have bridged the Rhine and Rhone,
  Yet worn the crown which Cæsar dared not take.

And yet, my sturdy boy, you soon shall see
   Youth's peerless poem dwindle into prose;
And soon your nimble feet, so wild and free,
   Shall bleed from thorns of each caressing rose.

Boy-Cæsar, in the Future's sullen shade,
   Some envious Casca plans his traitorous part;
Some lean and hungry Cassius whets his blade,
   Some much-loved Brutus waits to stab your heart.

Yet I salute you, ere your dreams go wrong;
   To you, young master, see my head bowed down;
O prince of romance, story, and of song,
   O lord of gladness, glory and renown!

THE WHISTLING BOY

So keen, so clear,
Falls on the ear
   The wild, sweet pipings of his lips,
So sharp, so tart,
I thrill and start,
   And Fancy tingles to her finger-tips.

The dingy town
With walls of brown,
   With grimy streets and pavements gray,
Its rush and roar
I note no more,
   And all its fierce commotions pass away.

Along the street
His brown, bare feet
   Remind me of a baby faun,
By fern-fringed pool
In shadows cool
   Leading a throng of fluting birds at dawn.

No hermit thrush
Through woodland hush
    Could trill a tune more fresh and free;
No mocking bird
More gladly heard
    Through verdant vine-clad swamps of Tennessee.

I feel a breeze
Through cherry trees,
    O'er dandelions wet with dew,
And on a rail
I hear a quail
    Gladden an old peach orchard through and through

Through hazy tears
I see old years
    When I too, happy as a bird,
By bubbling streams
Dreamed boyish dreams—
    The dear, dead dreams, so sweet and so absurd.

IN AN OLD LIBRARY

In this old farmhouse garret where I stray,
    A refugee from worries of the town,
I dig and delve the livelong summer day
    Through ancient volumes, dusty, worn and brown.

On dingy panes a hornet fumes and frets,
    A beetle thumps the wall with sudden thud;
A wasp hangs captive in a spider's nets
    A dirt-daub, singing, moulds his house of mud.

A mantel holds two antiquated clocks,
    Where scampering mice go playing hide-and-seek;
A wren, snug-nested in an empty box,
    Sits calm and quiet while her fledglings squeak.

Here, like a vein of purest virgin gold
  Deep-hidden in the desert rock and sand,
Are all the treasures of the days of old,
  Brought by the Great and Good from every land.

Here all the friends of youth (for youth alone
  Can make the friendships that are sure to last)
Soothe once again the heart half turned to stone,
  With old enchantments that I thought were past.

Here, like a pirate at his secret cave,
  I dig my buried ingots from the junk;
And, like a diver, from an ocean grave
  I raise the Spanish galleons that I sunk.

Here all the wise sit in serene array,
  Where Plato's words flow forth in honeyed sweets;
I see the face of Goldsmith and of Gray,
  I walk with Shelley and I talk with Keats.

O magic Past, you woo me from To-day;
  The frenzied world outside is lost to view.
Old friends are best!   I tread this quiet way,
  Forsaking not the old to win the new.

Like mellow wine in cobwebbed cellars stored,
  Here burn the suns of long-forgotten years;
To-day I revel in their precious hoard
  Of love and laughter, gladness, grief and tears.

OPPORTUNITY

They do me wrong who say I come no more
  When once I knock and fail to find you in;
For every day I stand outside your door,
  And bid you wake, and rise to fight and win.

Wail not for precious chances passed away,
  Weep not for golden ages on the wane!
Each night I burn the records of the day,—
  At sunrise every soul is born again!

Laugh like a boy at splendors that have sped,
  To vanished joys be blind and deaf and dumb;
My judgments seal the dead past with its dead,
  But never bind a moment yet to come.

Though deep in mire, wring not your hands and weep;
  I lend my arm to all who say "I can!"
No shame-faced outcast ever sank so deep,
  But yet might rise and be again a man!

Dost thou behold thy lost youth all aghast?
  Dost reel from righteous Retribution's blow?
Then turn from blotted archives of the past,
  And find the future's pages white as snow.

Art thou a mourner?   Rouse thee from thy spell;
  Art thou a sinner?   Sins may be forgiven;
Each morning gives thee wings to flee from hell,
  Each night a star to guide thy feet to heaven.

THE WORLD IS MY HOME

I travel to East, I wander to West;
Each land that I see is dear to my breast.
I greet the green hills as I float down the Rhine,
The vineyards of France I love as if mine.
With rapture the castles of England I see,
And Switzerland's peaks are old friends to me;
A freeman of Athens, a tribune of Rome,
All men are my brothers, the world is my home.

Let Sultans and Czars make war if they will,
But let their own blood on the battlefield spill;
For none but the Fool will lift up his arm
To murder the man who has done him no harm.
Let the bigot cry out for a bloody crusade,
To pierce heathen hearts with his sanctified blade;
From mosque of the Nile to Saint Peter's dome
All men are my brothers, the world is my home.

Wherever we meet, on sea or on sod,
We are brethren of Christ, we are children of God.
They may prattle of Codes, or prate of their Creeds—
I care not for these, but for brotherly deeds.
They may boast of their Church, their Clique or their Clan—
I but yearn for the touch of a true fellow-man.
So my heart still repeats, wherever I roam,
All men are my brothers, the world is my home.

OMAR IN HEAVEN

Year after year I wait, reposing here
    Among the Faithful, by the Prophet blest;
A stranger now to grief, remorse and fear,
    My one-time restless heart is wreathed in rest.

The years glide on, and still they find me free
    From every care that dogs the feet of men;
No sun on desert sand, no storm at sea,
    Shall ever come to vex my soul again.

No clouded skies on pages ashen-gray
    Reflect heart-breaking annals of the earth;
The Judas-kisses all have passed away,
    With all the madness that eclipsed our mirth.

[29]

Here all the year is April, May or June,
    With bud and blossom free from every blight;
Here all the day is everlasting noon,
    With glory never dimming in the night.

No thorns beset the beauty of the rose,
    No sweet is ever tinctured with a sour;
We pluck no fruits,—a heavenly zephyr blows
    And shakes the mellow apple from its bower.

No leaflet ever withers on the tree,
    No bulbul song on desert waste is lost;
From drought the date and olive flourish free,
    No tulip ever shudders from the frost.

No traveler's camel pants and kneels to die
    As hot siroccos fling their fiery dust;
No sun-scorched famine makes of earth and sky
    A brazen oven and a blackened crust.

Here bubbling fountains, cold as mountain snow,
    Refresh the pilgrim mad with feverish thirst;
Here verdant forests dim the noontide glow
    For caravans from white-hot sands accurst.

Songs can not sing the glories here on high,
    The white, white splendor of this blest estate;
One might rejoice ten thousand times to die
    To peep one instant through its jeweled gate.

No hunter here pursues the swift gazelle,
    The lad no longer here pursues the maid;
The fawn, grown fearless, knows her master well,
    The loved one by her lover's side is laid.

Around me, tripping with a dove-like tread,
    Are seven times seventy houris, passing sweet;
With oils of roses they anoint my head,
    And bring rose-water jars to wash my feet.

They bring me sherbets cool with creamy snow,
　　They scent my courts with frankincense and myrrh;
With peacock fans they make soft breezes blow,
　　And carol songs that set my heart astir.

Ah, they are fairer far than maids of earth,
　　And never flee the lover when he wooes,
They seek me dancing in delightful mirth,
　　And always come to kiss me when I choose.

They beg me think no more of loves of mine
　　In old-time Aprils there in haunts of men;
They bid me quaff their jug's mellifluous wine,
　　And never ask to see the Earth again.

Ah yes, they all surrender free of force,—
　　The bird comes captive though I set no snare;
Yet wines they hand me never bring remorse,
　　The love they lavish never brings despair.

And here in everlasting youth we stay,—
　　The youth of roseate feet and soft dark eyes;
Though fifty Sultans rule and pass away
　　The years flit soft as wings of butterflies.

Yet, Iran, in my dreams I feel again
　　Your dear temptations, your delightful snares,
Your bitter-sweets, your pleasures mixed with pain,
　　Your blissful sorrows, your divine despairs.

I long for Bagdad's mosques and minarets,
　　For Shiraz, with its fig-trees, vines and palms;
For dear old Ispahan my spirit frets,—
　　O sight more soothing than Arabian balms!

I weary of these everlasting Springs,
　　These gardens with their never-fading flowers;
O, bring the North Wind on his eagle wings,
　　To quench their glory in his sleety showers!

Who cares for youth where every one is young?
  Who values springtime life where none grow old?
All gold with iron in one heap were flung
  If every ship came weighted down with gold.

Where every man is wealthy, none is rich;
  Where bids no Evil, there can be no Good;
Without some valley's intervening niche
  No mountain ever stands or ever stood.

Though youth on Earth soon shatters like a rose,
  And love's fresh morning ends at last in night,
The song is sweeter for an early close,
  Love ten times dearer for an early flight.

Ah, sweet the prospect of a bliss pursued,
  Yet sweeter still the bliss we gained and lost;
O clutch it not with fingers fondly rude,
  Or else to-morrow we shall count its cost.

We slay the white swan for his peerless plume,—
  He falls, to splash in mire his snowy down;
We gather grapes,—our hands brush off their bloom;
  The creamy lily that we touch turns brown.

What though the damsel struggle from my arm?
  What though she laughs and runs beyond my reach?
The cherry's tartness proves its chiefest charm,
  The topmost bough witholds the reddest peach.

Only one game is ever worth dispute,
  Well won with ardors of an anxious day,—
To chase the prize, uncertain in pursuit,
  And having won, soon feel it slip away.

I envy Earth its secret, stolen bliss,
  Its fond embraces, half withheld, then given,
Its lovers' quarrels, crushed beneath a kiss,
  Its fond farewells, that makes a hell seem heaven.

I love the world,—its spice of doubts and fears,
  Its sugared fictions, hiding heartless truth,
Its silvery laughter, shining through its tears,
  The sweet, uncertain tenure of its youth.

I beg the Prophet from his judgment seat
  To let me steal to Earth from heights above,
Once more to test its wine-cup's dear deceit,
  And taste the bitter honey of its love.

THE PENITENTIARY

I

I see the convicts in disgraceful stripes
  Come homeward to their cells at set of sun,
The whole world's most despised, disgusting types,
  As hopeless as the day that now is done.

The penitentiary opens iron jaws
  To swallow up the mass of shame and sin,
The cages seize them in their rusty claws,
  And giant gates are locked to keep them in.

Their faces all are foul, their hands unclean,
  Their aching ankles drag the iron ball,
And two by two they bear a clanking chain;
  Their heads are shaved to show their hopeless fall.

One sings lewd songs, one tells a wicked jest,
  They laugh at honor and they laugh at shame;
All that on earth is sweetest and is best
  Is scoffed and blasphemed with a vulgar name.

Here comes a man who sought to make escape;
  Behold the swollen stripes of whip and rod!—
What shame to think that one in mortal shape
  Should beat and spit upon a child of God!

I pity them and feel a rush of tears,
   But not one creature there has tears to shed,
For none have ever sobbed since childhood years,
   As all their hopes and loves and joys are dead.

And then my heart is hardened as I hear
   How every virtue from their souls is driven;
I shrink and shudder as they come too near,
   Exiled from Earth and barred from hopes of Heaven!

II

And yet I feel all good is not yet lost;
   This man would share with me his crust of bread,
Would bring me water when with fever tost,
   Or share with me his narrow iron bed.

Or, if I told him some sweet tale of love,
   A smile would light his face's dull despair,
As radiant as the white wings of a dove
   Amid the darkness of a panther's lair.

Once more a tender touch his heart would feel
   To think of one he loved in years of yore,
Before the Law came, with its chains of steel,
   And bade him banish hope forevermore.

Or, if I traveled through a lonely land,
   In storms of midnight, when my feet grew sore,
Were he a hermit, he would take my hand
   And give me gracious welcome to his door.

Or, if a slave, I hid from haunts of men,
   Or fled in terror from pursuing hounds,
This thief would lead me safely to his den,
   And pour the oil upon my burning wounds.

If this be true of this poor convict now,
    How sweeter, happier might have been his fate
If chance temptation had not warped his brow,
    And friendly warning had not come too late!

And there are thousands in the world to-day
    Who never will be called to answer crimes,
Enthroned in wealth to rule with despot sway,
    Though viler than these clods a hundred times.

The shivering wretch who steals a tattered coat,
    Or crust to keep his starving soul alive,
A rusty penny, or a cankered groat,—
    That is the thief the world will not forgive.

But he who blights a maiden in her bud,
    Who snatches gold by force, or fraud, or might,
And he who bathes a nation in its blood,
    Walks forth as free as Heaven's own air and light.

Here treads a generous spendthrift, who at last,
    In evil moment, like a culprit fell;
His fawners and his flatterers of the past,
    All, all have left him in a convict's cell;

And as he treads in felon's stripes and chains,
    He learns the story told from sun to sun,—
Be generous; and men mock you for your pains;
    Be selfish; and your crown is surely won.

Here comes a poor old drunkard, weak and worn,
    His face all bloated, dark with leaden care,
His ashen eyes, once clear as skies of morn,
    Are dim and dull with unexpressed despair;

While he who held the bottle to his lips,
    Who robbed him of his last poor coin at play,
And she whose sweet lies made his soul's eclipse,
    Are roving free and happy far away.

Here comes a woman who was pure and young,
  A lily that was trampled in the dust,
Whose lover's treason like an adder stung,—
  Another victim to a foolish trust;

But while she pines in penitentiary walls
  Her false seducer never shares her doom;
He treads his measures in his gilded halls,
  She in the treadmill of this living tomb.

And she shall kiss no more the rose when red,
  And in her saucy sweetness laugh aloud;
A felon's couch shall be her bridal bed,
  A wreath of fennel rest upon her shroud.

Yet though the world may not believe me just,
  I pardon him who steals a loaf of bread,
But not the wretch who breaks my tender trust,
  And leaves me with aching heart of lead.

My soul forgives that poor old drunken man,
  That outcast, shivering through the cruel town,
But not the chieftain of a robber clan,
  Who steals my freedom and who wears a crown.

But then the world is strong and I am weak;
  You are the creatures of the powers that be;
So you must fester in your dungeons bleak
  Till Death shall come at last to set you free.

III

But midnight comes; each on a bed of straw,
  I see the two men and the woman lie;
Their servitude has satisfied the law,
  For now the time of death is drawing nigh.

Their fevered brains are swayed by fitful dreams,
    Their dim eyes glance through scenes of perished years,
And sweet, sad visions come in hazy gleams
    Beyond the realm of sin and shame and tears.

And then remember, in a broken prayer,
    With deaf, dull ears and dim and dying eyes,
How Christ once calmed the dying thief's despair,—
    "To-day thou meetest me in Paradise."

Who is this stranger treading by to-night,—
    A stranger coming from the far, far lands,
His sad face lovely with a smile of light,
    Who bears the print of nails upon his hands?

Behold, ye dying sinners! wake, arise!
    Ho, turnkey, jailer, open unto me!
For we shall meet to-night in Paradise,
    The King of Heaven Himself has pardoned ye!

"Behold, ye dying sinners! wake, arise!
    Ho, turnkey, jailer, open unto me!
The convict in his straw-strewn dungeon dies,
    For Christ Himself has come to set him free!"

THE POTTER'S FIELD

I

See the lonesome fields forsaken in their desolation spread,
Heaving with the silent grave-mounds of the nameless
    pauper dead.

Never blooms a rose above them, never peeps a violet
    here,
No one comes to sit beside them, no one comes to shed a
    tear.

No one speaks a word of pity, no one breathes a word of
love,
Earth around them shrinks with loathing, heaven recoils
with scorn above.••••••

Here are sleeping thieves and beggars, here the outcast
babes of shame,
Here the felon from the gallows, here the waif without a
name.

Here the suicide lies sleeping, with the madman by his
side,
And the drunkard and the spendthrift in the same strange
home abide.

Here the ruined woman slumbers, while her lover, far
away
In his revels, thinketh never of his victim in the clay.

Yet what vernal visions wreathed them in their childhood
long ago!
Ah, what aspirations perished in the pauper graveyard
low!

Ah, what happy mothers kissed them in their pink-white
boyish bloom,
Never dreaming that their idols thus should share the
felon's tomb!

Ah, what trustful maidens kissed them, gazing in their
eyes so brave,
Never dreaming that their lovers thus should share the
drunkard's grave!

And the ardent lover fondling this frail outcast's golden
hair,
Never dreamed that he, a traitor, should thus drive her to
despair,

Nor that this same trustful being, burning with a love
  untold,
Soon would sink and lie decaying in the pauper graveyard
  mould,

While their babe, scorned and deserted, soon would hide
  his shameful birth
Far below in dust polluted of the pauper graveyard's
  earth.

II

But amid the nameless outcasts sleep the good and brave
  and true,
They who lived and died for duty, they the world's Immortal Few.

For the palm to those deserving evermore shall be denied;
They must tread the earth with beggars, slumber by the
  beggar's side;

And the good and great and generous in a lowly grave lie
  down
Ere the fickle world rewards them with the sceptre and the
  crown.

Here are sleeping peerless poets, they who begged from
  door to door,
But whom Death has wreathed with laurels green and glad
  forevermore.

Here are sleeping brave old martyrs, they who strove to
  make us free,
Whom the flames consume to ashes for their love of you
  and me.

And they sleep as sweetly, calmly, in these pauper graveyard scenes
As the laurelled victor slumbers by the side of kings and
queens.

Here are sleeping countless heroes, whom the world
remembers not,
They who loved and toiled and struggled in their chill and
cheerless lot;

But while Earth has turned unheeding in its hurried stir
and strife,
Angels all their names have treasured in the Master's
book of life!

III

Now I dream I see the dawning of the awful Judgment
Day,
Far across the Eastern mountains, and the Eastern seas
away.

And the dull ears of those sleepers hear the trumpet in
their palls,
While their dumb lips strive to answer to its wild, soul-
stirring calls.

And from out their rusted coffins myriad bony shapes
arise,
While their dim eyes catch the glimmer in the vast vague
Eastern skies.

Then the beggar feebly totters from his grim and gaping
grave,
And he stands at last the equal of the great and strong
and brave;

Then the felon struggles slowly from his dark and dusty
  shroud,
There to face the last of Judges with the rich and high
  and proud;

Then the ruined woman rises with her infant from the
  tomb,
There to meet the trembling lover who at last must share
  her doom.

So the pauper graveyard's children unto endless life arise,
Now the equal of the haughty in the great Creator's eyes;

Still to live and live forever, when the myriad years have
  fled,
When the world is crushed to atoms, and the suns and
  stars are dead.

THE CHURCHYARD

Once I feared thee, mournful Monarch, with thy sad and
  solemn dells,
Haunted by the vesper shadows and the sobbing funeral bells;

Haunted by the ghostly roses, in their silken robes of
  white,
And the mock-bird's mystic singing in the dim and dusky
  night;

Haunted by the tombs of marble gleaming through magnolia leaves,
And the restless moonlight figures where the grave-mound
  dimly heaves.

But my loved ones gather with thee in the fading, fleeting
  years,
And I lay within thy caverns all my joys and hopes and
  fears.

Thou hast treasures in thy bosom richer than the ocean
    caves,
Where the peerless pearls are beaming and the coral for-
    est waves,

Where the mermaid gathers amber filled with mellow
    golden light,
And the silver-weighted galleons glimmer through the
    emerald night;

Thou hast hearts of gold within thee, hearts all priceless
    pearls above,
Rich with sweetness, rich with kindness, rich with never-
    dying love;

Thou hast dreams and aspirations sleeping with thy
    sheeted dead,
Wondrous visions, grand ambitions, from the earth for-
    ever fled.

Thou hast beauties in thy bosom blooming underneath
    our feet,
Lovelier than our purple lilacs and our jasmines soft and
    sweet;

Thou hast blue-eyed, dimpled children, with their mazy,
    golden hair,
Thou hast maids with brows of beauty, manly figures
    sleeping there.

Thou hast wisdom in thy bosom greater than the lore of
    earth,
Gathered by its gray-haired sages from the dim creation's
    birth;

Thou hast infants in thy bosom, learned in secrets whis-
    pered low,
Which our wise men seek forever, never find and can not
    know.

MARY

Of all the sweet names that ever were given
To mortals on earth or seraphs in heaven,
No matter if borne by milkmaid or fairy,
The sweetest of all must ever be Mary.

There's Helen, the star of song and of story,
Men perished to wreathe her ringlets with glory;
There also is Ruth, the true and the tender,
Whose meekness and faith make strong men surrender.

And Mabel's a name that ever sounds sweetly,
And charms and enchants a mortal completely,
While Katie suggests brown eyes and brown tresses,
Created for love and lover's caresses.

There's Maud, with a mouth as red as a cherry,
With kisses so sweet, with laughter so merry;
There's Edith, whose eyes are blue as the fountains,
With ringlets of gold like morn on the mountains.

There's Blanche and Adele, that sound autocratic,
Poor Sarah and Jane that dwell in an attic,
While Emma is dear, all dote upon Jenny,
And Annie is loved not least among many.

But never a name like Mary is spoken;
The dearest of dreams revive at that token;
Each other brings joy or brightness or sweetness,
But Mary alone has perfect completeness.

The lady high-born who reigns in a castle,
The widow forlorn, the spouse of the vassal,
The captive chained down in dungeon cell dreary,
The diademed queen, may bear the name Mary.

And Mary's the soul who opes the heart's portals,
A sweetheart, perchance, the dearest of mortals;
A sister, whose soul is dowered with beauty,
Or mother, who lives for love and for duty.

It was Mary who first shed tears of contrition,
It was she who was blest with God's greatest mission;
She stood by His Cross, she saw His tomb riven,
Her name shall be first on earth and in heaven.

TO ONE DEPARTED

Thy loving work is done forevermore,
Thy tender heart is free from all its cares,
For at the coming of the still, sad night,
Thy folded hands have won their final rest.
So thou art drawing near thy happy home,
With gladsome singing and with golden sheaves,
Fearing no foe amid the gloom of death,
Seeing beyond the radiant wings of dawn
The tufted palm trees of a paradise
With walls of jasper and with gates of gold.

Thy happy days, my dearest, have begun,
While we on earth are still amid our woes;
We can not dream of half thy boundless bliss,—
Our deepest joy would be a pain to thine.
Thou wert the fairest flower of the earth,
And now heaven claims thee as its loveliest star.

CONFIRMATION

The children, robed in spotless white, I see
Kneel for a blessing at the bishop's feet,
And, as I gaze upon their faces sweet,
As pure as doves, from stain of sin so free,
Before the priest whose sins unnumbered be,
Whose heart for selfish, sordid aims must beat,
I marvel why his blessing they entreat,
When he to them should rather bend the knee.

Dear little hearts, my soul adopts your creed;
Dear little feet, your pathway I shall share;
Dear little hands, my wanderings ye shall lead!
Dear little brows, guide with your golden hair;
Dear little lips, my God's forgiveness plead;
Dear little eyes, shine on my soul's despair!

ALONE IN NEW YORK

Far from familiar old-time haunts I tread,
  Far from remembered scenes of Tennessee;
A wilderness of walls I see instead,
  A surging ocean of humanity.

For leafy woods are piles of brick and stone;
  For grassy fields a million roofs arise;
For crooning winds, I hear the cable's groan;
  For lowing herds, I hear the huckster's cries.

No mocking-bird is singing to the breeze—
  I hear the roll of wagon wheels instead.
An iron eagle in his iron trees,
  The engine thunders swooping overhead.

Within the city park the sparrow cheeps,
  Consoling for the warble of a thrush;
Mechanic fountains make mechanic leaps
  To imitate the mountain torrent's rush.

The stiff, ungraceful walks, prim flower-beds,
  Show gaudy clumps of yellow, red or green;
The trim-clipped hedges lift their tawdry heads
  To vie with tangled wildwoods I have seen.

But here I came for sake of you, my Art,
  As I had promised in the long ago,
To follow you with ever-loyal heart,
  Though fame and fortune I might never know.

And though I tread alone, I feel your hand
  Slip into mine as in the dear old days;
And though a stranger in a stranger's land,
  I hear your footsteps all my crowded ways.

And though my heart aches as I go alone,
  And though mine eyes grow dim with unshed tears,
Although my bosom now is steel and stone,
  Unlike its old self of departed years;

And though at night I toss and toss awake,
  Within a garret, on a lowly bed;
Although my struggling spirit seems to break,
  When halcyon hopes and darling dreams have fled—

I hear you whisper: "Wait, O wait for dawn,
  When all heart-breaking anguish shall be through;
And should you win or lose, go on, go on,
  And still, brave heart, be true, be true, be true!"

ON RETURNING TO NEW YORK

Once more I see your towers touch the sky,
  And hear the sullen thunder of your street;
Once more I see your legions hurry by,
  And rush to join them with my restless feet.

I come not as I came in other days
  With ardent and enthusiastic soul,
When fame and fortune hovered in my gaze,
  And, near at hand, I thought I saw the goal.

Ah, surely things have sadly changed since then,
  When you were radiant with deceitful wiles;
A sorrow overclouds thy throngs of men,
  And sullen scowls erase thine olden smiles.

Plain and prosaic seem thy realms of joy,
O golden apple of my bygone themes,
O golden fleece that lured a foolish boy,
O priceless pearl, O diamond of my dreams!

Like Atalanta, fleetest of the fleet,
Thy lovers come to woo from far and nigh;
They run the race with thee, and in defeat
They bend the head beneath thy hand to die.

I shudder as I see thy crowded gate,
And outside, doubting and perplexed, I stand;
But now, I proudly come to face my fate,
With none to welcome, none to take my hand.

Yet, royal city, I have courage still,
A spirit that shall never bend the knee;
My soul is guarded with unconquered Will,
A sword I never shall surrender thee.

I give thee battle, and shall bravely smite,
For he who wins must woo thee with the sword;
My feet shall never safety seek in flight,
A coffin or a crown be my reward.

And there can be no abdication, save
When I throw down the sceptre that is mine;
If I should fall from glory to the grave,
My own hand must my own death-warrant sign.

He who relies upon his own right arm,
Nor fears his gauntlet at the foe to fling,
May drink of poisons, and they shall not harm,
And take up serpents, and they shall not sting.

ODE

FOR CHARTER DAY—NEW YORK, MAY 4, 1898

O Giant Empress of the Western World,
   Crown princess of the hopes of humankind,
What brilliant banners have thy sons unfurled!
   What gladsome garlands have thy daughters twined!
Resplendent at thy gateway of the sea,
   Thou holdest in thy hand the torch of Truth,
The greatest of the cities yet to be,
   In Oriental glory of thy youth.

The ancient East brings tribute unto thee,
   The pearls of Ceylon, spice of Hindu groves,
The silks of China, gums of Araby,
   The dates of Syria and Sumatra cloves.
France greets thee with the violet of her vines,
   And England with the fleeces of her looms;
Here palms of Cuba blend with Norway pines,
   And Greenland furs with Ethiopian plumes.

Yet all these glorious gifts shall pass away,
   Like Tyrian silver, Carthaginian gold,
And in some dim and undiscovered day
   Like fairy stories shall thy deeds be told.
In that far future none shall tribute bring,
   And none shall stand amazed before thy powers,
No poet shall thy strength and splendor sing,
   No monarch tremble at thy haughty towers.

So, stately city, ere thy youth be past,
   Let Goodness be thy daughter, Truth thy son;
Let Beauty be thy priestess to the last,
   Thy house their temple till the day is done.

Then in thy strength do deeds that can not die,
  Win honors that shall never pass their noon;
Let Art unite with Love to rear on high
  A palace like a lily 'neath the moon.

Lo! in thy million homes this very night,
  God sees thy children shed a flood of tears;
He sees the hungry stranger's piteous plight,
  And sees thee pass them by with deafened ears.
Though thou art rich, thine orphans cry for bread,
  Thy widows in their anguish weep aloud,
Thy wayward sons without thy palace tread,
  Thine erring daughters find thee cold and proud.

Take these upon their bosom, bind their wounds,
  And let thy boast be through the coming years,
"No man was ever hungry in my bounds,
  No woman wept, but that I dried her tears."
So then, O princess, bring thy cruse of oil,
  Like Mary, in her day of dark despair,
And wash His feet from dust of travel-toil,
  And dry them with the tresses of thy hair.

Then let years die and generations pass,
  Thy temples totter, palaces decay.
Though these may perish like the Summer grass,
  Thy greater glory shall not fade away.
For thou shalt raise an altar on this sod,
  Triumphant over funeral torch and bell,
O peerless daughter of the living God!
  O heroine who withstood the hosts of hell!

UNION SQUARE

I watch the water lilies in this pond,
  The white, the blue, the yellow and the red,
The sparrow tripping on their pads beyond,
  And splashing dewdrops on his wings and head.

The lotus, like a Cleopatra there,
  Reveals a bosom with a roseate glow,
As in her gorgeous old Egyptian lair
  She fascinated heroes long ago.

A-down the walk a throng of children goes
  With dewy eyes a-peep through hazy curls,
When years are poems, every month a rose,
  All morns are rubies and all noons are pearls.

Around these seats I see a motley crowd
  Of listless loungers, miserable and low,
With backs bent double, wrinkled faces bowed,
  Or, aimless, straggling by with footsteps slow.

With corncob pipes, these old men mumbling sit,
  Forsaken, friendless, waiting but for death,
When, like the dead leaves that around them flit,
  They fall to be forgotten in a breath.

And here a hard-faced girl reclines alone,
  Dreaming of dead days with their holy calm,
Before her happy heart was turned to stone,
  And slumber to her spirit brought no balm.

Here the young poet, once a farmer-boy,
  Who with glad heart unto the city came,
Sees manhood years his high-born hopes destroy,
  And slay his dreams of fortune and of fame.

When night descends, electric argent lamps
  Like radiant cactus blossoms blaze on high;
The city seems a world of war-like camps,
  While Broadway with its legions thunders by.

In gilt play-houses hundreds sigh to see
  The mimic woes of actors on the stage,
But not one tear for actual grief shall be,
  The snares for childhood or the pangs of age.

Around this Square rich men and women ride,
    Bedizened creatures in their fashion flaunt,
While this starved outcast, planning suicide,
    Steals back to perish in his dismal haunt.

Strange, while is known so well the sparrow's fall,
    Man heeds not when his brother's plaint is made;
Strange, that the brightest, whitest light of all
    Should cast the deepest and the darkest shade!

But still the world denies its helping hand
    To those most worthy of its love and care.
If Christ returned to-night, he too would stand
    Homeless and friendless, here on Union Square.

TO A STRANGER

Along a giant city's streets I go:
    Three million strangers right and left I see;
Three million faces I shall never know;
    Three million hearts, and not one heart for me!

O stranger passing by with careless glance,
    I long to greet you, long to know you well,
But still I falter, fearing to advance,
    My words of frienship in your ears to tell.

Your soul seems careless and your heart seems cold,
    Your eyes averted, lips a-curl with pride;
Yet half your secrets in your face are told,
    Your tragic story can not be denied.

Like you, such pride has made me lift my head
    When dull Despair was sitting in my heart,
Has made me smile when old-time friends have fled,
    And breathe defiance when my hopes depart.

[51]

Like you, O stranger, I have loved and lost,
  Like you, have seen my brave ambitions end,
Like you, on seas of sorrow have been tost,
  Like you, I seek a sympathetic friend.

Come, let me tell you secrets like your own,
  Till all your dull indifference shall depart,—
Truths that should melt a bosom wrought of stone,
  And bring the red sparks from a flinty heart.

For we were born to share this fleeting life,
  To tread the morning of one little day,
To feel the noontide sorrow, joy and strife,
  And in the selfsame twilight pass away.

Like mine, your heart is diamond clogged with clay,
  Your being dust and air and dew and fire,
And as you see earth's blossoms all decay,
  You gaze to heaven with untold desire.

For we are spirits manacled in sod,
  Two wandering heirs of all eternity,
Two exiled princes who are sons of God,
  Two blendings of the dust and deity.

A STRANGER IN LONDON

Here in the greatest city of the world
A hundred thousand people pass me by.
The old, the young, the rich, the poor I see,
All rushing on to different destinies.
I have no friend amid the swarming throng,
No man, no woman here gives thought to me.
I never saw one being here before,
Nor shall I see one being here again.

Alone, deserted in this stranger land,
I feel my utter insignificance,
And say, "It matters not what one may be,
What one may plan, his dreams, his destiny,
Since all his life is merest nothingness."

And then I turn, and hurrying swiftly by,
A careless stranger almost touches me.
I ask him to direct me to a place
Which I have sought an hour or more in vain.
Then all at once his half-impatient face
Breaks in a kindly and good-natured smile.
Not only does he tell me how to go,
Which way to turn, and where to find my place,
But suddenly he says: "Come, go with me;
I'll show the way myself." Though I protest,
He leads the whole way, till we reach the spot.

And so we part. A pleasant good-bye next,
A friendly smile from him and thanks from me,
And then I see him lost amid the crowd.
I never saw the stranger's face before,
And never shall I see his face again.

And yet, O stranger, you have taught me this:
All men are brothers! Though the nations fight
For fancied wrongs, and though the poor and weak
Must bleed and die to glorify the Great,
I feel that artificial boundaries,
Frontiers and outposts, cannot make us foes.
The little deed of kindness you have done
Shows all mankind are kinsmen unto me,
That you and I, contemporaries, friends,
Put here to share our portion of the earth,
And born to live the selfsame day and time,
Are children of the true and only God.

ODE

For the Semi-centennial Celebration of the Founding
of the Sigma Chi Fraternity, Oxford,
Ohio, June 28, 1905.

A half a hundred years ago to-day
   Seven youths joined hands to consecrate this shrine,
Where friendship's fires might never fade away,
   But glow forever with a flame divine.

Youth is the father of all fellowship,
   Begetter of the Brotherhood of Men.
Oh, when his suns in twilight darkness dip,
   The old-time thrills are never known again!

We drift on desert seas of selfishness,
   When cold Indifference steers the bark alone;
We heed no shipwreck's signals of distress,
   Forgetting others' miseries in our own.

But here we anchor for one happy day,
   And tread old memory-gardens of the past,
To pledge old friendships, made in morns of May—
   God grant them leal and loyal to the last!

Let Youth's pink roses twine through locks of Age;
   Come back, dear boy-hearts, from your tombs of yore!
Oh, let us read once more from this sweet page
   Of a lost volume we shall clasp no more!

Come, let us gather, old-time friends, again,
   Within the temple we have loved so long;
See here the old ideals, free from stain,
   The old-time precepts, sweet as heavenly song.

Here, like the seven golden candlesticks
   Beheld by John on Patmos long ago,
Seven lights are set, on which our eyes may fix,
   To guide our feet when darkness comes below.

One candlestick is Friendship, one is Truth,
　　And one is Faith, and Hope another yet;
And one is Peace, and one called Glow of Youth,
　　With Love high over all the others set.

Oh, be they not like torches quenched in strife,
　　Nor light of Laodicea, soon to wane,
But true as Smyrna, crowned with endless life,
　　And steadfast as the Philadelphian fane!

THE TREE IN THE CITY

Amid the fret and fever of the street,
Calm, peaceful and serene this giant stands;
Amid the strife, the worry of the town,
His mighty heart remains in deep repose;
Among the seething multitudes of men,
Their restlessness cannot disturb his rest.
I watch the emerald ocean of his leaves,
And every heaving billow speaks of joy—
The joy of living, joy of strength and health,
Of peace of mind, of duty well performed.
For he has kept the law with God and man,
Done well his part, nor sought to shun his lot;
So, hearty, hale and wholesome, he uprears
In green old age a tower of hardihood.
Like some old man whose youth was free from blame,
Whose temperate manhood brought him no reproach,
He reaps the rich rewards of goodly years,
Erect and strong in gray magnificence.

I see him, and I tread old times again,
A barefoot boy upon my father's farm.
I hear the warble of a wheatfield quail,
I gather sprays of dewy wilding flowers,
I breathe soft odors of the apple blooms,
And hear the cowbells tinkling in the lane.

A schoolboy in the old schoolhouse again,
I hear the children droning at their books,
I see my little sweetheart's soft brown eyes.

O patriarch of the multitudious leaves,
Content and calm amid this rush and roar,
Still uncontaminated in this strife,
Free from repining for the fields or woods—
Teach me the grandeur of thy deep repose,
Teach me the glory of thy goodly soul,
That I may walk with conscience undisturbed
Amid the struggle in the marts of men!

THE CHARMS OF THE CITY

Though misanthropes may praise the country more,
And turn from mankind to some rude retreat,
I seek the City, with its rush and roar,
Its eager and enthusiastic street.
I turn from fellowship of beast and bird,
The coarse backwoodsman and unlettered swain,
To where heart-blood of humankind is stirred,
To share my brother's pleasure and his pain.

I love the City's wilderness of stone,
Its flags, like scarlet poppies in the air,
Where Wealth erects a gold and silver throne,
And Fashion charms with silk and satin snare.
I love its splendid shops, where jewels blaze,
And crystals glitter like a starry crown,
With mirrors, plumes and laces, like a maze,
With furs and velvets, soft as thistle-down.

I walk its midnight meadows, and I mark
The flaming lamps of red and blue and white,—
Its dazzling daisies, come to cheer the dark,
Its morning-glories, born to bless the night.

O flaming flowers of the City's gloom,
You shine through Summer, Winter, Fall and Spring,
When snowflakes flutter on the tulip's tomb,
When leaves are brown, and birds have ceased to sing.

I turn from bobolinks in cherry trees
To sweet girl-faces dimpling in delight,
Their rosy ribbons flitting in the breeze,—
Seraphic doves in plumes of pink and white.
I love to pet these mischief-making boys
Whose eyes are twinkling stars in dewy dawns,
More nimble than the squirrels, full of noise,
More wild and wilful than a flock of fawns.

O, why should man seek soulless solitude,
From life and love to desert caves depart?
Nay, give me friends of sympathetic mood,
To share my spirit, understand my heart!
With friends like these I fill my pipe and smoke,
And brim the mug with brown Autumnal brew;
We talk together till the midnight stroke,
On themes delightful to the Chosen Few.

I see the play, and Shakespeare speaks once more
The masterpieces of his matchless art.
I hear the lecture; Science bids me soar,
And draw the mystic veils of God apart.
I read the papers, and I see all strands,
I live through peace and war, on field and flood;
I dwell in Europe, roam Sahara sands,
And all the wide world is my neighborhood.

I love the City's darkness and despair,
Its grandeur, grief, its glory and its gloom;
My brother's bliss and bitterness I share,
And with him march to meet the Common Doom.

I love the lights that glitter through its dusk
Like star-strewn skies downfallen from above;
I crave the fruitage of its iron husk,
Red-veined with life-blood from the breast of love.

Though buds may blossom, Autumn foliage flush,
This laughing girl is lovelier than them all;
More charming than a blackbird or a thrush,
The schoolboy's whistle and the newsboy's call.
Let hermit heed the babble of the brooks,
Let anchorites be comrades of the clod;
I turn from sticks and stones to read good books,
And study Man, the first-born son of God.

SUNRISE IN THE COUNTRY

I have grown weary of the noise and dust,
Weary of heat, and smoky, fetid air;
But now at last I walk in the country lanes,
And drink cool breezes of the flowery fields.

No more I vex to hear the trolley's gong,
I hear instead the bells of grazing cows;
The rattling and the rumbling hucksters' carts
Are now forgotten as I hear a thrush;
The shriek of locomotives now is still,
And in its stead I hear the crowing cock.
The clanging chimes of churches are forgot
In chirp of bluejays and in hum of bees.

I rise when dews bespangle fern and flower,
When farmer boys go whistling at the plow,
When mocking-birds are sprinkling showers of song,
And leaves are dancing for the joy of life.
How fresh, how cool, how pure the morning air!
I drink it as some rare elixir, brewed
To give my soul an everlasting life,
And give my body never-dying youth.

The bubbling spring from white Olympian snows
Leaps not more fresh for goblets of the gods.
O, let me watch the rising of the sun
With scarlet robe and diadem of fire,
Through roses dewy with the morning stars,
And clouds embroidered with a cloth of gold.
He comes in glory and in majesty,
He comes in splendor and sublimity.
Now, as I hear the wrens trill matin hymns,
And hear a million crickets chirp his praise,
As slender leaves pour forth libation dews,
And fields of corn salute with banners green,
My soul remembers old forgotten faiths
Taught in the tents by far-off Eastern palms;
With old ancestors on the desert sands
It bends its knees in worship of the sun.

O, let me drink this bracing morning breeze,
And fiery liquors shall my lips disdain.
I quaff the cooling goblet to its depth,
And hate the riotous revel yesternight.
Here is a brew that makes the spirit glad,
Yet never makes a misery shadow mirth;
Here is a cup to give the bosom cheer,
Without the poison of the serpent's sting.

I see this yellow primrose, and my heart
Forgets the bitter quarrel yesterday;
This dewy dandelion gives me gold
Worth more than that I lost in city marts;
This silver-throated quail shall drive away
My vain regrets for follies of the past;
This warbling grosbeak makes my heart forgive
The friend who proved me false on yesterweek;
This morning-glory, dangling with its dews,
Gives power to smile at scowls of enemies.

O, I have known the poignant pangs of love,
And felt its baneful fevers in my blood,
My heart has melted with its hot desire,
And grown delirious, fierce with passion-fire.
My soul has burned beneath seductive smiles,
And reeled from daggers of disdainful eyes.
Oft have I tossed in dreams of fancied bliss,
Only to wake with empty, aching arms.
My blood has boiled, impatient for its own,
And frozen when its loved one gave it scorn.
My limbs have wearied in a hot pursuit
Of clasps and kisses fraught with wild unrest.

Come to the country! See the sun arise,
And all ferocious passions then shall flee.
Behold this pied wood-lily, and be cured
Of poison that distills from dark brown eyes.
Wade barefoot in this brook, and you shall pine
Not for the fairest face in all the world.
Hark to the field-lark's note, and find release
From all the pangs of unrequited love.

MOUNTAIN BROOK

Mountain brook, wild mountain brook,
Roaring through this rocky nook,
Tell me why you twist and toss
On from couch to couch of moss?
Tell me why your spirit yearns,
Heedless of caressing ferns,
And the laurel's pleading look
As she begs you linger, brook?

Hear the murmur of the pines,
Heed the kiss of columbines:
How they call to you to stay
Ere you leap your headlong way!

Yet in foaming haste you go,
Far from parent peaks of snow,
Leaping cream-white cascades down,
Speeding to yon lowland town.

Pause, O, pause before you leap
Down this vine-entangled steep!
Linger here with peaks of snow
Flushed with morn's carnation glow;
Linger here in hemlock bowers,
Play with rhododendron flowers;
Linger here in youth and joy,
Like a bonny blithesome boy!

In that soiled and sinful town
Crystal waves are smirched with brown;
Soon your airy white attire
Draggles in the murky mire;
You shall curdle green with scum,
And your happy voice grow dumb.
Ere you leap, I beg you look,
Pure and peerless mountain brook!

But, you answer, "I must go
Far through panting plains below;
I must rescue fainting wheat
Drooping in the brazen heat;
I must bear to parching corn
Vigor of this mountain morn;
I must bring from melting snows
Blood for blushes on the rose.

"I must come to aid of men
In yon far-off huddled den;
Rush where huts and hovels scowl
Over alleys close and foul.

I must make the factory hum,
Though it curdle me with scum.
I must cleanse the sink and sewer
Though they make myself impure."

Mountain brook, wild mountain brook,
Heaven had planned the course you took.
Though the blossom soon must fade,
Though the leaf soon hangs decayed;
Though the star must sink in gloom,
Though I soon shall seek the tomb;—
Let us go with gladsome look,
God's hand leading, mountain brook.

BOHEMIA

Bohemia, Bohemia,
The land of verdant hills,
Of clustered vineyards, flowery fields,
Of blue and bubbling rills!
I love your orchards and your farms,
Your gardens neat and trim,
Your rocky rivers, crystal-clear,
With shouting boys a-swim.

Bohemia, Bohemia,
You give your charming name
To comrade-life, to fellowship,
To life that leads to fame.
And every woman, every man
Among the Faithful Few,
Bohemia, Bohemia,
Is always named for you.

Bohemia, Bohemia,
The Kingdom of Good Cheer,
Of tankards crowned with feathery foam,
From mellow golden beer.
The land that Shylocks ever shun,
That makes the dunces rage,
But where the Chosen People come
To live their Golden Age.

Bohemia, Bohemia,
The realm of poetry,
Of romance, story and of song,
Of love and loyalty!
The home of splendid girls and boys,
The land of dear delights,
Of happy morns, of blissful noons,
And passion-pulsing nights.

Bohemia, Bohemia,
Since first I loved your name,
Fond hopes have sped, sweet dreams have fled,
And youth has lost its flame.
Yet young and joyous, old and gray,
Your lover tried and true,
Bohemia, Bohemia,
Is faithful still to you!

Bohemia, Bohemia,
When I your flag unfurled,
The smiles of Fortune changed to frowns,
For you I lost the world.
But let the Gentiles go their way,
And let the heathen bawl,—
Bohemia, Bohemia,
You're ten times worth them all!

PASADENA

Pasadena, charming town,
Wears a fruit-and-flower crown.
There the tendrils, boughs and twigs
Bend with lemons, grapes or figs.
Purple bougainvillea vines
Interlace with palms and pines,
And the buff and crimson cannas
Wave beside broad-leaved bananas.

In the dallying ocean breeze
Swing the feathery pepper-trees;
Here nasturtiums, orange-red,
Wreathe the scarlet salvia-bed;
Here are lilies, pink or pied,
Spotted like a leopard's hide;
Here the marigold in yellow
Mocks the apricot grown mellow.

Morning-glories float and flow
Like a cloud of indigo;
Blooming eucalyptus trees'
Blood-hued clusters tempt the bees;
Rank geraniums fringe the ways
With a splendid sunset blaze;
Like a flame-robed Witch of Endor
Yon hibiscus shines in splendor.

Green pomegranates' blossom-stars
Glare and glow like angry Mars;
Here lantana clusters burn,
Trumpet-flowers with passion yearn.
Here are cactus, fuschia, rose,
Oleanders' fragrant snows,
Blue solanum, red tacoma,
Heliotrope with blest aroma.

[64]

Here are scattered on her slopes
Strawberries, melons, cantaloupes;
Here the golden orange clings,
Here the odorous grape-fruit swings.
Here are dangling in your reach
Olive, plum, and pear and peach,
Purple aster, red verbena,
Saffron poppy,—Pasadena!

CARROLL VANCE

We sigh because you passed away so young,
   Forsaking us, who wander still below,
When life was like a lute with strings unstrung,
   A-thrill with music Earth may never know.

But we, not you, deserve the piteous plaint,
   The sob, the sigh, the wringing of the hands,
Soul freed at last from every mortal taint,
   Among the lilies of enchanted lands!

For us, the slowly creeping steps of age,
   For you, the halcyon heart forever young;
For us, the garment soiled, the blotted page,
   For you, the glory of the songs unsung.

For us, the sad September's withered sheaves,
   For you, the peach-blooms of an April day;
For us, the numb November's hectic leaves,
   For you, the verdure of the morns of May.

Best is that death when Life is in its Spring,
   When morning skies are gowned in blue and gold,
Before one bird has ever ceased to sing,
   And not one forest leaf has yet grown old.

Ah, kindly Fate, forever thus to be,
　　When Love, the wild gazelle, treads not amiss,
When pearly-footed Youth forbears to flee,
　　And dimpled Joy defers his farewell kiss!

For you, assassin Autumn never comes
　　To stab white-blossomed Summer to the heart,
No winds of Winter beat their muffled drums
　　To bid the brilliant tropic birds depart.

You shall not see Hope's shattered roses strewn,
　　Nor golden locks flecked into frosty gray,
Nor learn the disillusions of the noon,
　　Nor see at last Affection's dull decay.

For you no fairy story came untrue,
　　No Gospel seemed unworthy of belief;
The peasant still will be king to you,
　　And every wisp of tares a golden sheaf.

Rest, calm and peaceful; you have naught to fear,
　　Who drove all hate and malice from your side,
Nor gave one being cause to shed a tear,
　　Until that day, dear boy, on which you died.

THE ALPS

Fresh air, green grass, and water crystal-clear,
　　Dew-sprinkled meadows, forests cool and dark,
These bid good-morning to the mountaineer
　　Who whistles as his waking watch-dogs bark.

Steep daisy-dappled pastures, grazing cows,
　　And scattered sheep with tiny bells a-ring;
A deep calm pool, with overhanging boughs,
　　Where early birds, from sleep awakened, sing.

An apple orchard, mossy, gnarled and old,
   Clings to a crag with bony-finger roots;
Wild flowers, pure as vestals, brave the cold,
   Their odors frail as notes from fairy flutes.

A peasant's cottage clutches to a cliff,
   A rocky pasture feeds a flock of goats;
And then a breeze comes in a sudden whiff,
   And over all a cloudy curtain floats.

A brawling brook with rustic bridge is seen,
   And girls with pitchers coming to a spring,
Far down below, the lake lies glossy green,
   With snowy sails like swans upon the wing.

Here, fragile as two airy wisps of lace,
   From mossy rocks twin cascades leap and call;
Another quivers with a plume-like grace,
   And others still in thundering torrents fall.

Some sparkle like a radiant shower of gems,
   And some are misty as a cloud of cream;
They grace the ferns with dewy diadems,
   And weave their rainbows like a seraph's dream.

The cascades echo to the hunter's horn,
   The cascades waft soft incense from the sod;
These are the goblets whence the hand of Morn
   Pours out libations at the feet of God.

Here lies the land from tyrant fetters freed,
   Where Liberty forevermore shall dwell.
Here every bird sings praise to Winkleried,
   And every mountain speaks of William Tell.

Far on the top of yonder stormy peak
   The unblest bones of Pontius Pilate lie;
In vain his ghost a resting place shall seek,—
   For in the tomb his memories will not die!

High over all rise peaks on peaks of snow,
   White-robed and silent, stately and sublime;
Their age, their birth, no man shall ever know;
   Their crowns shall glitter to the end of time.

O awful white-browed ministers of God,
   No storms can ever rend your steadfast thrones;
In vain the thunders shake your quivering sod,
   In vain the lightnings shiver through your stones.

The Cæsars and Napoleons all have gone,
   Dark Hannibal no longer roves at will;
Yet pure and white as at primeval dawn
   The day of judgment shall behold you still.

Like grateful Noah's smoking sacrifice
   On Ararat, when earth was flood-restored,
Your altars, clouded with their incense, rise
   In everlasting glory to the Lord.

THE BAY OF NAPLES

Here bends the road around a mountain-side,
   With laurels twined in myrtles like a hedge;
Beneath the cliff, in comes the ocean tide,
   And breaks in billows on a rocky ledge.

A sulphur-yellow crescent, sweeps the town
   Around the bay, as blue as indigo;
Vesuvius, smoking, lifts a cone of brown
   Above the terraced villas strewn below.

Here claret-colored dahlias fringe the wall,
   While cactus fattens on the ruined tombs,
And like a splendid purple waterfall,
   The morning-glories hang their heavenly blooms.

Here golden-globuled oranges swing low,
    With breath as sweet as songs of Paradise;
Pomegranate blossoms in vermilion glow,
    And mottled pansies open argus eyes.

A weeping willow overhangs the way,
    A eucalyptus rears toward the sky;
Pears, over-ripe, slow falling day by day,
    In scattered red and yellow clusters lie.

A herd of goats creeps trudging through the dust,
    An old hag prods them with a splintered beam;
An ancient water-wheel, a-creak with rust,
    Turned by a donkey, pours a little stream.

A friar, robed in black, and sleek and fat,
    Smiles forth a Pax Vobiscum passing by;
A purple tassel in his glossy hat
    Is dancing to the twinkle in his eye.

A mother in her peasantry finery dressed
    Smiles proudly on you like a festal morn,
As if to say the urchin at her breast
    Is finest of all babies ever born.

And now the beggars in battalions come,
    The old, the young, the crippled and the blind,
The halt, the lame, the deaf, deformed and dumb,
    Some running fast, some hobbling up behind.

As graceful as gazelles, with slender feet,
    With glossy curls, brown cheeks and dewy eyes,
The beggar boys and girls their woes repeat,
    And storm your heart with piteous smiles and sighs.

A lad sits here, a melon in his lap,
    Its crimson pulp is melting in his mouth;
Here figs in baskets ooze with honeyed sap,—
    The trickling sultry-sweetness of the South.

[69]

Some ear-ringed, turbaned sailors on a boat
   Dance while the vagabond musicians play;
The sounds of flute and violin afloat
   Soothe into dreams the eyes of dozing day.

O violin, chained in your fiery strings,
   Italia, like a bird within a cage,
Of all her woe, her grief and glory sings,
   Her love, her hate, her anguish and her rage!

A lovely barefoot girl before me stands,
   Her oval face like sunset-crimsoned dusk;
From tattered sleeves she lifts imploring hands,—
   A Queen of Beauty begging for a husk.

O barefoot beggar-maid, I fear your kiss,
   I fear the glory of your twilight eyes!
Thorns mingle in the blossoms of your bliss,
   You smite the strong, you stultify the wise.

Behind your smile I see the scowl of hate,
   Your dimple hides a dagger like a sheath;
Beside you is the warning face of Fate,
   To love you means to play at dice with Death.

For over there the hills of Capri swell,
   Like deep blue clouds afloat in pale blue skies,
Where dark Tiberius learned his lesson well,—
   All earthly joys and ecstacies are lies!

And, silent, over all Vesuvius looms,
   Like Gabriel waiting for the Judgment Day,
When Naples shall become a waste of tombs,
   And all this youth and beauty pass away.

THE LAURELS

Along the noisy city streets I go,
  Unknown, unheeded by the careless throng;
But in my heart I feel a morning glow,
  And on my lips the spirit of a song.

All unbefriended, I receive no smiles,
  And feel no pressure of a helping hand;
Yet I have journeyed for a thousand miles
  To win a triumph in this alien land.

But lo! Success awaits me as my bride,
  Crowned with a crown of gold, and robed in white,
And there I see my handmaids at her side,
  Fame on her left and Fortune on her right.

O high-born lady, I have come to woo,
  And I shall win you by the force of will;
Do not deny me! When I come for you
  No fortress can withstand my strength and skill.

What though the rabble turns away from me?
  What though my rights have been withheld for
    years?
That rabble shall my brilliant victory see,
  And change their servile hisses into cheers.

What though pretenders now usurp my throne?
  What though imposters now my sceptre wield?
I bravely come to battle for my own,
  And charlatans who trespass all must yield.

What though my heart has felt corroding care?
  What though I wince from iron fangs of want?
My soul will grapple with, and choke Despair,
  And strangle Hunger, though his jaws be gaunt.

What though I clutch with pinching poverty?
  What though the honors now are claimed by **knaves**?
All foes were raised before my face to flee,
  And all privations born to be my slaves.

Chance, stand aside! I do not bow to you;
  Success, strew laurels, and my triumph sings!
Behold, you now shall give me tribute due,
  And make obeisance to your rightful king!

THE SOLDIER OF FORTUNE

I seek for gold in Klondike mountain snow,
  And diamonds in the Transvaal waste afar;
I dive for pearls where Ceylon currents flow,
  And gather furs beneath the polar star.

I hook the spouting whale in seas to south,
  I gather corals by Sicilian strands;
I hunt for amber at the Baltic's mouth,
  And ivory far beyond Sahara sands.

A bare-foot boy, I leave the prosy farm
  To make my fortune in the marts of men;
With not a friend but one unconquered arm
  I beard the Monster, London, in his den.

In rags and tatters, seeking wealth and fame,
  I sweat, I struggle over all to rise;
I fight, I bleed, I win a noble name,
  And stab my Evil Fortune till he dies.

A beggar lad, I carve, I sing, I paint,
  Till laurel leaf and myrtle bough are mine;
Supernal Beauty, free from mortal taint,
  Beneath my brush and chisel wakes divine.

Unknown, disdained, I strike the poet's lyre,
    And maidens scatter roses in my path;
A peasant soldier, under fiercest fire,
    I snatch a red wreath from the brow of Wrath.

I am the slayer of the dragon Fear;
    The traitor, Chance, must cringe to me as lord;
All foes are frightened when my name they hear,
    All opposition flees before my sword.

Why should I quail because a woman frowns?
    Why should I whine because she turns away?
I am no trailer after girlish gowns;
    Maids were not born to rule me, but obey.

A world of women waits me to be won,
    And woman's kisses are the victor's right;
I cull the loveliest under every sun,
    Beneath the Southern Cross or Northern Light.

All things are mine.   I do not fear or flinch.
    All fruits, all flowers I claim by right of birth.
I fear no foe; I never yield an inch;
    I conquer all the kingdoms of the earth.

THE SLEEPING IDLERS

St. James Park

Stretched on the grass the weary outcasts lie;
    No one disturbs them in their heavy sleep;
Though London like an ocean thunders by,
    It leaves them stranded in its onward sweep.

These are the men who lost the game of life,
    These are the men whom Failure calls her own.
Success forsook them in the selfish strife,
    With broken blades and banners overthrown.

Here lie the vanquished on a battlefield
   More vast than any history's page can show.
Bowed in defeat, they drop the spear and shield,
   And only beg for quarter from the foe.

Yet ah, what hopes they had in youthful years,
   When marching proudly forth to fight the world!
Then came the toil, the sweat, the blood and tears,
   And foes in overwhelming columns hurled.

Where now the songs of triumph that they sung,
   Where now the blazoned banners lifted high?
Ah, who can sing with heart no longer young,
   And one is only waiting here to die?

Gone are the glories that they strove to win,
   Their dreams of fame and fortune all have fled;
They huddle here in misery, shame and sin,
   Their bodies living, though their souls are dead.

But still your jealous Mother guards your sleep,
   And bids you good-night when your sun has set;
Be sure a faithful vigil she will keep,
   For England claims you as her children yet.

Though she has sons who wooed and won success,
   Whose memories she records in bronze and stone,
Because you failed she does not love you less,
   But clasps you to her bosom as her own.

And it is well.   For some who fight must fail,
   Must play their part like those who fight and win.
Is not the price of bliss another's bale?
   Is glory not the flaming flower of sin?

Then let them sleep, and dream that life is sweet,
   That friends are firm, that men can never lie,
Forgetting Love hath wings on truant feet,
   That days will come when one may wish to die.

And when the feverish noon of life is past
  They reach the end appointed at our birth;
They gain what weary emperors crave at last,—
  A long, long sleep on breast of Mother Earth.

THE RIGHT TO WORK

There is work for all the millions, whether on the sea or
    land;
Every human being's birthright brings a task unto his
    hand.

Earth is ready for the toiler who may come to sow and
    reap,
Ready for the delving miner, for the sailor on the deep.

There are golden grains to garner, there are silver mines
    to dig,
There are gardens of the melon, orchards of the peach
    and fig.

There are pearls for every diver, corals waiting in the caves,
There is wealth of mellow amber in the sweep of ocean
    waves.

There are purpled-treasured vineyards, dangling with de-
    licious wines,
Hives that overflow with honey, woods of oaks and elms
    and pines.

There is work in forge and furnace, manufactory and mill,
Work in farm and work in foundry, street of city, country
    hill.

Work for poet, work for painter, work for him who carves
    and sings,
Coming with an inspiration like the touch of angel wings.

And that longing for their labor in the freeman's hearts
    shall be
Like the green blood of the springtime, tingling in the
    turf and tree.

They are coming not as beggars, but as men demanding
    work;
Not as vagabonds or vagrants, but as men who scorn to
    shirk.

They are mouthing not for mercy,—justice only they de-
    mand,
For the right to share the blessings of their great Creator's
    hand.

Not for alms these men are asking, but the right to share
    the earth,
Right to build, create, to chisel, right to claim their royal
    birth.

But the Masters of the Market, bloated with their sense
    of might,
Seek to wring from struggling brothers this their imme-
    morial right.

As in brutal barbarous ages, they have dealt in souls of
    men,
And humanity is bartered in these latter days as then.

In their train is heard the murmur of a thousand million
    slaves,
And behind them is a desert of a thousand million graves.

So the tramp, the prowling vagrant, maddened for the
    want of bread,
Makes the beggar, thief or robber, bends with shame his
    childrens' head.

So the homeless, hungry outcast, stealing sleepless through
     the night,
Seeks in suicide a refuge from a world where Might is
     Right.

So at last the ruined woman, once unscarred by brand
     of blame,
Walks the streets of wicked cities dealing in a life of shame.

Lo! the Masters of the Market dine from gold and silver
     plate,
Parks and palaces surround them in their insolence of
     state.

They have seized the fruits of labor, snatched the bread
     from those who toiled,
They have crushed the patient peasant, all his vineyards
     have despoiled.

While they seek their selfish pleasures, Lazarus at their
     gateway lags,
While their wives are decked with jewels, peasant wives
     are hung with rags.

While their darling dogs are petted, children cry from
     wasting want,
While their stables all are sumptuous, men go wandering
     pinched and gaunt.

They deny to manly merit this one right to manly toil,
They deny to God's own children God's own fruits of sea
     and soil.

Let them tremble! in the future looms the iron face of
     Fate;
Let them tremble! no intrenchments shall protect their
     guilty state.

For the wrath of millions gathers in an overwhelming
    flood,
And their march shall be resistless, and their cry be
    "Bread or Blood!"

THE KLONDIKE

I

Wrapped in a robe of everlasting snow,
Where icy blasts eternal revel hold,
Where gaunt pines shiver in the piercing cold,
Where mellow summer noontides never glow,
And sleety crags no springtime ever know—
Thus, like a miser, in his freezing fold,
The Arctic King has gathered heaps of gold
To lead deluded wanderers unto woe.

So in his radiant diamond palace there,
Amid white splendors of his thousand thrones,
Where keen auroras glitter, blaze and glare,
And like a wandering Jew the wild wind moans,
He smiles at wretches in their last despair,
Who dig for gold among their comrades' bones.

II

About my home I see the springtime bloom,
The sheaves of summer or the autumn fruits;
To make me glad, the robin lends his lute,
The lilies blossom, lilacs breathe perfume,
The red leaves flutter, golden asters loom.
Around me, tones of loved ones, never mute,
Are sweeter than the viol or the flute
Through June-time gladness or December gloom.

The daffodils their golden treasures pour
By lapfuls to my children as they play;
The vines, with clustered rubies at my door,
Gladden my good wife through the livelong day;
So in this humble nest, my wealth is more
Than all the gold and silver dug from clay.
  1897.

SUCCESS AND FAILURE

One is a maiden crowned with locks of gold,
  With cheeks like morning in the summer skies;
Around her, silken garments float and fold,
  And gems are gleaming with their peacock eyes.

The other is her sister, thoughtful-browed,
  With ashen tresses and with eyes of gray,
With shades of sadness lingering like a cloud
  Upon a visage like an autumn day.

One, like an empress, holds the world in thrall,
  And millions prostrate lie before her car;
Her subjects dwell in every hut and hall,
  And swarms of flatterers seek her from afar.

The other is forsaken by the world,
  Forgotten by the fickle sons of men;
Beside her, tattered conquered flags are furled
  That never in the skies shall float again.

One is attended by the rich and proud,
  Praised by the voice of princes, queens and kings;
To welcome her, the drum is beat aloud,
  The bell goes pealing, and the cymbal rings.

One is attended by the friendless poor,
    The sunburnt peasant and the burdened slave;
No callers ever knock upon her door,
    Her hearth is lonesome as an unknown grave.

One counts the smooth time-server in her train,
    The crafty courtier and the fawning friend,
Him, who like Faust, would sell his soul for gain,
    And him who filches means to win the end.

The other notes the unknown soldier's name,
    And gives the homeless poet sympathy;
She cheers the martyr on his couch of flame,
    And teaches countless heroes how to die.

The names they bear on earth need not be told;
    But God will crown the one we love the less;
He calls her "Failure," who hath locks of gold,
    And names her gray-haired sister there, "Success."

PRAYER BEFORE PLANTING TREES

Lord, we are setting in this chosen ground
These tender nurselings, trusting in Thy grace
To cherish them through infancy, to guide
Their tiny rootlets through the darksome earth,
To lift their boughs to heaven, and give them power
To yield their tribute unto grateful men
In fruit or flower or shade.   For who but Thou,
And Thou alone, O God, amidst the gloom
Of never-ending night beneath the sod,
Can weave the network of those fragile roots,
And make their long antennae feel the way
To nooks of moisture and fertility?

And who but Thou can pilot up the stem
The warm sweet sap, like green blood making glad
The veinlets of the utmost little twig?
And who but Thou, O Lord, in mystic wise,
With alchemy divine, can from the earth,
This sordid earth, extract pure essences
To paint the cheeks of blossoms, scent their breath,
To swell the fruits with lusciousness, and make
The leafy boughs one mass of heavenly green,
Haunts for the song-birds, cool retreats for men?

Yea, all these powers are Thine.   But on this day,
In lowly imitation of Thine own
Parental care, we plant these infant trees
To be a blessing in the far-off years
Unto our children and our childrens' children,
When we ourselves shall tread the earth no more.
Unselfish in Thy bounty, Thou hast strewn
Blessings around us, though partaking not
Thyself of that abundance which Thy hand
Alone created.   In the by-gone years,
To please us Thou hast reared Thy goodly trees,
Glowing with fruitage, spreading green with shade,
Or clustered with delightsome odorous blooms.
Shall we Thy largess take with selfish ease,
And not in some small way, though feeble, seek
To emulate Thy goodness, and bequeath
Unto succeeding generations, gifts
We never can share ourselves?   O God of Love,
Make us unselfish in this task: our hearts
Uplift; and move our hands to speed with joy
In this, our labor, whereby we shall seek
To bless the lives of others yet to come,
When we ourselves have mingled with the dust
Wherein we plant these trees.

In days to be,
When we are long forgotten, may these boughs
Rustle with gladness in the winds of Spring:
Amongst them let the thrush at dusk and dawn,
And the sweet mock-bird on moon-silvered nights,
Warble their wildwood lays: here let the dove,
Soft-cooing, woo his mate, and wooing, win,
So that the two together here may brood
Over their nest of love.   Upon these boughs,
From April unto April, June to June,
Hang the soft blossoms through the emerald glooms,
Wafting sweet odors, and with honey-dew
Burdening the murmuring bees.   Here let the sheep
And cattle through the fervid blaze of noon,
Chewing the cud, dozing and drowsing, rest
Free from the torrid glare.   Here hang Thy fruits,
Ruddy or tawny, apple, peach or pear,
To make the hearts of barefoot urchins glad
When school is over, and the lads go free,
Shouting and romping noisily: for they,
O Father, are Thy children, and we know
Their clamorous joyhood Thou wilt mark with smiles,
Pleased that these thoughtless ones are happy.   Here
Let gentle lovers in the friendly shades,
With scattered petals at their feet, and songs
Of sweet encouragement from sprays above,
Wander in joy, and vow the dear old vows
Of love that we ourselves, in our lost youth
Of forgotten years of long ago,
Were thrilled with bliss to hear.

And in those days,
Dear Father, when our names from minds of men
Have all been canceled, and we lie alone,
Forsaken and forgotten, dust in dust,
Perchance Thine eyes may look upon these trees,

Still hale and green and sturdy, and Thy heart
Incline to pity and to mercy: so
For sake of these, from records of our souls
Thy hand may blot some past transgression.   Then,
O Father, as Thou liftest up to heaven
The tree in verdure and in flower and fruit,
Uplift us likewise from our dungeon-cell
In the dark earth, and in the radiant skies
Let us rejoice to see Thy Light again.

TO MIKE CONNOLLY ON HIS 62nd BIRTHDAY

Mike!   You have lived to see another Spring
Coming in joyous triumph as of old,
And you shall hear once more the red-bird sing,
And see the hyacinth sprouting from the mould.

Yes, we are still here.   But the friends we knew
In many a happy scene of youthful days,
Have left us.   Though a thousand trumpets blew,
None could recall them to our earthly ways.

Yea, though the Springtime pours her gentle showers,
And bids the ice-bound rills of Winter flow,
Though all her songsters greet her opening flowers,
She wakens not the sleepers there below.

But we, the friends still left thee by the years,
After thy long life's double share of pain
Rejoice to see thee spared the fatal shears,
Not young indeed, yet not upon the wane.

Not perfect thou!   No, not a tiresome saint
Sent to reproach us with thy faultlessness,
And chain good fellowship in dull restraint,—
Wert thou less faulty we had loved thee less!

[83]

Not on a snow-clad peak, whose wintry gale
Stings keenly, and whose white waste blinds the eyes,
Thou dwellest, but within a lowly vale
Often in shadow, yet with lovely skies.

Thine is the word of cheer, the kindly hand,
The loyal friendship and unshaken trust,
And thine the voice that in a weary land
Uplifts thy fallen brother from the dust.

Long flourish!   But when quitting haunts of men
To greet old comrades on some happier shore,
O mayest thou, Michael, blithe and young again,
Rejoice to greet the Springtime as of yore!

A GIFT OF FLOWER SEEDS

To the Boys of a Reform School

Dear boys, the gift I send you is but small,
A trifle men and women might disdain;
Yet with it I have sent my heart to all,
Hoping the poor remembrance not in vain.

Your lives have never known their rightful share
Of sweetness or of beauty or of joy;
Before your time, man's heavy load of care
Has weighted down the shoulders of the boy.

You have a right divine to happiness,
To claim just measure of this world's delight,
And shun acquaintance of the soul's distress
While heaven-born Youth forbears to take his flight.

Perchance you strayed from duty; but in truth
I love you all the better as you are:
God gave you that impassioned heart of youth,
And the wild wayward feet that roved afar!

These walls must never be your boyhood's tomb:
Your days not all delightless, you shall know
A little portion of the splendid bloom
That sets the Spring and Summer fields aglow.

Old-fashioned flowers you shall have, like those
That once, perchance, in lost years far away,
Around the doorway of your home arose,
Beaming upon you in your happy play.

You shall have pansies, purple, golden, pied,
And fragrant sweet-peas, white and pink and red,
While tawny tiger-lilies in their pride
Shall lift behind the pathway where you tread.

Nasturtiums there shall be, of orange hue,
And brilliant poppies, flaunting scarlet flame,
While morning-glories of celestial blue
Shall be as lovely as their lovely name.

White lilies you shall have, sweet as the days
Before your feet in banishment were driven,
And they shall breathe of long-untrodden ways,
Of mother, father, and of home and heaven.

So, when the lowly earth-strewn blooms you see,
Or those that cluster in the vines above,
Your hearts may turn one moment unto me,
Remembering that I sent them with my love.

THE LIGHTS OF THE CITY

Here in this quaint old farmhouse, late at night,
Soft pillows woo me vainly: slumberless,
Tossing unrestful, weary eyes I turn
Unto the window by my bed, and gaze
On the dark skies without.   Faintly I hear
Whispers of wandering winds through leafless trees:
A lamb, housed with its mother in the fold,
Bleats pleadingly, and then is still: a cow,
Dozing beneath her shelter, stirs a little,
Half rouses, and breathes deeply; but ere long
She too is quiet.   Through the ancient house
Lie all the other inmates, fast asleep:
I only am awake.

                        With all this peace
And restfulness about me; in this calm
That Nature, like a benediction, folds
Around me, and around the little world
Of simple beings where I stay to-night,—
My soul will not be soothed to harmony
With scenes reposeful.   For without, I see,
Like a great silvery Moondawn in the North,
Lights of the far-off City, and my heart,
Forgetful of this homely humdrum life,
With all its sober joys and sorrows, turns
To you, O haunts endeared and unforgot,
Ways where my brothers tread in grief or joy,
And where in triump or in ruin sweep
The tidal-billows of humanity!
Yea, beast and bird and tree, when I have fled
To arms of Nature from the noisy crowd,
May yield me solace; but at last I turn
To you with deepest and sincerest love,

O City, wilful, wild and passionate,
O City, kind yet cruel, warm yet cold,
Dread masterpiece of cunning hands of clay,
Boast, beauty and brilliance of Mortality,
The gloom-enshrouded glory of the world!

My heart hath wandered back to thee, O scene
Of splendor and of squalor, bliss and pain,
Laughter and jest and singing, dance and play,
Of moaning and of misery and despair,—
Owner of all things but Contentedness,
Giver of all things but the pearl of Peace!

Like gorgeous poppies, purple, yellow and red,
Thy varicolored lights are blooming; there,
Dazzlingly white, a star-rayed Cereus
That blossoms only in the fields of night,
Glitters the great electric flames. Athwart
Thy radiant world, what scowling shadows fall
From those resplendent lamps!

                                    Stretched on a cot
In a dark room, where a pale candle's beam
Flickers as feebly as the wavering life
Beneath it, one is dying. Not afar
Is heard a childish wail, whereby we know
Another soul has entered into the world,
To take the dead man's place. In festal halls
Are mirth and wine and music. In a cell
Stone-floored and iron-grated, cowers a wretch
Who gaily danced and feasted through his day,
And now, clanking his chain, the debt repays.
Here the young painter in his attic loft,
Despite the mean surroundings, labors on,
Hopeful of fame and fortune. In the parks
Lounge the old derelicts, who, long ago,
Likewise had plans for conquest of the world,

But subjugated now in dark defeat,
Devise brave schemes no longer.   Through the night
Bedless and supperless, the vagabonds
Mumble and drowse and grumble. ˙Strange indeed,
That though the sheep are gathered safe in fold,
And herds of cattle all are snugly housed,
Still the great herds of fallen humanity
Wander unshepherded, unloved and lost!

Rambling these streets, the rustic lad, whose heart,
Burning with high hope, scorned the prosy farm,
Now seeks his fortune in the town.   Ah, boy,
Hast ever, in secluded fields at home,
Or in dark wildwoods there, felt loneliness
As deep as in this human wilderness?
And yet, if thou art lonely, lonelier still
Is the gray scholar, who in that vast throng
Is known of all men, yet misunderstood!
His face men recognize; they call his name:
And yet he roams a stranger still.   He speaks,
But none will hear, or hearing, comprehend.
O deep-souled, pensive wise man, how profound,
How hopeless is thy solitude!   The cave
Of the lone hermit in the desert waste
Keeps not its tenant further from mankind
Than high thoughts in the heart of one who roves
A wanderer through the frivolous multitude.

Here, nimble-footed, happy-hearted, trips
Youth, with the downy cheeks and dewy eyes,
Youth, with the frank face and the eager air,—
Fresh as the Springtime, radiant as the dawn!
All the world wooes thee with insidious arts,
Careless, wild-bosomed Youth!   Snares it hath woven
To trip thy feet.   Yet I, who fear for thee,
While warning thee, have not the heart to chide.
God gave to thee that flaming spirit: He
Surely will guide thee to the rightful way.

Here the frail sister, who in sweet slain years
Was gladdest of all gladsome bonnibels,
Strays now bedraggled in the mire of sin,
Haunting the night-time like an evil dream.
And yet, poor outcast, fallen as thou art,
Still art thou daughter of the King of Kings,
And sister of the pure and stainless Christ.
Nor ever will that Father, erring child,
Disown thee: and upon this very night,
Thine Elder Brother calls thee, claims thee still,
And knocks upon the portals of thine heart.

But now, O turbulent City, midnight comes:
My weary eyes must turn away.   Forget
In gentle sleep thy sufferings and thy sins,
Thy vain ambitions and thy fleeting joys.
With God's hand resting on thy fevered brow,
Be as a little child that sinks to rest:
Peace, peace, wild-hearted City,—rest in peace!

THE DYING TREE

Old veteran who hast fought three hundred years,
Three hundred winters with their sleets and snows,
And welcomed back from exile, Spring by Spring,
The South wind as thine ally and thy friend,—
At last thy great campaigns are over; now
Nears to its end thy long and blameless life.

Dear old companion of my boyhood hours,
Our neighbor on that day when I was born,
Our neighbor on that day my father died,—
You knew old friends of mine who past away,
Gone to the churchyard—scattered over earth;
Now comes thy summons, and my list of friends
Shall lessen as thou goest on before.

Ah, thou wert true in many, many things,
And never wast thou false to aught on earth;
Ah, thou hast showered blessings many times,
But never have thy branches waved a curse.
Gift after gift hath fallen from thy hands,
Though no one ever brought a gift to thee.
The bluejay from thy branches, like a shrew,
Hath fumed and fretted at some crawling snake;
The crow hath croaked and quarreled from thy limbs,
The owl hath cried, the whippoorwill complained;
In Summer, doves have mourned among thy leaves,
In Winter, winds have moaned among thy boughs;
But never, in the seasons foul or fair,
Hast thou spoke ill of any living thing.

Through fiery noons the patient sheep have lain,
Cud-chewing, dozing in thy grateful shade;
The squirrel found a home within thy trunk,
Thy boughs were free for nest of every bird;
Thine acorns fell to please the chuckling swine,
The chipmunk scooped a lodging at thy roots;
The raccoon and opossum, close pursued,
Found refuge from the hunter and his hounds.
Yet not one bird that ever flew through heaven,
And not one crawling creature of the ground,
Gave thanks for shelter, refuge, or a home,
Or brought thee gold or silver for thy pains.

There too, a boy, I dreamed my foolish dreams
As long, long Summer days would wax and wane;
Lost in the pages of some magic book,
I fancied for myself its glorious deeds.
Thou sawest when my wild, impatient feet,
Left the old farm to wander through the world;
Thou sawest me when I left thee, full of hope,
And then, long after, in defeat return.
Then lying at thy feet, mine aching heart
Learned its hard lesson,—patience with its lot.

No wise man ever said thou hadst a soul,
No creed hath promised thee a hope of heaven;
Yet thou, without inducement of reward,
Eschewed all Evil, giving only Good.
The artist dreams of palms of Paradise,
The poet sings of meeting friends in heaven;
And thou, fast-rooted by the stream of life
Shouldst be at home in Eden, as on earth.
Then, since no man can rend the secret veil,
Who knows that you and I shall never meet again?

THE AGNOSTIC'S CREED

At last I have ceased repining, at last I accept my fate;
No longer I beat at the Portal, I have ceased to knock at
    the Gate;
I have ceased to work at the Puzzle, for the Secret I have
    ended my search,
And I know that the Key is entrusted to never a creed or
    church.

They have threatened with lakes of fire, they have threat-
    ened with fetters of hell;
They have offered me heights of heaven with their fields of
    asphodel;
But the Threat and the Bribe are useless if Reason be
    strong and stout,
And an honest man can never surrender an honest doubt.

The fables of hell and of heaven are but worn-out Christmas
    toys,
To coax or to bribe or to frighten the grown-up girls and
    boys;
I have ceased to be an infant, I have traveled beyond their
    span,—
It may do for women and children, but it never will do for a
    man.

They are all alike, these churches, Mohammedan, Christian, Parsee;
You are vile, you are curst, you are outcast, if you be not as they be;
But my Reason stands aginst them, and I go as it bids me go,
Its commands are as calls of a trumpet, and I follow for weal or woe.

But O, it is often cheerless, and O, it is often chill,
And I often sigh to heaven as my path grows steep and still.
I have left behind my comrades, with their prattle and childish noise;
My boyhood now is behind me, with all of its broken toys!

I have renounced my dream of heaven, with its siren song of hope,
And I know that beyond the darkness no vision of man can grope.
I am treading the mountain heights alone, through the silent flakes of snow,
And I long for the hut of the herdsman, far down, with its hearth aglow.

They may sing in the lowly valleys, where the milkmaid flirts with her swain,
But he who would scale the mountains must stifle in silence his pain.
Let the girls and the boys go churchward, and let them believe and receive,—
The Thinker may envy the thoughtless, but Reason he cannot deceive.

He must seek the Good for the Good's own sake, and not for the hope of heaven,
He must flee from Wrong from dislike of Wrong, and not by the devil driven;

He distrusts the virtue that works for reward, the virtue
    that clamors for pay,
And spurns the piety spurred by fear to depart from the
    evil way.

He is friend of every religion, of Socrates, Buddha or Christ,
There is good in all of the dogmas, though none of them
    ever sufficed;
The evil that cankers among them he tosses away to dust,
But he seeks and he treasures the jewels he picks from
    their charnel rust.

He may pray not, public or private, a hypocrite plea for
    his foes,
But he never longs for Gehenna to swallow them in its woes;
He would welcome annihilation, where the dawn comes
    never again,
Rather than behold one foeman condemned to an endless
    pain.

He never pretends acquaintance of a God he never knew,
Nor pretends to receive revelations not given to me or you;
Though he loves the summit's grandeur, and the forest's
    holy hush,
He pretends no one-man message from mountain or burn-
    ing bush.

He boasts of no Royal Favor, of no deity friend at Court,—
He knows on his own weak merits he must find his only
    support.
He cares not for circumcision, baptism, Atonement or Fall,
For the Jew and the Mormon and Brahmin are but man-
    kind, after all.

He has carved no hideous idol, and said it was God that
    frowned,
He has mapped no petty province and declared it Holy
    Ground.

God lives not alone for the Hindoo, nor the Congo blacka-
  moor,
But alike for every nation, and alike for the rich and poor.

That God has no holy cities, for in all there is evil and
  good;
In Paris, Jerusalem, Mecca, alike have His temples stood.
That God has no chosen people, no heathens to slight or
  scorn,
For they all are His lawful children, to His royal house-
  hold born.

Oh, that God of gods is glorious, the emperor of every land;
He carries the moon and the planets in the palm of His
  mighty hand;
He is girt with the belt of Orion, He is Lord of the suns and
  stars,
A wielder of Constellations, of Canopus, Arcturus and Mars!

I believe in Love and Duty, I believe in the True and Just;
I believe in the common kinship of everything born from
  dust.
I hope that the Right will triumph, that the sceptred
  Wrong will fall,
That Death will at last be defeated, that the Grave will
  not end all.

I believe in the martyrs and heroes who have died for the
  sake of Right,
And I promise, like them, to follow in my Reason's faithful
  light;
If my Reason errs in judgment, I but honestly strive as
  I can;
If a God decrees my downfall, I shall stand it like a man.

THE UNION OF THE SEAS

On the Completion of the Panama Canal.

Athwart the Isthmian realm,—that slender band
Wherewith God holds two continents in leash,—
We lay this thread of ocean, and with eyes
Averted to the past a moment, then
Turned forward, make a forecast of the years
Yet hidden in the voiceless future.   Here,
Four hundred years ago, that sturdy knight,
Balboa, striding through the yellow sands
Marging the vast Pacific, reached the waves
Of the gray King of Oceans, and with feet
Adventurous braved the flood, till round his knees
The surging waters murmured.   On the beach
Behind him, Spanish veterans, browned and scarred
From savage warfare under tropic skies,
Stood with the dusk barbarians of this land,
Naked like graceful porphyry statues,—all
Gazing intently on their leader's form
As it strode onward.   From above, the sun,
In his prime glory, deluged all the sea
With molten gold.   At last the Knight stood still,
In shining armor panoplied, with plumes
Nodding above his brows, a glittering sword
Uplifted in his right hand, while his left
Upheld the banner of triumphant Spain,
Gorgeous in saffron and in scarlet hues.
Then rearing high that banner and that sword,
The Great Sea, with its golden continents
And palmy isles unnumbered, one and all,
He called on heaven to witness, hence should be
Domains forever of Iberia's King.

[95]

For two long savage centuries from that day
The history of this fated land but seemed
A chronicle of groans,—mildewed with tears,
And writ with sword-points dipped in human gore.
Here was it that Piazarro first imbibed
His lessons in the school of cruelty,
And from these shores he swooped upon the south
To be its modern Attila.   Here Drake,
That Tamerlane of ocean, scoured the shores
With torch and steel.   That king of buccaneers,
Morgan, here burned the palace, robbed the hut,
Sacked cities, clogged the streets with slaughtered men,
And wrought such havoc in the Spaniard's house,
As more than paid in vengeance all the wrongs
Of Aztec or of Inca in the past.
But we, unlike that western Chief of Huns,
And those grim Tartars of the sea, come not
To pillage, burn or slay: nor even yet
Like stout Balboa, do we come to claim
A lordship over continents or isles
Or oceans.   For we come with peaceful hands
To raise a trophy not baptized in blood,
But in the sweat of generous toil; to rear
A monument, not to ourselves alone,
But all humanity; to dedicate
A high memorial, not to kings or queens,
But unto patient Labor and to Skill.
Yea! it shall be a fane for all the world,
Offered to God, and all the sons of God.

This modern wonder of the world we raise
Not for caprice, or pride or vanity,
But daily use; prosaic it may seem,
Prosaic as our daily meat and bread,
And yet, God grant it may ever be
A blessing like that good but homely food.

Here are no Hanging Gardens, reared aloft
To please some idle princess: here arise
No monstrous pyramids, like hills of stone,
Costing innumerous lives of groaning slaves,
Yet cumbering earth, and useless unto Man:
Nor have we here a mausoleum, raised
To keep alive some deedless name, that else
The indifferent world had canceled from its mind.
This is the work of free men, made to bless
No pampered favorite, but the multitude,
A highway for the living, not a cave
With dusty catacombs for mummied forms
Of long-forgotten despot Pharaohs.

Here all the argosies of all the world
May pass in peace.   A worthy sequel here
The voyage of Columbus finds; and here
We see a climax to the glorious deeds
That Vasco and Magellan gave mankind.
And here is found a work that typifies
The race of Morse and Fulton,— that same race
That made the vapor's fragile wreath become
A chained leviathan to draw great ships
Over long leagues of ocean; that compelled
The lightning's flash to bear its torch, uplift
Its burdens like a willing slave, and speak
Its message unto Iceland or to Ind.
But still, with hearts regretful we confess
That seeking for the Useful, we have oft
Passed heedless by the Beautiful.   Our sires,
Felling the gloomy forests, and at war
With wild-beast or with savage, might not pause
To heed the thrush's lyric; nor have we,
Building the city, tunneling through the mount,
Or interveining barren desert sands
With fruitful man-made rivers, ceased from work
To learn the violet's mission.   Yet the toil

Of plain Utility shall build the bridge,
And pave the highway to the fane of Art,
Where all the noblest lessons of this life
Our children shall be taught.   And may our God
Soon send that purple age!   For now we stand
No longer pioneers; raiment and food
No longer are our only needs.   The True, the Good,
The Beautiful,—that Trinity of Earth,—
Must be the end of all enlightenment;
And as the traveler circling round the globe
Only returns at last from whence he came,
So all true Progress, with these three beginning,
Though wandering far, must yet to these return.

Oft have we stumbled on our forward course,
And oft shall stumble yet, ere we attain
Our white ideal.   In the past our sins
Have led our feet astray, and coming years
Shall see us stray again.   And yet, O God,
We pray Thee, lift and lead us onward still,
Hopeful though erring.   Ever hallowed keep
Within our hearts the memories of those
Who made our country great,—men of the mould
Of Washington, of Lincoln and of Lee.
And in our lapsings, let us not forget
That never yet hath Springtime come to bring
Her joyance to the world, without dark days
Of frost and winds of Winter that delayed
The leaf and blossom: that no man may climb
The mountain by a straight unvarying path,
But by a labyrinthine trail that winds
And twists and turns, upward and downward leading
Ere it attains the summit of the peak:
That never yet hath saint arisen to heaven
Without some sin that burdened down his wings,
Or soiled the whiteness of his heavenly robes,
Keeping in doubt his victory to the end.

That nation can not stray afar that keeps
Ever before its mind the simple worth
And courage unadorned of those plain men
Who freed this land from pestilence,—those men
Of unromantic lives, in days of prose,
Who yet braved death, giving themselves to stings
Of poisonous insect pests that bore the seeds
Of the foul plague.   Not pompously they went
Into the jaws of Pestilence, and yet
How glorious was their battle!   Overthrown,
The enemy they met shall nevermore
Reap his dread harvest.   And these heroes died,
Or, hovering near the iron-gated tomb,
Were snatched from death by heaven.   Their names
    obscure
No poet sings: no magic legendry
Is woven round their story.   In their lives
No bugle urged them on, no banner streamed,
No high-born lady from her castle-tower
Waved them adieu.   Above those who are gone,
No marble cenotaph, no eulogy
From lips of oratory, and no shout
From fervent multitudes, uplifts in praise.
Yet never rode a knight through Arthur's realm,
Seeking the Holy Grail, that wore a plume
Whiter than their devotion: never a king
Taking his throne on Coronation morn
Wore ermine that was purer!

       Then, O Lord,
Make us esteem their names forever!   Make
Thy servants ever emulate their deeds;
Make us unselfish, striving for the good,
As they strived, hopeless of reward.   And make
Thy servants seek to purify the world
Of all uncleanness of the heart, as they
Saved pure men's bodies from the unclean plague!

All these things grant us, Lord.   And speed that day,
That day desired through long millenniums,
When man is truly worthy of his Sire.
And as we now in wedlock shall unite
These mighty oceans, grant that all the tribes
And kingdoms of the world shall soon be one,
Blest with one common hope, one end and aim,
One stainless flag, one Fatherland, One God.

TO A JUDGE

O thou who wieldest for one fleeting day
The power that belongs alone to God:—
O idol moulded out of common clay,
To sway one little hour an iron rod,—

Dost thou not tremble to assume thy seat,
And judge thy fellow-travelers to the tomb?
Dost thou not falter as thy lips repeat
Thy Comrade's downfall, thy Companion's doom?

A word from you, and Fortune flies away,
While silks and satins tatters into rags;
The banquet revellers scatter in dismay,
And Pride and Pomp haul down their flaunting flags.

You sentence, and your brother, lost to light,
Sits crouching in a dungeon dark and damp;
No stream can ever wash his brow to white
From inky impress of your iron stamp.

He bids farewell to all things fair and sweet,
Exiled from fields and forests, blooms and birds;
He hears no more his children's pattering feet,
Their liquid lisping of their mother's words.

Your hapless fellow-man must heed your call
To mount the scaffold,—you have power to kill,
And Life, the greatest miracle of all,
Is ended in obedience to your will.

Your softest speech may smirch the fairest name,—
What reputations hang upon your breath!
Your fiats may translate from fame to shame,
Or bring dishonor blacker-hued than death.

Then be so wise, so merciful, so kind,
The words "Well done!" may never come begrudged;
For thou, the master, shalt a Master find,
And thou who judgest soon shalt be adjudged.

THE LAD IN HANDCUFFS

Being Carried to Prison

Thy fault was trivial, but our man-made law,
    Which lets the strong break through, yet holds the weak,
Hath clutched the captive in its vulture-claw,
    And fed thy young heart to its vulture-beak.

Thy very vigor urged thee on to harm;
    Thy courage bade thee snatch forbidden fruit;
Walls tempted thee to use that lithe young arm;
    Those slender, swift limbs yearned for Joy's pursuit.

That vigor made thee wild and spirited,
    And planted mischief in thy boyish breast—
Youth will be youth, as long as cheeks are red,
    As long as Spring is sweet, or Life has zest!

Green fields and groves were made to feast thine eyes,
    Big brother unto Puck and all the elves!
And they should mirror back the Summer skies,
    Not bluer and not brighter than themselves.

Those nimble feet were formed to wander free,
  Caressed and kissed by daisies drenched in dew,
To wade the brawling brook, to climb the tree,
  And lead thee where thy darling dreams come true.

Those downy lips should whistle like a bird
  In vine-clad woodlands of the month of May—
O boy, to think some man may speak one word,
  And brush the beauty of thy life away!

Those strong brown hands, fast-fettered in their shame,
  An eaglet's cunning talons locked in steel,
Were made to govern flood and frost and flame,
  And bring all Nature underneath thy heel.

God gave dominion unto thee, my man,
  To take the silken leopard in a snare,
To hurl the harpoon in leviathan,
  And seize the raging lion in his lair!

Yet thou art doomed to mope behind the bars,
  And bend thy proud young neck beneath a rod,
O Son of Him who rules the Suns and Stars,
  O splendid youthful image of thy God!

THE SOLDIER BOY

O soldier boy, my soldier boy,
I see you march away
While fifes and bugles play,
Bright, brave and debonair,
With Springtime in your clear blue eyes
  and in your sunny hair.

O soldier boy, my soldier boy,
There in the morning sky
The brilliant banners fly,
And in the shouting street
Are lovely maidens who are scattering
  flowers at thy feet.

[102]

Yet soldier boy, my soldier boy,
Soon shall yon flag be torn,
Yon bugle peal forlorn,
And not one lonely bloom
Of all that scatter on thee here shall
 grace thy lowly tomb.

O soldier boy, my soldier boy,
Yon eager-hearted maid
When thou in dust art laid
Tearful, shall pine alone;
O bonny lad, the Queen of Death shall
 claim thee for her own!

HAD LINCOLN LIVED

Had Lincoln lived, the aftermath of war,
More terrible than war itself, had lost
Half of the miseries of its harvesting.
But Lincoln passed away, and there the South
Lost her best friend! I seem to hear him say:
"Now, boys, the War is over: stack your arms:
Let us be brothers once again. No, no,
My friends, don't strike them when they're down! They
 fought us
Fairly and squarely, and they gave us all
We could well stand, I tell you! But we won,
And having won, why not be satisfied?
Come, come, let us shake hands, forget the past,
And let old grudges die." Such words indeed
He uttered, but the shock of sudden death
Thwarted his kindly purpose, and deferred
The era of good will and brotherhood
Through a dark age of virulence.

But still
I love to think of Lincoln living on
After the roar of conflict long had past.
Had he thus lived,—the martyr's aureole
Encircling not his brows, the martyr's doom,
Shedding no awful grandeur on his name,—
I feel that none the less would we to-day
Yield him our hearts.   For, not mythologized
Beyond all recognition, he would stand
The simple, homely, gentle soul he was,
Faithful and honest as the plain old sod,
And good and wholesome as the daily bread
That plain old sod produces.

So I seem
To see him living to a great old age.
White are his locks with years, but still his form
Rears vigorous.   In a little country town,
Under an old green leafy tree, before
Some village lawyer's office, sits the man
Who freed the bondman and restored the State.
For now he comes to visit well-known scenes
Of boyhood, and we see him seated, calm,
Peaceful and cheerful in an easy chair,
Whittling a stick.   Round him, a throng of friends,
Old comrades of the long-lost years, is drawn.
His lank and rugged frame, his awkward limbs,
And his quaint, kindly face, we easily know
As we first see him.   At his feet, a dog
Lies peacefully dozing.   Hitched to the same tree
That shades the group, a farmer's horse and wagon
Are waiting; for the owner of the team
Has left the driver's seat, and stands with awe
Viewing the man who was once President.
As Lincoln slowly whittles on his stick,

And tells his anecdotes, in loud guffaws
His friends respond: or, now and then one speaks,
Asking a question, or familiarly
Bantering "Old Abe," as they all fondly call him.
But though he loves his jests, his every thought
Is sound and weighty: simple are his words,
Yet terse and wise, and true as truth itself.
And though he loves the sturdy sound of laughter,
In his worn face and in his patient eyes
One reads the story of those weary years
Of suffering, when he stood and steered the ship
Of his great Nation into port again.
Ah, never was he happy in those times,
With all that weight upon him, as he now
Is happy in this little country town,
Among his old friends of the long ago!
Like Diocletian with his cabbages,
Dalmatia he prefers to purple Rome!
So we will leave him in these sunset years
Soft and reposeful, and a while believe
The picture true to history.   And I like
The picture better than the rigid Fact.

         They tell us that the pure white ray of light
Is woven of the seven prismatic hues
That deck the rainbow.   To the weary eye
Longing for rest, those hues are lovelier
Than all the dazzling radiance of the noon.
So, Lincoln's memory I would not enrobe
In the white, blinding light of Saintliness,
But in the tints that wed to make that light,—
The colors of the noble heavenly arch,
Spanning our dark clouds after dreadful war,—
The tender vernal green of joy, the calm
Celestial blue of prudent thought, the gold
Of wisdom's mellow age, the violet

Of sweet humility, and the warm red
Of glowing human kindness.   And although
This memory of the Martyred one may lack
That other memory's lofty dignity,
Be sure the world had known and prized his worth,
And loved him none the less,—had Lincoln lived!

THE GREEK BOY

To this cheap restaurant I sometimes come
And see him working.   Now he scrubs the floor,
Now sets the chairs, now with a nimble step
He waits here at my table.   As I look
Upon his poor surroundings here to-night,
I mutter, "Evil days have come to thee
And thine, O boy of Hellas!"   But I muse
Deeply upon him, and his fine young face
Allures me more and more.   That pure white brow,
Shadowed by glossy, jetty hair; those eyes,
More softly brown than brown Autumnal woods
At twilight; and that curving boyish mouth
Smiling so sweetly,— youth of Hellas, while
I gaze upon you, these environments,
Sordid and low, evanish, and with thee
I seem to wander in a happier land,
And in an age more glorious.   Here the peak
Of Helicon arises, forested
In paradisal green, with crystal springs
Gushing from out of its bosom.   On the steep
Of Latmos, with thy flocks, a shepherd lad
Thou roamest, and when moondawn in the east
Silvers the balmy night, thy Cynthia comes
To clasp and kiss thee, her Endymion.
On Lesbos, thine own Sappho strikes her harp
To flaming lyrics as she pines for thee

In all thy fresh young beauty.   Under the snows
Of smoking Aetna, from the bending vines
Thou pluckest the purple grapes, and from the shades
Of cypress and of pine thou gazest forth
On yellowing wheat-fields with Theocritus.
Athens arises with her marble fanes
In all their olden splendor.   Corinth wakes
From ruins into stately palaces,
And Argos, loved of Hera, lifts again
The walls long leveled by barbaric hands.
Yea, in thine eyes I see the Spartan fire
That flamed in glances of Leonidas
Facing the Persians at the dreaded Pass.
But now I start, and look about me.   Gone,
All gone, those visions!   Once again I see
Only the mean appointments of this place,—
Low walls and dingy ceilings, battered chairs
And rickety tables: now I hear alone
The clatter of plates and knives and forks and spoons,
Yells of the waiters, and the noise of crowds
Talking but never thinking: and I sit
An exile in an unfamiliar land,
Unnoticed,—dazed and silenced by the din,
Babble and jargon of an age of prose.

THE REBEL

You were known of old, Johnny Rebel, to soldier, to prince
     and to priest,
In the aeons ere Egypt had risen, or the Aryans tramped
     from the East;
Antedating dynasties of China, more ancient than Gypsy
     or Jew,
Religions, languages, empires, are of yesterday unto you.

O yes, well I know they denounce you; you have long been
      under the ban;
I know that they hunt and they hound you, and they
      crucify when they can;
For you is the fetter, the fagot, and for you is the dungeon
      cell,
And for you in another existence are provided the torments
      of hell.

Ah, the prince and the priest and the soldier, how they
      yearn to possess your head!
Ah, the prince and the priest and the soldier, how they
      chuckle when they think you dead!
For you flout them all and defy them, with their mitres
      and sceptres and swords,—
These owners of earth and of heaven, these heirs of the
      Lord of Lords!

But you look on them all as upstarts, their threats as but
      bluster and brag;
To you the crown is but tinsel, and the royal robe is a rag;
They may boast of their arms and escutcheons, of succes-
      sion from Peters or Pauls;
You remember their fathers as butchers, or as keepers of
      cobblers' stalls.

You remember their little beginnings in the scramble to
      reach the top,
How they grabbed and they gouged and they elbowed to
      palace from tailor-shop;
Your memory is vilely tenacious; old foemen you seldom
      forget;
You fought them while climbing the ladder,—on the roof
      you will fight them yet!

On the wild, bleak Steppes with the Tartars, you defied the
    Chief of the clan;
On the sands of Arabian desert you rebelled at the sheik
    and the khan;
You clinched with the robber-barons in the teeth of their
    castled crags,
And you face the Yankee moguls on their ramparts of
    money-bags.

This world of the men who are living is controlled by the
    men who are dead;
This age of the vital present holds the past in a nameless
    dread;
We may boast of our strength and cunning, and scoff at the
    folk of the dust,
But the beings who make us or mar us, lie under the
    mundane crust.

The catiffs, freebooters and pirates of the mediaeval gloom
Still stalk in their ghostly armor, and decide for us still our
    doom;
The medicine-men and witch-doctors, in a time when men
    are called free
Still set up their icons and idols, where we mumble and bend
    the knee.

We may boast of our modern freedom, but the thoughts
    that we think we think
Were exhumed from the charnel and coffin,—you can trace
    them link by link!
O yes! we are free, we are footloose, but a dead hand pokes
    from its hole,
And we find, when we seek to struggle, we are bondmen,
    body and soul.

If you look for God, you must search him out in the fables
    of barbarous folk,
If you hunt for Truth, you must swallow the myths
    Mohammed or Moses spoke;
If you seek the Law, think not for yourself, for a priest a
    thousand years dead
Will tell you the right, and will tell you the wrong,—so
    nothing more need be said!

But you flee not, Johnny Rebel, from the spooks of a
    bygone day;
You will not be made the lackey of a master turned to clay;
You believe in living people,—that the living should own
    the world;
You would leave the mummies quiet, in their catacombs
    snugly curled.

You have stood for the rights of "the people," but "the
    people" are a sorry lot;
They hoot you, abandon, betray you; when you warn them
    they heed you not;
You love them, and yet you loathe them, gross creatures,
    half-gorilla, half-god,
These crawlers, half formed from the star-beams, and half
    from the dunghill sod!

You fight and you flay their master, and you bend and you
    break their chains;
But the helots turn on you in frenzy, and they quarter you
    for your pains;
Barabbas they choose to be pardoned, and Pilate they
    place in the chair;
They ridicule, curse and belie you, and they nail to the
    cross in air!

You lead them to lands of promise, where the manna and
      quails are showered,
But they whine for fleshpots of Egypt, the onions and leeks
      once devoured!
You free them from devilish despots,—they return to the
      nabob and duke,
As the sow returns to her wallow, as the dog returns to
      his puke.

You've been hung by the thumbs, old fellow; they have
      made you a galley-slave,
Bastinadoed, beheaded and burned you; they have rushed
      to spit on your grave;
And then in their maudlin repentance they have raised
      you a tablet of brass,
And have dubbed you a prophet and hero, whom living
      they had jeered as an ass.

But still, like a good old phoenix, you arise from your
      ashes once more,
And the prince and the priest and the soldier you fight
      as you fought them of yore.
I drink to your health, Johnny Rebel! There is worth in
      your honest eyes;
You're the only knight-errant still roaming in a world
      enamored of lies.

THE DRIED-UP STREAM

This poem has reference to the old swimming hole on the
Malone farm, where the boys of the neighborhood used to gather to
go in swimming.

O you who wander by this shallow bed,
All dry, except one tiny, dwindling pool,
Remember me, who knew you when a boy,
Who bore you on her bosom in the past!

[111]

How changed, how shrunken I am now, you say,
Choked up with sand and overgrown with weeds;
O you who knew me in those far-off years,
My glorious, gladsome youth will come no more!

Ah, then the mosses velveted in green
The gentle banks that sloped to pet my waves;
The brilliant cardinal flowers, white button-balls,
And blue-eyed ageratums wreathed my ways.
The red-bud and the dogwood hung above,
To find a mirror for their bloomy boughs.
Great elms threw twisted roots in monstrous coils
To drink my dews, and gather giant strength;
Huge oaks have blessed me as they raised on high
Their chaplets of a myriad million leaves.
Here mocking-birds have flitted down to drink,
And thanked me in a rain of silvery songs,
And here the redbird fluttered in delight
To see reflections of his breast of fire.

But most of all I loved the Summer days
When bathers came to wanton in mine arms.
Then gathered groups of slender fair-haired lads,
With youths as splendid as the morning stars,
And glorious young men, shapely, strong and tall,
To leap and dive and swim the hours away.
Disrobing on my tufted banks of fern,
And parting leafy boughs to plunge below,
Their marble feet, their graceful curving limbs
Beamed white as moonlight through the sprays of green
Revealing unabashed to all my world
Such living charms no sculptor cuts from stone,
But frankly naked like the happy gods
Who tripped through woods of Doric hills at dawn,
O, then I thrilled from trembling wave to wave,
To drink their youth, their beauty and their joy.

Ah, all those comrades of the past have gone,
And left me here to dwindle day by day.
First came the woodsmen, and they felled my trees;
Then blazing sunshine drank my dews away.
Drought followed, so the thirsty cattle came
And left a trickling stream half choked with mud.
Sands gathered weeds and rushed on my way,
Till only this poor tiny pool is left.
The birds and blooms have all deserted me,
With all the other friends I made in youth.
But most of all I pine to see again
The lovely boys who swam me long ago.
Ah, they are boys no longer!   Grizzled men,
Grown gray with years, and stooped and warped with
        toil,
Uncouth and rough from strife and grief and sin,
They hobble on, and hobble, hobble still,
When all the world is weary of the sight.
You, too, have changed! the wrinkles on your brow,
The restless eyes, the light hair flaked with frost,
The lips that ever seem to breathe a sigh,
All tell me that your fate and mine are one!
Come, see your image in my mirror here!
Do you recall your laughing boyhood face,
And would you know it if you saw it there?
Ah, old-time comrade, we have come to grief,
The boy grown wrinkled, and the stream gone dry!

SLEEP

In bygone years I sought to win renown,
And longed for titles, riches, pomp and power;
But Fate with hand relentless held me down,
And gave a hovel for a castle-tower.

In later years, Love came to share my path,
Yet bruised my bosom as he thrilled my heart;
His April morning died in clouds of wrath
As I beheld his dove-like wings depart.

I sought to drown my anguish deep in wine,
But saw the serpent in the goblet's wreath;
I roved from Tropic palm to Arctic pine,
Yet in my heart the Sword still found its sheath.

I dreamed of heroes, of contending powers,
Of daring deeds on far-off strands and seas,
Yet feared those troubled isles of blood-red flowers,
Where Glory plucked from bitter-fruited trees.

So now I come to be your humble guest
When selfish, vain ambitions find surcease,
O gentle Sleep, whose other name is Rest,
O golden Sleep, whose other name is Peace.

With you my feet shall cease their wandering
In fragrant fields besprent with dews of Morn,
O magic wine without the serpent's sting,
O fleckless pearl, O rose without a thorn!

When youth is dead, one seeks your dulcet rest,
And roams through gardens of undying bloom;
Though loved no more, he sinks upon your breast,
And One he loved rejoins him from the tomb.

O soothing Sleep, the mother of all men,
You bring back childhood with your lullabies;
The graybeard wreck becomes a babe again,
And feels a parent's kisses close his eyes.

Time, distance, chance, misfortune, end in thee;
What means the desert waste, the ocean foam?
With you the captive from his chain goes free,
The broken-hearted exile wanders home.

You stay all judgments; you blot out all sins;
Your pardon comes at nightfall swift and sure;
The Best and Worse lie side by side like twins,
All felons guiltless and all sinners pure.

O balmy Sleep, you wipe out all disgrace,
You ease all anger, end all thirst for blood;
You level every wordly rank and race,
You right all wrongs, and make all evil good.

THE SON OF ADAM

They have sung the depths of the ages past
    of the beauties of sea and sky,
Of the forests and fields in their robes of green,
    of the peaks of snow on high;
They have sung of Summer and sung of Spring,
    of the hush of the twilight hour,
They have sung of the star, of the seaside shell,
    of leaf and of fruit and flower.

And the bards have sung from forgotten times
    of the glorious gods in heaven;
They have called them good, they have called them kind,
    have thanked them for sins forgiven;
They have grovelled, and covered their heads with dust,
    in ashes and sackcloth lain,—
They have begged for an answer ten trillion times,
    but have always begged in vain.

They have sung of childhood's golden hair,
    of the patter of childish feet,
Of the liquid lisp, of the dimpled cheek,
    of the love-words softly sweet;
They have sung of lovers with eager eyes,
    of the care-free boys and girls,
They have harped and harped of the beauteous brows,
    and the wealth of their clustering curls.

They have sung the praises of woman, too,
    from Winter to Summer sun,—
From the dawn to dusk, from the dusk to dawn,
    that worship is never done.
They have sung of her beauty, her goodness, her grace,
    they have sung of her faith and truth,
They have sung with the blind devotional hymns
    of a blind and headstrong youth.

But they never sing in their puny strains
    of the grand and good in Man,
Of his masculine soul, that has led the race
    from the day that it first began.
He is called a worm which crawls in the dust,
    which never looks up, but down;
He is theme for the penny-a-liner's screed,
    he is butt for the jest of the clown.

And yet he has fathomed the ocean depths,
    he has measured the orbits of stars,
He has tunnelled the Alps and the Andes peaks,
    rode the clouds in his railway cars;
He has conquered the desert and jungle and marsh,
    he has bridged the chasm and flood,
And has sent his message on lightning wings
    through the air and the deep-sea mud.

He has weighed the earth, the planets, the sun,
    he has mapped the face of the moon;
He has dived far down in the coral grove,
    he has sailed in the light balloon;
He has bulwarked the land from the tidal wave,
    exploded and shattered the shoal;
He has found the source of the Niger and Nile,—
    he will find the Northern Pole.

The great behemoth and mammoth he slew;
    he has slaughtered the spouting whale;
He has trapped the fox and the beaver and wolf,
    he has followed the panther's trail;
He has captured the lion and tiger and bear,
    unmindful of hurt or harm,
And condor and ostrich and eagle and hawk
    succumb to his stalwart arm.

He has reared the castle and palace and tower,
    he has laid out the road and the street,
He is planter of corn, of cotton and rice,
    he is reaper of barley and wheat.
To the daughter of Eve is given one task,
    and that one task alone,
But the Son of Adam has the whole world's weight
    on his sturdy shoulders thrown.

But he seeks not alone for the Useful Device;
    he is lord of the works of the heart;
He is master of sculpture and painting and song,
    he is prince of the poet's art.
He has strung the lyre of Homer and Keats,
    to Shakespeare given a stage,
He has written the book of Dante and Poe,
    he is glowing in Byron's page.

He has reared the marbles of Phildias, too,
    the Cathedral of Angelo;
He is Rembrandt's mind, he is Raphael's soul,
    he is heart of Correggio;
He is heard in the storms of Beethoven's bars,
    and in Mendelssohn's magic notes,
With Mozart he sings in a heavenly choir
    of a thousand nightingale throats.

He has given us Newton and Darwin and Morse,
    Confucius and Plato and Paul,
He has given Aurelius, Isaiah and Job,
    and Jesus, the gentlest of all;
Though he fights for his rights and holds to them fast,
    and rebels at the chastening rod,
He is author of all religions and creeds,
    creator of every God.

They say he is selfish and heartless and cold,
    but he plows through the flood and the field,
And for those he loved he has fought and bled,
    till Nature was forced to yield;
He sweats in the tunnel and furnace and mine,
    he is toiler of toil that is scorned,
He digs for the gold and he dives for the pearls,
    that the Daughters of Eve be adorned.

He plods through the swamps and the barrens and bogs,
    over steppes and Saharas accurst,
And he calls aloud through the ocean storm, "Save the
    women and children first."
He plunges to death at the engine brake,
    burns to death as the boat strikes shore;
He has mortgaged his head and his body and soul for
    the wife and the child she bore.

And his very faults are the sure result
    of his courage, his might and skill;
If he strikes and smites, if he takes by force,
    he does it for loved ones still.
If he stifles with gas in depths of the pit,
    if he falls on the battle-line,
He has sold his life for the ones at home
    with never a whimper or whine.

There is beauty in woman, there is grace in the child,
    there is charm in the leaf and flower,
But the Son of Adam is strong and sublime,
    he is Glory and Grandeur and Power;
He is broad as the seas, he is kind as the sun,
    as useful as homely sod,
He is next in rank to the Cherubim,
    he is wrought in the image of God.

ANNIE LAURIE

For you the lover spake his fondest vow,
For you the poet breathed his sweetest sigh:
To twine your myrtle wreath around her brow
The fairest empress might rejoice to die.

And yet your loyal lover sued in vain;
You proved unfaithful to your "promise true,"
And never did he kiss your face again
On green Maxwelton banks at fall of dew.

O lass, your lad was bonnie, brave and grand,
If you but willed, had "laid him down and died";
None other had the right to claim your hand,—
How could you live to be another's bride?

The lyric of your love is never done,
But speeds forever, on from soul to soul;
The traveler hums it in the Afric sun,
And sings it as he seeks the Northern Pole.

Yet through the solemn nights and silvery noons
Your fickle heart hears fond reproaches fall;
Your story to her babe the mother croons,
The schoolboy's whistle tells the tale to all.

As long as Scotland's mountains pierce the skies,
And green Maxwelton banks are gemmed with dew,
Your broken vows shall cause the lover's sighs,
And maids shall weep to hear you proved untrue.

Far from your gentle lover's side to wend,
Your heart must miss him as you fare alone.
The ghost of Love shall haunt you to the end,
O loveliest ingrate that the world has known!

THE SONG OF THE FROGS

When the soft south wind is blowing, and the melted
    streams are flowing,
It is then I hear a croaking in the marsh;
By and by the notes grow stronger, and the little strain
    grows longer,
Though the music still is just a little harsh.
Oh, you little hump-backed hero, you defy the Winter Nero,
And a thrilling message of delight you bring;
O, you quaint amphibious satyr, in your ever welcome
    clatter
You have brought the first glad tidings of the Spring.

Soon your brethren join your singing, till the tangled
    swamps are ringing,
And my heart is bounding blithely at your call.
Soon the swaying reeds and rushes shall be thrilled by
    notes of thrushes;
But your bagpipe made the summons first of all.
Soon shall come the swift song-sparrows, like a flight of
    feathered arrows,
And the mocking-bird and redbird and the wren;
Then shall come the rose and lily, hyacinth, crocus, daf-
    fodilly,
And the old, old world shall then be young again.

Soon yon bleak and barren highlands, wreathed in green,
      shall kiss the skylands;
Soon their old Arcadian sports begin once more.
In the breast of every virgin love shall bud and love shall
      burgeon,
And the youth shall flush and quiver o'er and o'er.
Under beams of mild-eyed Venus, friendly myrtle boughs
      shall screen us;
We shall tell the old, old story at her fane;
There young lovers shall be treading, there'll be wooing,
      there'll be wedding,
With the old, old painful bliss and blissful pain.

We shall hear the hosts of Bacchus through the verdant
      woodlands track us,
Old Silenus on his donkey in the rear;
We shall hear their shouting shepherds, we shall see their
      gliding leopards,
We shall hear their loud and boisterous hymns of cheer.
We shall see gold-haired Apollo in a vine-clad, ferny hollow
Come with all the muses back to haunts of men.
For the frogs say Winter's over, they predict the bloom of
      clover,
And they say the world shall soon be young again.

EDGAR ALLEN POE

1809–1909

Far through the hazes of a hundred years
We see him, wrapped in solitude and gloom.
Enchanted gardens, haunts of pallid bloom,
Amid the desert shadowland of Tears,
Girt by the dark, wild wilderness of Fears,
Glow pale as moongleams on a hoary tomb:
There roamed he, sealed to melancholy doom,
Fate whispering "Never, never!" in his ears.

Death bade the Raven of his soul depart,
With all the aching and unrest of yore;
The stainless marble fane he reared to Art
Shall be his mausoleum evermore;
And there the anguish of his eager heart,
Shall find surcease in love of lost Lenore!

WHENCE AND WHITHER

O River, from where dost thou come?
By what peaks of snow,
Pink orchards a-blow,
By what lakes and lawns,
Green forests of fawns,
By what castles and cots do thy rivulets hum?
O tell unto me,
What far distant sea
You hasten to join through dusks and through dawns?

O ship say from where dost thou hail?
From what fronded palms,
From what tropic calms,
With gums and with spice
From what far paradise,
From what blissful isles hast thou trimmed thy sails?
To where will thine oars
Bear thy fragrant stores,
Thy honey, thy fruit, and thy silken bales?

O babe with thy prattle so sweet,
What seraphs have blessed you,
What cherubs caressed you?
What heavenly singers
Have fondled your fingers
What lilies of Eden have fondled your feet?
And where will you go
From this world of woe
By what strands where billows of Eternity beat?

O barque with thy mystical lore,
From what far-off lands,
From what shining strands,
From what stars have you brought
The wisdom you taught
To Enlighten the darkness of this earthly shore?
For what home dost thou yearn
At last to return
When the day of thy detention is oe'r?

FROM LOW BEGINNINGS

No thing on earth can be contemptible in Wisdom's eyes.
This brown mud-spattered bulb a splendid lily may arise,
This freckled egg may be a peacock or a bird of paradise,
This peasant boy a Shakespeare or a Cæsar in disguise.

THE CONQUEST OF CHINA

"Be *Christians* in the cheerful endurance of sufferings. May *honor* and *glory* follow your army and flags. * * * *No quarter is to be given, prisoners are not to be taken.* * * * Preserve your military discipline, and may *God's blessings* be with you. The *prayers* of the people and my best wishes accompany you. Open a way for *civilization* once for all.

Emperor William.

None now but heathens heed the voice of Christ;
The Poor In Spirit all have learned to shoot;
The Sinner, not the Saint, is sacrificed;
The Meek and Lowly have their turn to loot.

We thrust the Gospel in a sabre stroke,
We search the pockets of our erring brother;
We ease him of his coat,— he gives his cloak;
We smite his right cheek,—and he turns the other.

[123]

We long to lead this Gentile to the fold,—
We kindly kick him if he dares resist.
We love our neighbor,—and we love his gold;
Our hand of fellowship is now a fist.

We come to give the pagan Church and School,
His burning home shall light his barbarous gloom;
The Gatling Gun shall preach the Golden Rule,
And Joyful Tidings in the Bombshell boom.

No quarter!   Let him kick and squirm alone!
None but the Righteous have the nerves to feel.
The poor blind heathen bows to Wood and Stone,—
We'll make him bow to Sulphur and to Steel.

The Christian-Up-To-Date, with prayer for pelf,
Has made his heel tramp human hearts in mud,
Made him burn incense at the Shrine of Self,
And belt the whole world in a zone of blood.

And so this pious Pharisee hath set
The snares once woven by bloodthirsty Rome,
And come with brandy, bible, bayonet,
To rob the naked native of his home.

But China flourished in Creation's gloam,
Before the gods of Syria were adored,
Ere Abraham and Sarah left their home
To pitch their tents in deserts unexplored.

She mapped the earth, she named the stars above
When Gaul and Teuton burrowed with the Mole;
She taught forgiveness, preached the law of love
Before the Briton thought he had a soul.

In that far time, no ship sailed Tyrian Seas,
No Roman banner in the breeze unfurled;
The Southern Cross shone on the Hebrides,
Another pole-star glimmered on the world.

She saw old Thebes and Tadmor pass away,
She saw the god-built Trojan towers fall.
She saw her foeman flourish,—then decay;
She knelt to conquerers,—yet outlived them all.

The Kings may crush her, but they cannot slay;
She shall survive their puny petty spite;
For they are but the upstarts of to-day,
Toadstools and mushrooms sprouted yesternight.

IN PRAISE OF RIGHTEOUS WAR

I am coming not in a weakling's verse, with a milk-sop's
feeble whine,
With uplifted hand and with pious drawl, aghast at the
battle-line;
But I come to praise the fight that is fought for the sake of
Truth and Right,
The fight that is fought for God and for Home, that will
mate the Right with Might.

Yes, patience is good, and humility, too, and so is the pipe
of peace;
But the time will come when forbearence ends, and your
sugary smiles must cease;
Then either your hand must grip at your gun, and brighten
the sword from its rust,
Or your slavish neck must bend to the yoke, and your
mouth must chew the dust.

You must fight for the fire that toasts your feet, for the
roof that shelters your head,
For the herd that yields you its milk or meat, for the field
that gives you bread;
You must fight for bed, you must fight for board, for the
woman you love the best,
And O, you must fight with a ten-fold will for the baby at
her breast.

When a mad-dog comes down your village street, with the
    green foam in his jaws,
Do you greet him with bibles and hymn-books, and lovingly
    bid him pause?
When a rattlesnake rises amidst your path, alert with his
    fiery sting,
Do you pet him, and pat him, and wish him well, and a
    song of welcome sing?

When a big-armed bully among the Powers says the folk
    of a little land
Must sprawl in the dirt, and confess to a crime that never
    besmirched their land,
Do you blame that people that rises up, a pigmy ready to
    fight,
A David, aroused, with only a sling, defying Goliath's
    might?

When a vain war-lord with a swollen head, and inflamed
    with a brute desire,
Through a little state that was lapped in peace, comes
    tramping with blood and fire,
Despoiling the fields and looting the towns,—do you blame
    that blameless state,
For rousing in godlike righteous wrath, and hitting with
    righteous hate?

And war is the great Arouser; it silences whimpering
    tongues;
It toughens the muscles, it hardens the fist, and brings
    fresh air to the lungs;
Though it comes with torch and it strikes with steel, and
    shortens life's petty span,
That life it exalts to heroic heights, so a man is twice a man.

Yes, patience is good, and so is peace; but he is not
    worthy of good
Who will not rush forth when the spoiler comes, to defend
    it with his blood:
When that Spoiler comes with his bandit crew, to shatter
    with shot and shell,
Let the good man rise, with a fervent prayer, and give him
    hell for hell!

THE HAUNTED HOUSE

Thou art a haunted house, my heart,
Where joys have lived and died,
And stealing back to olden scenes,
Like pallid spectres glide.

There haggard wraiths of ancient griefs
Pace the old ivied walls,
And ghostly triumphs and defeats
Stalk through the ruined halls.

At twilight, round the lonesome hearths
Gather dead hopes and fears,
And there Repentance and Regret
Sit bathed in phantom tears.

Old hates are there; and sweet lost loves,
After youth's days depart,
Wander with white unresting feet
That haunted house, my heart!

EPITAPH FOR A FRIEND

Stranger!   A Man of men sleeps here in dust:
Life he made lovelier in the days of yore:
Now Death he makes less dreadful, since we trust
That Death will lead us to his side once more.

TO A MOCKING-BIRD

Singing in October

Dost thou not know, sweet bird, that Spring hath fled,
Taking the youth and joyance of the year?
That Summer's gladsome hours of gold have sped,
Leaving the fields and wildwoods sad and sere?

Above, through melancholy skies of grey,
The red leaves flutter on the chilly breeze,
And birds of passage, calling, wing their way
From Norland shores to strands by tropic seas.

Yet still thou singest; and thy presence bright
Cheers the lone bowers beneath a faded sun
Like the sweet spirit of a lost delight
Haunting old scenes when life's best days are done.

O teach me, noble songster, how to wend
My life's autumnal pathway, strong of heart
When youth and youthful fervor have their end,
And all the old ambitious dreams depart.

Teach me to sing when dim October skies
Are flecked with dead leaves on the north wind whirled,
When the rose, shattered, by the pathway lies,
And Sorrow, like a shadow, walks the world.

Teach me to sing for sake of song alone
As I go unapplauded or unheard,
When laurels that I longed to call mine own
Encircle not my brow, celestial bird!

MOTHER AND CHILD

I pass the two upon this crowded street,
And mark their strong resemblence at a glance,—
One like a living Poem, freshly sweet,
One like the spectre of some slain Romance.

How strange it is, each seeming like the other,
Yet differing as the dawn from chastening dusk!
The happy, heedless child, the care-worn mother,
The pink-white blossom and the faded husk!

Yet in that lovely child's cerulean eyes
I see the mother's girlhood ere its wane;
I see the springtime of purpureal skies
Which never in her world shall be again.

The golden tresses on that pearly brow
Were filched from sunshine of forgotten years,
The bloom upon that face plucked from a bough
In long-lost isles beyond a sea of tears.

Pale, care-worn mother with the beauteous child,
In those old days thou, too, wert wondrous fair,—
Thy step as joyous and thy heart as wild
As that of one who trips beside thee there.

Relentless years have tamed thee to thy fate,
And made thee patient with thy prosy life;
Long hast thou ceased to batter at The Gate,
And wage with powers of heaven unequal strife!

Men have forgotten thou wert once a swan
That soared above the snow-peaks, white like thee;
That close-clipped wing no more shall cleave the dawn,
With rose-wreathed clouds to bear thee company!

But not afar, pale mother, need we seek,
The blossoms that were rifled from thy bower;
Thine own heart's blood incarnadined that cheek,
And made those child-lips seem a scarlet flower.

For, like some glowing rose in years long past
Twined by a lover in his loved-one's tress,
Which, dying, bound the man and maiden fast,—
Thy brilliance paled, another's life to bless.

And blest of women art thou in thy doom,
O thou unselfish one, O true Life Giver,
Who fadest that another's cheek may bloom,
Whose beauty dies, yet dies to live forever!

THE EARTHQUAKE

Judge Malone, of Memphis, Tenn., author of the remarkable American epic poem, "Hernando de Soto" (just published by G. P. Putnam's Sons, New York), from which the following impressive and peculiarly timely passage is extracted, has put forth several earlier volumes of lyrics, including the famous lines on "Opportunity." Alfred Austin, the English Laureate, writes of this American contemporary's work: "I find in it deference to the best traditions of English poetry, and a rare power of continuous yet never tiresome narrative."

Bells toll in steeples where no human hand
Puts forth to ring them; great cathedral walls
Fall crashing to the ground, and overwhelm
Under their ruins frantic multitudes
Whose shrieks they smother into silence.   Birds
Are stifled by the ashes and the fumes,
And fall like dead leaves headlong from the skies.
Wild beasts forsake their highland fastnesses
In rocky dens and caverns, or their lairs
Amidst the forest's deep untrodden glooms,

Trembling with terror, and into homes of men
Creep tamed and whining.   Everlasting hills
Seem sick men writhing in convulsive spasm;
The mountains rock and quiver; ocean waves
Dash wildly on the promontory's brow.
Keen lightnings round the lofty craters glitter;
The sun turns red, grows murky, disappears.
With wrench on wrench and frightful quake on quake
The heavens and the earth seem gulfed together.
Stupendous chasm yawns; in awful pangs
The hoarse-voiced subterranean thunder roars;
Explosion on explosion rends the peaks
With great concussions that the mariner
Feels on his bark an hundred leagues at sea.
Amidst the din of houses tumbling down,
The sickening shocks, the suffocating dust,
And the deep darkness veiling earth and heaven,
Women and men, bewildered, agonized,
And lifting feeble rushlights in their hands,
Rush to and fro, crying the names of friends
Now lost or dead.   But through that sulphurous pall
Their tapers glimmer but a cubit's length,
And none can find his comrade.   On their heads
They scatter dust, or on their shoulders bear
The weight of heavy crosses for their sins.
And quivering through that midnight of despair,
One hears the deep-toned chanting of the priest,
While frenzied mortals, barefoot, grimed with soot,
In rags and tatters, with disheveled hair,
With white lips, and with wild distended eyes,
Delirious in their terror, supplicate,
And shriek to God to save them from their doom.

THE HEART'S DESIRE

From Hernando De Soto

Give me, O Fate, some one to love
   And one to love me in return;
To win this blessing Saints above
   For old-time earthly haunts might yearn.

Oh, for the touch of gentle hands,
   The spell of accents sweet and low!
One cannot crush the heart's demands;
   Nature will not be cheated so!

Man's bosom ever seeks its mate;
   No soul that lives can live alone
Unloved, the king in kingliest state
   But banquets on a crust and bone.

The dream, I dream may be in vain,
   My idol be with earth alloyed,
But shield me from this deadening pain
   Of seeing faith and trust destroyed!

The disenchantments learned from truth
   Fall blotting life's unsullied page;
Better sweet follies born of youth
   Than bitter wisdom bought of age!

Reft of its plumage sinks the dove,
   Reft of its dewdrops droops the fern;
Give me, O Fate, some one to love,
   And one to love me in return.

SOLACE

From Hernando De Soto

When I am bowed with grief, let me not say,
"Lord, I am cheered in mine adversity
To know that countless thousands in this world
To-day are bowed with burdens heavier
Than those allotted unto me."   Let not
The selfish thought that hearts of others ache
With pangs more poignant than mine own, be made
A balm to soothe me to contentedness.
No, rather let me say, "Though I am thrall
To sorrow, it is comfort unto me,
To know that countless others at this hour
Are glad of heart.   I thank Thee that my gloom
Eclipses not the noontide of their joy."
O, brother, though my heart be desolate,
Lonely and dreary, let my solace be
To know that in thy house is warmth and love,
Dancing and feasting, and the sound of mirth:
Yea, brother, let my worthier comfort be
To know thy path is bright though mine is dark.

TO AN ENEMY

From Hernando De Soto

Although I love my friend, still let me yield
This tribute to thy worth, mine enemy!
Unjust thou art, perchance, no doubt unkind,
Yet much I owe to thee, stern monitor!
Faults though thou hast, due honor shall be thine.
Close, keen-eyed critic, oft thy scrutiny
Hath made me blush defenseless, and in shame
Turn from my darling idols.   Thou hast set

Full oft in paths of righteousness my feet,
That else had wandered in forbidden ways,
Lovely yet treacherous, and thy censure harsh
Hath oft rebuked my days of dalliance
In pleasant fields where pitfalls hid in flowers
Awaited me with secret perils.   Yea,
Thy sneer hath been a sword to prod me on
To duty; it hath been a goading spur
To make me win a race I counted lost.
Thy jeer hath oft aroused me till I swore
To reach success despite thy prophesies
Of my defeat; thy challenge, like a blast
Of trumpets when the battle hangs in doubt,
Hath nerved my hand to snatch the victor's wreath
That else had never graced my brows.   Again,
Amidst my paeans sung by parasites,
Thy frown from mien austere remindeth me
That I am merely mortal, child of dust,
Soon summoned unto strict account.   Stern friend,
Not thine to soothe with silken flatteries,
Nor gloze with unctuous phrases; it is thine
To do much more—to save me from myself!

THE RELIGION OF BROTHERHOOD

From Hernando De Soto

There is a great day that is yet to come,
A morn more glorious than all morns before.
Far, far away I see that marvelous time,
Though we shall never live to greet it here.
In that blest day all nations shall be one,
And one resplendent banner wave for all,
Frontiers and boundaries then shall be no more,
And Fatherland shall mean the Whole Wide World.

To-day we count that man an enemy
Because he dwells beyond a fancied line;
We only call him friend whose span of life
Is rounded by the colors of a map.
We slay the man who never did us harm
Because his monarch and our own are foes;
We rob the maiden of her heart's own boy
For fancied wrongs from dusty archives dug;
We part the widow from her only son
To bring some mounted soldier to renown.
Our hates are fixed by planes of latitude,
And longitude has governed laws of love.

Because the heathen in his blindness bows
To gaping idols hewn from wood and stone
We wade the green scum of tropic swamps,
We drink the fevers of its fetid air,
We rouse the tiger and the hooded snake,
To force the naked savage from his gods,
With crash of bomb and thrust of bayonet,
And all for what?   Because his simple faith
Was handed from his fathers down to him,
While we accept the faith our fathers taught
Yet blind ourselves we seek to lead the blind,
While still the Great Unknown is hid from all.

O brothers, let the Lapland peasant dream
His snow clad forest is a paradise;
Still let the Congo native loudly boast
His snaky jungle is the realm for kings;
Still let the huddled Chinese millions claim
Their yellow rivers lave celestial fields.
Let us remember there are other lands
Beyond the hilltops of our boyhood home;
Let us remember other men have hearts,
Although they march beneath another flag,

O let us not forget that pious souls
Will bow to-night to other gods than ours
In awe, in reverence, and in living trust,
Which shame us in the boldness of our sins.

Who knows that God will spurn the heathen's prayer
Because he calls Him by another name?
What matter, when that idol, wood or stone
Is merely symbol of the Great Unknown?
Men seek Him by a thousand different names,
Yet all those names are titles of The Lord.

That swarthy savage in the trackless woods
Who leads the famished hunter to his hut,
And shares his little store of food and drink,
Is brother unto me, is Son of God.
That Hindoo mother, who, when famine comes,
Dies that her child might eat the crust and live,
Is sister of the meek and lowly Christ
Although her ears have never known His name,
Although in death she bows to wood and stone.

O brother of that far-off glorious time
When only Love is Force, when Right is Might,
O brother of that undiscovered day
Which sees the Lion playing with the Lamb,
Remember us your brethren of the Past,
Who groped in darkness and in doubt and fear!
Our rude ancestors rose above the brute,
And stumbled slowly up to higher things,
To-day we struggle for a better life,
Although your glory we shall never share;
Remember how we strove, and fought, and bled,
While still the old, old Adam clutched below,
And sought to stay us as we climbed the height,
All this remember in your glorious age,
And breathe one word of kindness for us here,
Who prophesied and hailed you from afar!

FRANK FAWCETT McKERNAN

Died March 6, 1902.

In a great city, where my friends were few,
 Where myriads struggled in life's selfish race—
Amid those days of darkness first I knew
 The perfect poem of your fine young face.

When shrouded Sorrow sat within my heart,
 You came to meet me in the stranger's land;
Though all forsaken, thou didst take my part,
 And though deserted, thou didst hold my hand.

Long have I wished to see your face again,
 But you have left me in the gathering gloom;
Death must have loved you, for he eased your pain,
 God must have loved you, for he called you home.

Ah, you will make new friends where you have gone—
 Friends free from faults you knew in me of yore,
And they may bid you to forget the one
 Whose shadowed life is linked with yours no more,

But, O, if new companions take your hand,
 If splendid seraphs greet you there on high,
Forget me not in this far-distant land—
 For none will love you half as well as I.

And though your heart may never miss its mate
 Among the lilies there in Paradise,
Remember old times, when we fought with Fate,
 And wandered homeless under scowling skies.

Though still I wander through this desert dearth,
 Where hopes prove false, where tears are never dried—
Remember still your old friend here on earth,
 Whose heart and soul were darkened when you died.

WILL HUBBARD KERNAN

Thou art the poet of the realms of Night,
Of anguish, desolation, and despair.
Like stern-browed Orcus leaping from his lair,
While Enna's blossoms withered in their fright,
Thou treadest through the earth with blast and blight,
The sweet muse from her gardens glad to tear,
That she thy mournful kingdom's gloom may share,
A bride enrobed in funeral garb of white.

She roams our fields when Spring is rich and green,
And when the golden Summer crowns the years;
But when the Autumn's haggard face is seen,
And icy Winter's stormy brow uprears,
Returns to be Death's sad and solemn queen,
With thee, weird king of terrors and of tears.

ANNIE COOK

Died September 11, 1878

Your life, in youth, was written all in wine,
   You gathered poppies of the poisoned breath.
Sin was so beautiful she seemed divine,
   Thou daughter of the Devil and of Death.

But soon you saw her loveliness depart,
   You saw her splendor and her glory dead,
And you were left with bruised and bleeding heart,
   When all the comrades of your youth had fled.

Yes, all had fled, sweet youths of long ago;
   Where now their fruity lips, their clustering curls,
Their May-morn eyes, their dimpled cheeks aglow,
   The peach-bloom boys, the morning-glory girls!

Yes, all had left you to your bitter fate,
    To walk the highways of the wicked town,
To hear your heart cry out "Too late, too late!"
    Amid the darkness when the sun went down.

The City's noises seemed to mock your pain;
    The iron engine like Prometheus groaned,
Like drowning Sappho sobbed the midnight rain,
    And like King Lear the winds of winter moaned.

Then fell the plague on men with poisoned breath,
    And weakling saints were scattered far in flight.
But you were firm, you would not flee from death;
    You dressed the dead, you nursed the sick at night.

Deserted and abandoned by them all,
    When even God seemed frowning from the skies,
You would not shirk the sufferer's piteous call,
    But faced the Terror with unflinching eyes.

Where death was strongest, thou wert sure to be;
    Where hope was weakest, thou wert sure to come.
Then He who knew thy sorrows pitied thee;
    Thy kind eyes closed, thy faithful hands grew numb.

What Priest, what Sage, can solve life's mysteries?
    We know not whether hope died in thy pall,
If thou dost tread to-day in Paradise,
    Or whether in thy grave was end of all.

Yet I would lay a lily on thy tomb,
    O thou who in the steps of Jesus trod,
O heroine who defied the voice of doom,
    O daughter of the true and only God!

PAST AND PRESENT

You said you loved me, when my heart was gay,
　When Fortune was a guest within my door;
But will you love me in this gloaming gray,
　When others, whom I cherished, love no more?

Who needs a friend when Fortune is his friend?
　Who needs a guide through sunlit fields a-bloom?
But when disaster gathers in the end,
　Where is the hand to lead me through the gloom?

Love, how I need you!　As the Summer grain
　Needs benediction of God's golden light,
As fading foliage needs the rippling rain,
　As wan moonflowers need the soothing night.

I ask you, "Do you love me?"　Not as then,
　When Life was laughing, wreathed with roses red,
But now, when darkness drapes the world of men,
　And all the splendors of my youth have sped.

Then, like a brilliant cactus blazed the noon,
　And twilight flitted like a brown-eyed fawn,
Then, like a white swan sailed the May-night moon,
　And like a purple poppy flamed the dawn.

Young April, in her girlish frock of green,
　Blonde August, with her glory-gleaming eyes,
Brunette October, like an Arab queen,
　And gray December, with his gloomy skies,—

These with their flowers and snowflakes strewed the ground
　In jest and joyance through the years of yore;
Love's lilies blossomed all the year around,
　His birds went sweetly singing evermore.

But like Aladdin when he lost his lamp,
   I saw my childhood's palace pass away;
So then, forsaken, I was forced to tramp
   All weary, worn and footsore, day by day.

Yet as I grope through ebon glooms of night
   And know a jasmine by its rich perfume,
So, sweet, I know you in this fading light,
   A princess, come to share a peasant's doom!

And like a crystal palace in the heart
   Which keeps through Winter warmth of Summer noons,
Love's tropic splendors never shall depart,
   Still glowing through their everlasting Junes.

Then come to me, O precious, as of old,
   Bring back the brilliance of the perished years,
Bring back the glory of my age of gold,
   And end my exile in the realm of tears.

Then we shall lose the false for real bliss;
   True love turns not when fickle youth forsakes;
A fairy prince, beneath his ardent kiss,
   The Sleeping Beauty of the soul awakes.

SOLITUDE

He who ascends the cloud-encircled peak
And gropes along through mist when twilight comes,
When all the rocks are veiled in gloomy gray,
Has trembled in a fearful Solitude.
He who has trod the trackless wilderness
Where giant trees turn noontide into night,
Where monstrous vines are twisting coil on coil,
Where unknown birds chirp through the loneliness,
And unknown beasts are crying from afar,—

Has felt an awful silence in his soul.
He who, shipwrecked, a thousand miles from land,
Drifts on and on, and never sights a sail,
With but a stormy petrel flitting by,
Has longed to clasp a helping hand again.
He who has wandered through a foreign land,
And trod a giant city's crowded streets,
And knows no one amid the myriad throngs,
And only hears an unfamiliar tongue,—
He, too, has known the depths of loneliness.
He who imprisoned in a dungeon cell,
Sees no one, but beholds a stealthy hand
Slip through the iron grating day by day,
And leave a cup of water, crust or bone,
And cowers in that dungeon thirty years,
Yet never knows his captor or his crime,—
He, too, has craved a comrade's sympathy.

But, still, my soul, your awful solitude
Is more than his who climbs the mountain peak,
Than his who treads the trackless wilderness,
Than that of him adrift upon a spar,
Than that of him lost in a foreign town.
More lonely than the prisoner in his cell
Are you, O soul, whom no man ever knows.
You strive to speak, but none will understand,
You call for help, but no one ever comes.
No friend can ever share your confidence,
No spouse the secret chamber of your mind!
Wise men may read the ruined monuments
Which tell the stories of forgotten kings,
May read the parchment or the papyrus,
And learn the legends of forgotten years,
But none may translate from the secret book
Locked in the dungeon seen by you alone.

O Soul, you sail strange oceans like a ship
Steered by a pilot whom you never see,
Ruled by a captian you have never known,
Bound from a land you cannot recollect,
And destined for a harbor never told.
Come, tell me, are you seeking for a strand
Where tufted palms wave under blissful skies?
Or, are you only speeding on your way
To wreck your cargo on a desert shore?
Or, are you only hastening after all
To sink forever in the ocean waves?
Sometimes I see another ship afar,
And clap my hands and cry, "A sail! A sail!"
I wave a signal, never understood,
And then the bark fades swiftly from my sight.
O soul, amid your awful solitude
You sail without a compass or a chart.
No consort cleaves the ocean by your side,
You know not whence you came, nor where you go.

THE QUEEN OF THE VALENTINES

I

"Little bird, little bird, coming back from the South,
    Where spring-time's youth never dies,
With a melody sweet in your passionate mouth
    To gladden our gloomy skies;

"Little bird, little bird, in the days long ago,
    A prince you lived and you died,
And you flit like a leaf through the sun and the snow,
    Over earth and ocean wide.

"You have seen in the days that forever have fled
  Full many a fair, fair face,
And to-day you behold merry maidens that tread
  With gladsomest fawn-like grace;

"Will you say, little bird, if you've seen in your flight
  A maiden as fair as mine;
With a smile half as sweet, with a step half as light,
  Or eyes, like her own, divine?"

II

"Never, O never, in sunshine or shadow,
  Never, O never, on mountain or meadow,
  Never, O never, in legends of glory,
  Never, O never, in song or in story,

"On the glad, green earth or the ocean wide,
  Has a maiden lived or a maiden died,
  In the huts below or the halls above,
  As sweet as the sweet, sweet maid you love.

"There were proud, proud queens in the days of old,
  With their white, white brows and their locks of gold,
  So stately and tall, so witchingly sweet,
  That the heroes died at their lovely feet;

"There were maids beloved by the bards of yore,
  Whose beauty is treasured for evermore
  In the songs still sung as the bards sang then,
  And ever shall be by the sons of men;

"Though the heart regrets, and the memory lingers
  On the vanished queens and sweethearts of singers,
  O lover, O lover, the maiden thou greetest
  Is fairest of all, and brightest and sweetest."

III

All things that are fair at night and at noon
   Are blent in the face of my sweet,
From the stately orb of the full white moon
   To the bluebell low at her feet;

From the diamond crown of the evening star
   To the dew on the pansy's plume,
From the blush in cheeks of the dawn afar
   To the blush on the peach tree's bloom

Fairer than them all in the ages fled,
   In the banished or vanished scenes,
Than roses living or the lilies dead,
   Sweetest of sweethearts, queen of queens!

FOR MILDRED

O lovely maiden of the peach-bloom face,
   So artless in your morning mirthfulness,
O maiden tripping in unstudied grace,
   This weary world to beautify and bless;

You bring strange memories to my callous heart,
   Forgotten fancies from forsaken years,
Old joys, that long ago I saw depart
   Amid the hazes of regretful tears.

You bring to mind those dear departed Springs,
   Those Summers that vanished evermore,
A halcyon youth, whose head and feet had wings
   In lost rose-gardens of the years of yore.

You bring to mind the days of dead romance,
   When my young heart was like a dewy flower,
When song and story centered in a glance,
   And pain was but a passing April shower.

How all is changed!   The fairy stories close,
　The fields are faded, dull the skies above;
The life that once was poetry, is prose;
　None seek me now to bring me gifts of love.

I do not wonder as I gaze at thee,
　How Helen thrilled the nations far and wide,
How Cleopatra weaved her witchery,
　Till heroes for her glory bled and died.

For such as you were leveled walls of Troy,
　And Actium's ships were wrapped in sheeted flame,
With fire and sword were ravaged realms of joy,
　Leaving great cities but a storied name.

So then, remember that thy subtle power
　Is like a magic sceptre in thy hands,
To rear to God upon a rock a tower,
　Or scatter hopes like houses built on sands.

So, when the One of All shall come to woo,
　Remember thou canst make him or canst mar,
His love in ashes and in dust to strew,
　Or fix his aspirations on a star.

Within thy heart, ere youth has flitted by,
　Let Love, the Rose, its blossoms never cease,
Beneath it place the Violet, Modesty,
　And high above them all the Lily, Peace.

Amid the blessings that to thee are given,
　Let Self upon thy shrine be sacrificed,
Becoming then the blessed bride of Heaven,
　Daughter of God, and sister unto Christ.

FIRESIDE FANCIES

Here, hand in hand, we sit to-night,
Flushed in the logwood's ruddy light,
While red coals glow and blue flames leap
And hot sap sings and crickets cheep.
Outside we hear the wild winds call
And down the pane see snowflakes fall,
While Winter, like a hungry hound,
Hunts over hills with bay and bound.

A palace in the brilliant fires
Rears garnet walls and golden spires,
And many a labarynthine maze
Bedecked with opal hearts ablaze.
The smoke, an azure banner, curls
O'er halls of rubies and of pearls;
Blue sapphire turrets flame and flare,
And jasper columns glow and glare.

Here, hand in hand, my love and I
List to the wild winds whistling by;
We hear the sap sing, crickets cheep,
And see the lithe blue blazes leap.
And then, as chill winds whistle on,
We talk of youthful days long gone;
Of love that laughed through summer days
Then left us treading thorny ways.

To-night, our hearts, like brands aglow,
Are burning in a world of snow;
For in your love is summer peace
And summer joys that never cease.
I kiss you, take your hand in mine,
And feel my sordid soul divine.
Let worldly wealth and glory be,
But leave you, precious, still with me!

So here we sit, still hand in hand,
And tread a wonderous fairy-land—
The kingdom of a lover's dreams,
With bloomy woods and murmuring streams.
Still let the wild winds shriek and shout,
Still set the flying snows to rout;
I care not where my feet may be
When God has put you, love, with me.

AN UNSENT LETTER

Yellow and worn after long, long years,
Hiding its treasures of smiles and tears,
Breathing soft odors from days of old,
Sweetest of stories, yet still untold!

Whispers I hear from the faded sheet,
Saying, "I love you, I love you, sweet!
Foolishly fond though my words may be,
Tell me, O tell me, if you love me!"

Love then was light as the feet of a fawn,
Brilliant of brow as dazzle of dawn,
Jocund as June, unwearied of wing,
Hearing his heart like a goldfinch sing.

Life was as sweet as a seraph's bliss,
Youth was a dream, a dimple, a kiss,—
Beautiful girls and beautiful boys,
Jubilant smiles and jubilant joys!

Tattered alone in the garret here,
Breathing its tidings of hope and fear,
After the writer grows old and gray,
After his passion has passed away.

Did the maiden watch with anxious eyes,
Pining away with her secret sighs,
Treading alone with her dead, dull pain,
Waiting your coming, but still in vain?

Never, O never, love's clasp and kiss,
Never, O never, love's honeyed bliss,
Never, O never, love's Summer sun
Came to the hearts that should have been one.

Over the earth he wanders alone,
Callous and cold and cynical grown;
She who should be a mother and wife,
Faces alone a long, loveless life.

Silent in dust you will sleep at last,
After dull years of waiting have passed.
Shall you meet some day in God's own fold,
And the words of love at last be told?

LA PALOMA*

O Peerless love-song of the golden South,
  Melodious lyric of the lands of light,
Warm as the kisses from a wooing mouth,
  As brilliant as the dawn and sad as night!

I see the vine-clad tropic mountains there,
  The birds of gorgeous plumage flitting by,
The tangled forest and the panther's lair,
  The dark-blue ocean and the dark-blue sky.

I see the star-eyed Spanish damsel there,
  A blood-red cactus on her beauteous breast,
And dazzling diamonds in her dusky hair,
  Like a proud peacock's iridescent crest.

And close beside the daughter of old Spain,
    I see her lover of the years of yore,
I feel the fierce heart-hunger of his pain,
    When peace and rest have fled forevermore.

O lover, lover, cease thy sobs and sighs!
    Soft sleep deserts us when our souls adore;
For those who love not are the truly wise,
    And those who love are happy nevermore.

O lover, lover, she must soon grow old;
    Her stately step will be no longer proud;
Her heart will crumble in the churchyard mould,
    And dewy dark eyes vanish in her shroud.

O lover, lover, in her coffin low,
    The pure white flowers will wither on her breast,
That fair, fair breast whose love you longed to know,
    Forgotten like a swan's forsaken nest.

But still thy passion leaps to mine own heart,
    Thy grief, thy joy, thy clasping and thy kiss,—
Love's honeyed whispers and his poisoned dart,
    His thorns among the roses of his bliss.

And when I hearken to thy melodies
    I feel thine anguish in my bosom burn—
The pangs of gazing into dark brown eyes,—
    And pine to love and be loved in return.

O lover, lover, though thy heart and hand
    Are crumbling clay amid the charnel rust,
They come to haunt me in this Northern land
    Till I, like thee, am ashes and am dust.

Yet, lover, lover, cease thy sobs and sighs;
    Soft sleep deserts us when our souls adore;
For those who love not are the truly wise,
    And those who love are happy nevermore.

*"The Dove," a Spanish-American love song.

A PORTRAIT OF HENRY TIMROD

Strange eyes gaze sadly from that weary face,
　Beneath a brow that shows the seal of care;
Defeat and Disappointment leave their trace
　Upon the youthful visage pictured there.

The same old story here is handed down—
　The true-born poet and the same old doom—
The bard who starves while rhymesters wear the crown,
　Who finds his throne erected in a tomb.

Gone are the glories of your halcyon days,
　Gone are the heroes whom you sung of yore;
Their banners in the skies no longer blaze,
　Their fervent shouts are stilled forevermore.

No more their white steeds paw the bloody field,
　No more their trumpets rouse the raptured soul,
No more their ranks in fiery fight are wheeled,
　No more their drums like sullen thunders roll.

Yet as I view your old-time picture, all
　The proud past blossoms, though your day has fled;
Once more I hear your Stuart's battle-call,
　And see your Stonewall rising from the dead.

I see their blazoned banners float like fire,
　I hear their shouts sweep down the perished years;
I hear once more the throbbing of your lyre,
　Ecstatic with a nation's hopes and fears.

And foes with friends now come to honor you,
　O poet, free from blemish and from blame.
A wreath is yours as long as men are true,
　As long as Courage wins the crown of Fame.

[151]

THE PORTRAIT OF MICHAELANGELO

Here, painted by himself with rugged force,
The master's likeness gravely gazes down;
    A man advanced in years, in garments coarse,
Is limned in sober gray and black and brown.

See here the firm-set mouth, the shaggy hair,
The bushy beard, the high, determined jaw,
    The knotted hand, as though from out his lair
A dreaming lion stretched his mighty paw.

High over all, his many-wrinkled brows
Lift like a thunder-smitten mountain dome,—
    A head to wear Athenian myrtle boughs,
And laurel chaplets of Eternal Rome!

As in a rough brown bulb with ragged husk,
A splendid starry lily has its birth,
    His genius groped to dawn amid this dusk,
And brought from heaven new glories for the earth.

Here, in this Winter landscape, white with snow,
With naked rocks, bare trees and shivering herds,
    The Springtime slept, to wake in godlike glow,
With new-born blossoms lulled by songs of birds.

In melancholy majesty he stands,
Alone, and all bereft of earthly ties.
    No maiden ever kissed those rugged hands,
Or lured the love-light from those solemn eyes!

Born of no mother, save a marble sheath,
His offspring, waiting for him, slept alone;
    His Moses and his David first caught breath,
Begotten by their father out of stone.

Like one who roams at twilight, lone and late,
A mountain peak, where winds of Winter moan,
    The truly wise can never find a mate,
The truly great must always tread alone!

Down in deep vales he hears the herdsman's cries,
The cowbells faintly tinkling far below,—
   But all around him as the daylight dies,
Eternal cold, and everlasting snow!

ON A BEAUTIFUL PORTRAIT BY AN
UNKNOWN ARTIST

A sweet face smiles upon me from this frame,
   A high-born beauty, reigning long ago;
But not a record gives the artist's name;
   His home, his country, none shall ever know.

O what an art, to triumph o'er the tomb,
   To keep that lovely face forever fair,
To keep that youth in everlasting bloom,
   Defeating Death, and bidding Time despair!

Old age can never fade this virgin rose,
   Nor mar that smile, which flits but never flies,
Nor fleck those tresses with December snows,
   Nor dim the glory of those splendid eyes.

The peaches of those cheeks are blushing still,
   As in enchanted orchards long ago,
When some forgotten Autumn felt a thrill
   Of mellow honey through its fruitage glow

The cherries of those lips are ripe and red,
   But still unplucked, and free from all decay,
Though poaching birds and bare-foot truants fled
   As seasons came and pined and passed away.

Yet Artist, Artist, in thine ecstacy,
   Thou hast forgotten all the world holds dear;
Fame, fortune, power, all eluded thee,
   No acclamations thou shalt ever hear.

Upon thy brow shall never rest a wreath,
    No princely palm thy hand shall ever hold,
And thee, victorious over envious Death,
    Oblivion's mantle ever shall enfold.

Day after day, mayhap, thy feet have gone
    In weary, weary search for daily bread,
Or thou hast labored from the dusk till dawn,
    And tears of anguish in a garret shed.

Yet Artist, Artist, in thine eager joy
    Of toiling lovingly and toiling well,
Like some enthusiastic, ardent boy,
    Thy thrill of triumph none can ever tell.

For he who saves from death the works of God,
    Upon his shoulders feels the bud of wings,
Has plucked a blossom never sprung from sod,
    Is greater than the greatest of the kings.

POE'S COTTAGE AT FORDHAM

Here stands the little antiquated house,
    A few old-fashioned flowers at the door;
The dead past leaves it, quiet as a mouse,
    Though just beyond a giant city roar.

See here the curious porch, the attic there,
    The quaint square window with its awkward blind,
The weather-beaten wall, so blank and bare,
    And shadowed by an apple tree behind.

Within this room Virginia lay when ill,
    A black cat nestling there to warm her feet;
And so she languished, growing paler still,
    And shivering as the winds of Winter beat.

And here her mother through the long, long night
  Watched ever by the poor consumptive's side.
Here by the smoky lamp's low flickering light
  They looked upon Virginia when she died.

And here it was they wrapped her in her shroud,
  And hence they took her through the falling snow.
So on this old house closed at last the cloud
  That haunts it still with griefs of long ago.

And here the poet's life grew darker still
  As dream by dream had vanished into air;
Here day by day grew weaker yet his will,
  As golden hopes were rusted in despair.

But here were born those strains that can not die,
  Romances that shall rule the human heart.
Here Fame, whose summer hears no autumn sigh,
  Shall rear immortal marbles to his art.

Here Ligeia haunts us with enchanting eyes,
  We catch the rustle of Morella's gown;
Here Usher treads, and William Wilson dies,
  And Israfel sings Poe's supreme renown.

HOMER

What earthly King who envies not my name?
  What century shall behold my honor dim?
As virile and as vigorous is my fame
  As when mankind first heard my morning hymn.

Cæsar has come, has conquered, passed away;
  Young Alexander's empire is a dream;
Napoleon shared my sceptre for a day,
  Then saw the snapping of his cobweb scheme.

But I, who living begged my daily bread,
    Found death the gateway to a golden throne;
I rule the living, though they call me dead,
    And time to me is but a term unknown.

I see new poets come to take my place;
    They can not lift my lance or bend my bow;
If in their lines be loveliness or grace,
    I said the same three thousand years ago.

So Babylon and Ninevah have gone,
    While I rejoice in everlasting day;
Paris, Manhattan, London, had their dawn,
    And I shall see their splendor fade away.

The dear old gods I knew in ancient days,
    Of Egypt and Assyria, Greece and Rome,
Have lost their crowns, and strange new idols gaze
    Across the desert and the ocean foam.

The golden-haired Apollo is no more,
    But songs I sang him still have power to thrill;
Though Pallas pass, I keep my strength of yore;
    Great Pan is dead, but I am living still.

Lo, by the everlasting throne of God
    Sits Gabriel with his trumpet in his hand,
Waiting that far, far day, when sea and sod
    Give up their dead, before that Judge to stand.

Not till that trumpet bids the sun grow black,
    Shall breath of God blow out my radiant flame;
Not till the earth shall wander from her track,
    And there is no more sea, shall die my name.

BYRON

His heart was moulded in the weakness of the crumbling
    dust and clay,
Yet mighty as the summit of some granite mountain,
    old and gray.

His fancy twined the blushing roses round the crystal cup
    of mirth,
Then like a fleeting phantom wandered through the des-
    ert's parching dearth;

Within his portals Love was throned in richest Oriental
    state,
While at his doorway flourished thistles, thorns, and loath-
    some weeds of hate;

His spirit knew not Spring-time's songsters, nor her dewy
    waking flowers,
But loved the sad magnificence of Autumn's gorgeous
    dying bowers;

His feet were strangers to the purple morning's palaces of
    light,
But haunted vistas where the twilight's tearful eyes grew
    dim with night.

The world hath grander, purer bards, like Alps enthroned
    on spotless snow,
While he, like raging Aetna, flames forever with a fevered
    glow;

But round their chilly crowns of ice the timid blossoms
    fear to twine,
Whilst through his lavas spring the olive and the purple-
    clustered vine.

The world hath poets who from tears and thraldom rose
      to royal fame,
While he from state descended to assume the bard's and
      patriot's name;

They with the spell of old Timotheus raised their muses
      to the sky,
While he, like Saint Cecelia, drew his seraph earthward
      from on high.

His name, though mark for fling of despot, and the blinded
      bigot's thrust,
Shall live when Europe's tongues are silenced and the lips
      that spake them dust.

NAPOLEON AND BYRON

Two names together linked for evermore;
    Their onward march no kingdoms can retard;
Their banners flame on every sea and shore,
    Immortal chieftain and immortal bard.

Napoleon's name no longer awes the world;
    His legions long ago have shared his doom,
His stately empire in the dust is hurled,
    His aspirations ended in a tomb.

And Byron lost the fickle praise of man
    Amid the blossom of his youthful grace;
So then Death came to drag unto his den
    The classic beauty of that perfect face.

And yet they live triumphant o'er their shrouds,
    In song and story, legend and romance.
One, like an eagle, soars above the clouds,
    One, like a lion, rules the soul of France.

Sons of the mountains and the stormy sea,
    With souls of thunder, and with hearts of flame,
The czar of heroes, prince of poesy,
    The Spouse of Beauty, and the King of Fame.

THE BYRON CENTENARY
1788—1888

A hundred summers since his first birthday
Have shone in splendor, then have drooped and died;
Earth's fond old heart has throbbed with joyous pride
To greet them with their garlands green and gay,
And ached with anguish as they passed away.
But brightest summer decked her kingdoms wide
When unto Byron's lyre her mounts replied—
He perished, and her fields were sere and gray.

Her sweetest buds were blooming when he came,
But faded as his footsteps turned to leave.
Among her sons is many a mighty name,
But none like him, the reckless, bright and brave.
He died, like music in a glorious dream,
And Love's own heart was laid in Byron's grave.

SHELLEY
1792—1892

He came amongst us, wandering from on high,
Like golden-haired Apollo, long ago,
To share with us our lives and labors low,
And gaze with longing on his native sky;
To sing sweet songs whose strains shall never die
For weary mortals on their paths of woe;
To cause a golden city's walls to grow
By magic of his heavenly harmony.

But now the singer hath forever flown,
And left us beating still our prison bars;
His spirit over midnight's jeweled zone
Returned to reign with Mercury and Mars,
With Cassiopeia on her dazzling throne,
And dusk Orion crowned with flaming stars.

TRIBUTE TO SHELLEY

He was the son of Beauty and of Love,
Born in the lilies of the land of dreams;
A blithesome boy, who wandered from his home
In all his sweetness and his innocence,
And brought to earth mellifluous melodies,
Sung by the song-birds in its wondrous woods.
The gladsome singer of the summer hours,
The fair-haired playmate of the budding blooms,
Who flitted like a shadow from our sight
Amid our Autumn's waste of withered leaves.

O wondrous child, thine innocence hath power
To soar to heights where sages can not tread,
Thy sweetness thrills the cheerless heart of earth,
With strains triumphant of a starry lyre;
Our poets bring us fading flowers of earth,
Thou bearest blossoms from the fields of heaven.

His heart was deathless, but his form was dust,
His breath is still, and he will sing no more!
It seems the fire that smouldered in his heart
Should warm his breast within the frozen ground,
So that the Earth would throb within her womb
And give new birth unto her fairest son,
Just as the violets of the fragrant spring
Are withered but to rise as fair again.
But only humblest buds again can bloom;—
When angels fall they fall to rise no more,
And stars once darkened, never beam again.

But he shall dwell in lovelier lands than this,
Low Earth he leaves to reign in Paradise,—
A land of lilies and a land of love,
Rich with the glories of eternal day,

Beyond the woes of this poor world of ours,
Beyond the splendors of the radiant morn,
Where Love doth live unchanged, unharmed by time,
And where the canker touches not the flower.

I am left here in loneliness and pain,
Condemned to sing such humble songs as this,
To yearn for power that is all his own;
Where all our best songs crave for nobler things,—
Whose mortal rage, chained down, laments our fate,—
The common wailings of all hearts together.
But I am happy if my loving hands
Add one poor leaflet to his laurel wreath.

THE TOMB OF GALILEO

I have grown weary of the idle show
    Of pompous Castle and pretentious Court,
Of Churches—dingy wrecks of long ago—
    Of swords and guns in arsenal or fort.

I sicken at the sight of tarnished toys,
    Of dead-and-buried mistresses of kings,
Of spears of warring barons—bearded boys
    Who fumed and fought for cheap and childish things.

I care not for the saint of mythic fame,
    Who wore brass haloes on an empty haed,
The so-called patriot, who in Freedom's name,
    Heaped neighboring lands with hillocks of the dead.

But here lies one, the brave, the great, the good,
    Worth all the kings and queens the whole world round;—
Make bare your head in reverential mood,
    For here indeed you tread on Holy Ground.

His life, from selfish earthly motives purged,
 Was consecrated unto you and me;
He took the blow, that we might go unscourged,
 And wore the chains, that we might wander free.

He found the long-lost Pleiad, Saturn's band,
 And brought Jove's moons to yonder Tuscan hill;—
The second Joshua, at whose command
 The heavens ceased turning and the sun stood still.

The moon in starry-frosted skies of night
 Shall write in splendor Galileo's name,
And sun to sun at noon and morning light
 Shall blazon heaven with Galileo's fame.

MELBA

In radiating circles all aglow,
 The galleries glitter like a Northern light;
Electric torches wreathe the stage below
 Like royal gems of some Arabian night.

I see the silks and satins swirling by
 With misty laces and aerial plumes,
And diamonds palpitating far and nigh
 Through bowers of a paradise of blooms.

Blue eyes outbeam the sapphire's bluish spark,
 O'er feathery fans like doves a-flutter there;
Tiaras glimmer over tresses dark,
 And moon-like pearls on moon-like maids more fair.

The curtain rises on a splendid scene
 Amid the plaudits of that splendid throng,
And then She comes, of queenly beings Queen,
 World-famous Empress of the world of song.

O stately singer, from thy magic voice
    The present, like a dreary dream, hath fled,
In glories that have perished we rejoice,
    And transcendental splendors that were dead.

I hear a wild swan's piercing melodies
    At shrine of Venus, on the Cyprian shore,—
Dying in glory under diamond skies
    When Venus, Queen of Beauty, reigns no more.

In Persian gardens, under golden moons,
    I hear the nightingale still woo the rose,
Though faded are their far, forgotten Junes,
    And twice five hundred years have healed their woes.

By mediaeval castle, thrilled with bliss,
    I see the lovers trysting through the dark;
In odorous dewy dusk I see them kiss,
    Till startled by the lyric of the lark.

O thou hast suffered, peerless Queen of Song,
    And thrilled with keener than terrestrial joy,
Hast loved and languished, borne the yoke of Wrong,
    And seen stern Fate thy noble hopes destroy.

Upon thy brow the white swan lives again,
    And in thy lips the perished Persian rose,
Within thy heart the nightingale's own pain,
    And in thy soul the dear dead lover's woes.

The music ceases, and I wake to find
    The dull, dry story of our sordid life,
The same old ways, where blind men lead the blind
    Through all the selfsame sorrow, toil and strife.

Alas, to think that voice must pass away,
    And leave no marvel of thy matchless art,
And never, never, after this short day,
    One breathing being shall those strains impart!

Alas, to think those lips shall then be dumb,
  That glorious name be graven on the tomb,
And never, never, through the years to come
  Those notes divine shall vibrate through the gloom!

But, peerless lady, like thy silver songs,
  The stateliest empires soon must pass away,
With all the murmur of their mighty throngs
  Like chirp of insects on a Summer day.

Then princely Paris, radiant realm of art,
  Shall be abandoned in a waste alone,
Manhattan but a long-forgotten mart,
  And lordly London but a heap of stone.

Yet perfume cannot pass to nothingness.
  No blush on blossom ever come to naught;
In some far Spring, beneath a beam's caress,
  They live again, with soulful sweetness fraught.

No song, no poem ever thrilled in vain,
  Nor word of kindness, lover's smile or sigh:
The True and Good and Beautiful remain,
  And Love lives on, though lovers all must die.

So no thing beautiful is lost in death;
  All that returns for which our souls repine;
Fadeless thy laurel and thy myrtle wreath,
  O peerless Empress of the voice divine!

HOLLAND

A land of straight canals, of quaint old towns,
  Fat cows, fine horses roaming level leas;
Of poplar-bordered roads, of dykes and downs,
  And fisher-boats a-sail on misty seas.

A land of windmills and of wooden shoes,
 Stork-trodden marshes, meadows white with sheep,
Where salt sea winds their vital forces infuse,
 And salt sea billows rouse the soul from sleep.

A land which, hating sluggards, drones and slaves,
 Faced tides and tyrants since its life began.
Brave little Conqueror of the ocean waves,
 Brave little Champion of the Rights of Man!

SAINT AUGUSTINE

Saint Augustine, Saint Augustine,
What memories come to me,
While treading down your quaint old streets,
Along the tropic sea!
Where old Fort Marion rears his walls
Of mouldering shells and sands,
And green against an opal sky
The tall palmettos stand.

Here mocking-birds entrance the air
With keen and quivering notes,
And through the long gray Spanish moss
The redbird's love-song floats.
Here orange gardens scent the breeze
With wreaths of starry blooms,
And citrons with the lemons hang
Like gold in emerald glooms.

Like Ponce de Leon, I have come,
Old town, forever young,
To find your bubbling Fount of Youth
For ages sought and sung.
Alas! I find you fresh and green,
Blithe in your old-time joy;
But man, for all his plaints and prayers,
Is only once a boy.

SAN GABRIEL MISSION

A long, low building, reared of brick and stone,
  An iron railing running up its side;
A churchyard with its graves weed-over grown,
  And epitaphs which tall geraniums hide.

A plumy pepper-tree hangs billowy boughs
  To shade the portals of the ancient church;
On crumbled walls the droning hornets drowse,
  And now and then some pigeon finds a perch.

Two swarms of bees have found a quiet home
  In hollowed niches of the Mission's side;
Here they have treasured honey, hung the comb,
  As years have flourished, pined away and died.

Here in the chapel hang the old-time saints,
  Brought centuries past from convent-cells of Spain;
Stern-browed and formal, in their vivid paints
  They hold their own as empires wax and wane.

This quaint baptismal font of copper here,
  Old monks beat into shape for pious need;
Here fired with zeal, yet half in doubt and fear,
  Three thousand red men chose the white man's creed.

Around the rectory door frail roses twine,
  In pink and yellow clusters faintly sweet;
Lantanas glow like red and golden wine,
  In brilliant sprays that hang from head to feet.

Flame not, lantana, with too bold a red,
  Flush not, young rose, in vanity or pride;
Remember how your loving Master bled,
  Remember how your loving Master died!

Without these walls one hears the mighty world
   Rage like an awful ocean in alarm;
Here in this haven every sail is furled,
   And every sailor safe from every harm.

Without these walls let revolutions roll,
   Let epochs march, let progress never cease;
Here seek the balm that soothes the weary soul,
   That gives the broken-hearted wanderer peace!

THE EVERGLADES

Vast, watery fields of slender waving grass;
Near by, a green and matted mangrove swamp;
Huge live-oak limbs where verdant creepers romp,
And orchids hang red flowers in a mass;
A river in a bramble-tangled pass,
Where trumpet blossoms swing in scarlet pomp;
Great bamboo thickets, oozy, dark and damp,
And starry lilies in a green morass.

White cranes on yonder cypress boughs alight,
An old gray heron stalks demure and slow;
Then gliding through the gray-mossed forest's night,
A water-snake dives in the dim bayou.
I wonder, as the reptile sinks from sight,
What monster shapes are swimming down below.

NOON IN THE TROPICS

A violet ocean and a violet sky;
A glistening beach of red and yellow sands;
A promontory where one palm-tree stands;
Green orange groves, gold-fruited, far and nigh;
Here clumps of cocoanuts soar to the sky,
Here spreads the sugar and tobacco lands;
Here, deftly tilled by swarthy negro hands,
Pineapple fields in burning sunshine lie.

Ah, what relief, should summer pass away,
And bring this gorgeous pageant to a close!
Once more to see a dark November day
Shake down his dead leaves while the north wind blows!
Once more to see December, cold and gray,
From leaden clouds sweep swirls of fluttering snows!

A MEXICAN WAYSIDE STATION

A red-hot sun is blazing fiercely down
    On red-hot hills of dreary desert sand;
The ragged sage-brush all is scorched to brown,
    And gray with dust the mesquite bushes stand.

Like grizzled ghosts the cactus thickets lift
    Their gaunt, gnarled fingers, barbed with spines for claws;
Thorn-girdled, thrusting from a rocky rift,
    Are serried teeth of aloes sharp as saws.

A stockade wall surrounds a hut of mud,
    Where naked urchins romp with mangy curs;
Dumb as a painted post, with scarlet hood,
    A mongrel native stares but never stirs.

An ancient bucket hangs above a well,
    The well-rope dangling from a crooked stick;
Here beggars swarm, their harrowing tales to tell,
    Where hobbling hunchbacks crowd the maimed and sick.

And here a broken wooden plough is left,
    Discarded with a battered wooden wheel,
And here like shipwrecked seamen, all bereft,
    Two oxen by a shattered wagon kneel.

On brazen zinnias withering blazes beat,
    The hollyhock in thirsty anguish dies;
The prickly-pears, a-blister in the heat,
    Ooze out their sickly syrup for the flies.

But here a-swing from cracks of mud-built walls,
    There blooms a peerless lovely yellow rose;
Her sweetness all the Northern Spring recalls,
    New-born at melting of the northern snows.

And here, like Patience, still she waits and waits
    In burning suns that doom her soon to die,
Yet never breathes a murmur at the fates
    Who forced her exile from her native sky.

The railroad trains pass thundering North and South,
    And bear rich gifts to others far away;
But here she lingers in the land of drought,
    Forgotten as she fades from day to day.

Here one by one her golden petals fall,
    Yet hear no sighs borne on her fragrant breath;
O Rose of Patience!   Life soon takes your all,
    And leaves you to an unregretted death.

And so, my heart, in patience still you wait,
    While fame and fortune come and pass me by;
The great world rumbles on in pomp and state,—
    It would not answer though it heard you cry.

So, glorious dreams, here I can only sit
    With folded hands and watch you fade from view;
I smile in silence as I see you flit,
    Yet all my life is lost in losing you.

AT THE CATHEDRAL OF MEXICO

Here gold and silver glimmer everywhere,
    Through gracious twilight, down the solemn aisles;
A cloud of incense dims the dreamy air,
    As up yon stair a long procession files.

[169]

They reach the altar; priests and chorus-boys
  Are all enrobed in scarlet draped in white;
How quiet!   Not the shadow of a noise
  Disturbs the pious meaning of the sight.

Then like a constellation, star by star,
  The golden candlesticks have burst in bloom;
Now like great winds from Paradise afar
  The glorious organ pipes begin to boom.

The sweet, sharp voices of the bird-like boys
  Respond to deep-toned chantings of the priest;
O what a call to heaven's transcendent joys
  Beside the Bridegroom at His wedding feast!

Yon sculptured angel with the golden wings
  Seems beckoning to a blissful realm above;
Ah, is it true, that song the choir-boy sings,
  Of endless life, of everlasting love?

And then my gaze falls on a wooden saint
  Whose wooden feet long in this niche have stood;
Poor little doll!   Your lips, through gaudy paint,
  Seem saying "I would help you if I could."

O wooden saint, outside, on yonder square,
  The Inquisition fixed its fearful stake;
O whisper not the horrors that were there,—
  And all enacted for Religion's sake!

Down yonder street, housed in yon rambling pile,
  Are hideous Aztec idols, all a-grin;—
Nay, do not shrink my question with a smile,—
  Those Gods, like yours, presumed to pardon sin!

There stands the Aztec sacrificial stone;
  Above it frightful Aztec idols scowl;
They heard ten thousand human victims groan,
  And heard a million maddened votaries howl!

Perplexed, confused between the warring creeds,
  I can not tell which way to turn, in sooth.
My anxious soul, beset by sorest needs,
  Like Pilate, still is asking "What is Truth?"

O, breathe me, wooden saint, one precious word!
  Come, tell me, as we two forever part,—
Will all these prayers in heaven at last be heard,
  Or end forever at your wooden heart?

IN A TROPICAL GARDEN

Here every honey-hearted sweet
In fruits of gold and red
The heavy-laden tropic trees
With rich profusion shed.
Here buff and scarlet blossoms hang
From vines of glossy green,
And humming birds, with ruby throats,
Like floating flames are seen.

Here pink and purple passion-flowers
Hang scarfs of airy silk,
And claret-clouded orchids bloom
By orchids white as milk.
Here red and yellow mangoes cling,
Here citrons bend the twigs,
Here green and golden melons trail,
Here swing delicious figs.

What gorgeous flowers, what luscious fruits
Unknown to me before!
I gaze in wonder on them now,
But soon shall see no more.
Their blaze of glory stills the speech,
Their brilliance blinds the eyes;
What Tyrian tints, what heavenly hues,
Like flaming sunset skies!

No Northern violet opens here
Its baby eyes of blue;
No daisy lifts from tufted grass
To drink the morning dew.
No oak tree ever quivers here
In wanton winds of heaven;—
Ah, I am but a stranger, too,
Here for a moment driven.

Yet, Beauty ever hand in hand
With Sadness still is met;
These glories only fill my heart
With longing and regret.
What sorrow haunts this scented air
For bliss once all my own;
Yes, Love and Joy should both be mine,
Yet here am I alone!

BESIDE THE DANUBE

Beside the Danube let me sit
    And view the scene before me,
While olden griefs and olden joys
    On spirit wings flit o'er me.
This is the stream in song renowned,
    Far-famed in storied pages,
Whose shores are haunted by the dreams
    Of lost romantic ages.

And yet, O Danube, as I muse
    Beside your rippling waters,
I think not of your chivalry,
    Your splendid sons and daughters.
Forgotten are your mounts and vales,
    Your peasant-cots, your castles,
Your Kings and Queens, your peace, your wars,
    Your noblemen, your vassals.

I think of one who sang to me
　　In years gone by forever,
Of lovers, who one night in June
　　Rowed on you, Danube River.
O, I remember still that night,
　　Your city lights a-glimmer,
And how the mellow moon arose
　　And made your wavelets shimmer.

Ah, in those days we never thought
　　We ever would be parted;
We thought to wander side by side,
　　Forever single-hearted.
How strange!　Beneath her churchyard grass
　　She dreams no more, O, never,
Of one, six thousand miles away
　　Beside the Danube River.

AT THE PARIS MORGUE

Behind a glass, all in a ghastly row,
　　We here behold the loathsome pauper dead;
Sick at the sight, our horror bids us go;
　　We shudder, start, we turn away the head.

Shocked and disgusted at those staring eyes,
　　Those blue-white brows, lips withered, pinched and
　　　　　brown,
We quail at hideous Death without disguise,
　　And like a leaden lump our hearts sink down.

And yet, poor creatures, you have loved and laughed,
　　And known Parisian glory in your prime;
The cup of passion and of mirth you quaffed,
　　Before the days you fell to want and crime.

Old woman, in your girlhood long ago,
  Some lover's fingers fondled through your hair;
He breathed sweet words no other ears might know,
  And clasped you close, and swore that you were fair.

Old man, your mother would not know you now,—
  Her blue-eyed boy is now a shocking sight!—
God! who would think a man could fall so low,
  That such a dawn could die in such a night?

Young woman, trusting hearts are seldom wise!
  You here forsaken in the Morgue alone?
Man's sweetest vows are oft but honeyed lies;
  Youth's tender heart may sometimes turn to stone!

Young man, you loudly swore to win the race;
  Hither you came in all your boyhood bloom;
See, glorious Paris turns away her face,
  And leaves you in the horror of this tomb!

O Paris, Paris, you have slain them all,
  Your foolish lovers, snared within your spell;
You sit enthroned, robed in a funeral pall,
  Your face a heaven, and your heart a hell!

THE DESERT

Streched helpless on the burning sands I lie,
  While scorching suns beat on me as they pass.
Day after day I watch the glaring sky,
  A fiery furnace reared like burnished brass.

Spread like a tawny lion's shaggy hide,
  The yellow plains reach hillocks red and brown;
See here the bones where dogs and men have died,
  While imp-faced rocks in hideous hate looked down!

No living thing will come to share my grief,
   Save when at night the famished coyotes howl,
Or, coiled at twilight by some withered sheaf,
   The rattler hisses at the screeching owl.

Ah, if I only once could hear the birds
   Trill songs of joy in woodlands fresh and cool!
Ah, if I only once could see the herds
   Wade, lowing, knee-deep in some dark-green pool!

Ah, if I only once could feel the tide
   Come thundering with its giant foaming waves;
Through all my burning veins cool streams should glide,
   And raise the corpses from my world of graves!

But year by year I wait and wait and wait,
   And year by year I linger in despair;
Yet still I hear the stern decree of Fate;
   "No rain, No rain!" through white-hot noons a-glare.

O God, remember I was dear to Thee
   In green, glad mornings ere I felt Thy frown.
I am Thy daughter; hear and pity me,
   Accurst and fruitless, withered, barren, brown!

A gray-haired virgin, still unwooed, unwed,
   I waste away unloved and all alone;
My bosom is a dried-up river bed,
   The heart within it but a dusty stone.

O, all Thy gifts are held beyond my grasp;
   I am a woman; let me sweetly rest,
To feel a lover's arms around me clasp,
   A tiny infant cooing on my breast!

No rain, no dew, from cruel sky or sea;
   In restless, raging passion here I lie.
Like Rachel I am crying out to Thee,
   "God, give me children, or else let me die!"

[175]

DOVE OF THE DESERT

Dove of the desert, so wild and so free,
   What nook in this waste is dear unto thee?
Around you I see the dead cactus stand,
   And brown, withered weeds on hot hills of sand.
Here yawns the red gully, here burns the dead plain,
   Here hangs the sharp rocks, all thirsty for rain.
O dove of the desert, so wild and so free,
   What spot in these barrens is blest unto thee?

Dove of the desert, around thee are spread,
   In the alkali dust, the bones of the dead.
No spring can be seen, no blossom uprears
   Through the bayonet-bush with its porcupine spears.
No cloud cools the brow of the hot, fevered plain,
   Unbaptized, unblest, with the patter of rain.
O dove of the desert, as meek as a child,
   What charm brings thee here to this death-haunted
      wild?

Dove of the desert, you find a sweet rest
   When sinking at night to sleep on your nest.
The desert is barren, and sterile and hot,
   Yet it gives to your heart a consecrate spot.
I traverse great cities, yet I find no home,
   On the crowded streets I in solitude roam.
There out in the desert, you mate with your own,—
   Dove of the desert, I fare forth alone.

THE BLUEBIRD

When the bluebird comes in the days of spring,
With a sweet, soft note and swift, wild wing,
When the redbirds blush and the dogwoods bloom,
And the daffodil comes from her chilly tomb,

When the fox-glove peers through the tender grass,
And the bluet peeps like a roguish lass,
When the south winds with a swirl of showers,
And a bugle blast through the budding bowers,

Then I hear the moan and the pensive plaint
Of his throbbing throat, like a love-song faint
From the far, far lands where the dear ones go
When they leave us lorn in a world of woe.

So the primrose knows of his secret well,
And the brown bee learns from the lily bell,
And the wrens have heard from the friendly doves
That the violet is the one he loves.

And they say his heart is forever true
To the one wee maid with the eyes of blue;
At his songs she wakes in the morning light,
And they fold her lids at the fall of night.

In the days of old, so the wild flowers say,
When the world was young as an April day,
When the red man roved through the Western Wild
With a heart as free as a wilful child,

Then the bluebird came as an angel white
From the lands of love and the lands of light,
Where the blasts never blow and the skies never snow,
And he trod with men through the world below,

Till his eyes were cast on the damsel sweet,
With her flower-like face and her fawn-like feet.
And they loved so well that the birds and bees
Would repeat the tale to the gossiping trees.

Of a mortal race was the lovely maid,
And the day would dawn when her face would fade,
While the angel came from a world on high,
Where the night falls not, nor the blest ones die.

In her youth and joy was the arrow sped,
And they laid her low with the dreamless dead;
So she passed away from her loyal brave,
And his clasp and kiss to the silent grave.

So the fleet days fly and the years pass by,
And the centuries fade and the ages die,
And he pines away in his passion true
Till his raiment white is an ashen blue.

So the bluebird sings to his long-lost love
Through the fields below and the skies above,
From the noon to night, through the misty morn,
Through the summers, the springs, till the falls forlorn.

And she loves him so as he pours his notes,
And the dear, dear call through the forest floats
In her moulded shroud, after long, long years,
She awakes at last and her loved one hears.

When the springtime comes through the sleet and snow,
She trills at his call in her grave below,
And returns to him with her dear, dark eyes,
So a violet blooms under April skies.

But the bluebird sings, and her lips are dumb,
And the bluebird calls, but she cannot come.
And the one reply she makes from her tomb
Is her soft, soft breath, with its frail perfume.

When he sings love-songs she but sobs and sighs,
And her sweet, sweet breath in its dumbness dies;
As the dew-drops fall she is faint with fears,
And her blue, blue eyes are bedimmed with tears.

But the wild flowers hear what the lovers say
Through the ardent hours of the April day;
They have told the words of their songs to me,
And so I will tell of their secrets to thee.

The Bluebird

"Violet sweet, with the eyes of blue,
Violet sweet, with the diadem dew,
Violet sweet, the dearest to me,
Violet sweet, I am waiting for thee!

"Lying alone in thy dungeon gloom,
Parted from me in thy mournful tomb,
See, I await with a heart of lead,—
Listen to me, and wake from the dead!

"Violet sweet, I am filled with fears,
Violet sweet, I am blind with tears,
Violet sweet, awake to my trill,
Violet sweet, I am faithful still!"

The Violet

"Beautiful bird, I have waited long,
Beautiful bird, I have heard thy song,
Beautiful bird, so faithful to me,
Beautiful bird I love none but thee!

"Waiting for years under dank, dark sods,
Shrouded and still under hard, cold clods,
Numb with despair, my hopes had all fled,
Scattered and lost with the dreamless dead.

"Beautiful bird, bringing life unto me,
Beautiful bird, I am searching for thee,
Beautiful bird, from death I depart,
Beautiful bird, to thy sweet, sweet heart!"

The Bluebird

"Loving thee still when the redbirds call,
Loving thee still when the red leaves fall,
Loving thee still when the blue-bell blows,
Loving thee still through the chill, white snows;

"Loving thee still in the radiant noons,
Loving thee still under ghostly moons,
Loving thee still as the days go by,
Loving thee still as the dim years die."

The Violet

"Dreaming of thee in the bleak, black earth,
Dreaming of thee in the dim, dark dearth,
Dreaming of thee in the morning light,
Dreaming of thee in the mournful night;

"Dreaming of thee through the winter gloom,
Dreaming of thee through the springtime bloom,
Dreaming of thee as I ope to the sky,
Dreaming of thee as I wither and die."

The Bluebird

"And the wild rose singeth her songs to me,
Seeking, O precious, to woo me from thee,
And her proud head bends from her stately seat
In scorn upon thee far down at her feet;

"The marsh lily sayeth she is fairer by far,
With her white, white breast, her face like a star,
She begs me, O sweet, to flee from thy side
And make her, O sweet, my love and my bride.

"But never shall I grow faithless to thee,
O fairest and sweetest and truest to me!
My heart and my soul forever are wed
To the one lost love in realms of the dead."

THE HUMMING-BIRD

I flit through the bowers of April flowers
    And the mellow skies of June,
O'er sparkling floods and bloomy woods,
    From orient morn to radiant noon.
From the fairy cells of budding bells
    I suck the golden honey;
They sway and they swing at the wave of my wing,
    And my fires make shadows sunny.
Unknown to pain and to earthly stain,
    I glitter near and far;
My courses I run, like a beam from the sun,
    Or a midnight shooting star.

In the torrid zone my fires are sown,
    And in northern worlds of ice,
Over wizard strands in the Arctic lands
    And the palmy isles of paradise.
Where the awful night, in winter bedight,
    Shrouds desolate, boundless seas,
I glint through the glooms with butterfly plumes
    When the mariner despairing flees.
The dark-eyed maiden of the Southern Eden
    Far, far from the kingdom of snows,
Will give me a smile as I bask awhile
    In the heart of a tropic rose.

No mortal sorrow, no fear of the morrow
   Can darken my rainbow hours;
Though the bale be thine, the bliss shall be mine;
   I live forever in budding flowers.
When the buds I cherished have pined and have perished,
   I fly to the younger blooms.
I know not the dearth of this lonely earth,
   Nor the shades of its silent tombs.
By the seraphs given, I flutter from heaven,
   I can not abide in a cage;
I beat at my bars a-bleed from my scars,
   Till I die in restless rage.

THE MOCKING-BIRD

From an Indian Legion

I

I gazed at a mocking-bird high in a tree,
And this was the song he warbled to me:

II

Thou wonderest why, as aloft I soar,
I sing to thee not the same strains o'er,
And marvel much that the notes I pour
By other blithe birds were thrilled before,
And every sound on the sea or shore
I mimic and mock forevermore.

III

Far beyond the mystic mountains,
   Far beyond the sunset's throne,
Where the crystal western fountains
   Bubble through the forest lone,

Lived an Indian tribe now perished,
    I their prince in days of old;
Yet a maiden sweet I cherished
    In a neighboring nation's fold.

But our tribes were foemen ever,
    So our love we dared not tell,
And I saw her sweet face never
    Till the twilight shadows fell.

Then with stealthy steps I sought her
    With a signal sharp and shrill,
Till the foeman chieftain's daughter
    Joined me by the woodland rill.

I would mock the thrush in flying,
    Or the katydid at night,
Hooting owl or panther crying,
    So her steps were guided right.

Then we two would roam together,
    Kissing in the friendly gloom,
Till the blooming stars would wither
    And the night sink in her tomb.

But together once they found us,
    And they doomed us both to die;
To the stake they dragged and bound us,
    Where the cruel flames streamed high.

But the great God heard our sighing:
    In the sky a storm upreared;
From the smoke two birds came flying,
    And the lovers disappeared.

Yet we thoughtless twain had ever
    Gazed but in each other's eyes,
Impious souls, had worshipped never
    Him who rules within the skies.

So he saved us but to doom us
    Through the moons to roam apart,
While despair seeks to consume us,
    Reigning in each breaking heart.

I, a mock-bird, fondly singing,
    Robed in sombre ashen gray,
She, with gorgeous plumage, winging
    In some forest far away.

IV

My tongue must twitter through all the hours,
Still mocking each sound in woodland bowers,
The wail of winds and sobs of showers,
The cricket's shrill chirp in fading flowers,
The night-hawk's cry in her pine-tree towers,
The bark of the wolf when midnight lowers.

But then at last, in a dim, sweet year,
When gray with despair and gray with fear,
And mocking still at the sounds I hear,
I shall trill the true note that strikes mine ear,
The song that is sung by my long-lost dear,
And then her sweet face shall reappear.

Till then this song over forests wide
I sing as I seek my banished bride:

V

I am seeking for thee ever through the emerald woods of
    May,
I am seeking for thee ever through October's fields of
    gray;

I am seeking for thee ever through the June-time's golden
    glory,
I am seeking for thee ever through December's twilight
    hoary;

I am seeking for thee ever where the morning buds are
blooming,
I am seeking for thee ever where the vesper shades are
looming;

I am seeking for thee ever through the dazzling tropic
noons,
I am seeking for thee ever under wan and wasted moons;

I am striving still to find thee through the green magnolia
trees,
I am striving still to find thee by the misty northern seas;

I am striving still to find thee in the palmy Indian Islands,
I am striving still to find thee in the chill and trackless
highlands;

I am striving still to find thee on the crimson cactus blossoms,
I am striving still to find thee in the white lake-lilies'
bosoms;

I am striving still to find thee with the Aztec meek and
mild,
I am striving still to find thee with the Huron's savage
child.

So I seek thee, always faithful, seek thee, sweetest, thus
forever,
But I find thee in my roamings, banished, vanished darling,
never.

VI

Hear the blackbird, silver-throated, calling me to meet him
in the breezy boughs,
Hear the bluejay, blithe and buoyant, bidding me to join
him in his mad carouse;

Hear the redbird, wild and wilful, teasing me to aid him
    in some curious quest,
Hear the bluebird, sweet and soothing, bidding me to come
    and see his happy nest;

Hear, amid pink-blossomed orchards, wooing, cooing of the
    fond enamoured dove,
And the oriole, her rival, begging me to bless her with my
    love.

But my heart is ever faithful; never shall another love be
    known to me;
Though the myriad ages wither, in my visions only one
    sweet face I see.

VII

I burn,
I long, I yearn,
Through autumns chill and red,
Where blasted, burning deserts spread,
To see once more thy precious, loving face,
And hear once more thy wild, sweet, fawn-like tread of
    grace.

I've not
Thy love forgot;
Then wilt thou let me pine
Far from thy starry eyes divine?
Return, return! then like a blithesome boy
I'll sing forever for thee thrilling tunes of joy!

VIII

Indian wigwams, Indian camp-fires from their ruthless
    pale-faced foes have vanished,
And the red men, like the red leaves, on a hoary winter
    blast are banished.

[186]

All our sacred groves have fallen, all the trophies of our
   tribe have perished,
All our legends long forgotten, and our mother-tongue no
   longer cherished.

But amid the desolation, ever vainly for thy presence
   pining,
Never in my tearful visions have I seen thy glorious plumage shining.

Yet another love can never make me drink from out his
   bubbling chalice,
And no other maiden woo me to abide within her blissful
   palace.

I shall love thee till the springtime thrilleth not the earth's
   breast with emotion,
I shall love thee till the dew-drops all have vanished from
   the desert ocean.

Though I find thee, beauteous being, not till all the mountains burst asunder,
And the judgment trumpet rouses all the earth's dead like
   a peal of thunder.

THE ORIOLE

I

Oriole, swift oriole,
All the Orient glories stole
In the splendor of your sable and your orange plumes,
Come from tropic lands of fire
In your royal, rich attire,
Like the dazzle of a dawning through the ebon midnight
   glooms.

Oriole, swift oriole,
Like a fiery-hearted coal,
Or a blazing topaz in the darkness of a mine,
Like a blossom black as night
With a breast of burning light,
Or the jet and saffron banners of an autumn day's decline.

Like a meteor's yellow spark
In the bosom of the dark,
Like the flaming treasures of some old Arabian cave,
Like the gems a gypsy wears,
Tiger eyes in lurid lairs,
Or a crown of flashing jewels in a dead king's gloomy
        grave.

Oriole, swift oriole,
Like the fierce and fiery soul
Of a sinful seraph who is doomed forevermore,
Come from tropic lands of light
Unto Northern lands of night,
Over palms of peerless islands, over ocean's sullen roar!

Oriole, swift oriole,
You are like a shining scroll,
All the tropic glories burnished on your brilliant wings,
And our tender Northern blooms
Waken from their chilly tombs
As you flame above our forests in the summers and the
        springs.

II

In the ages that have fled,
In the generations dead,
Far away in richest regions of the Southern land,
You were eldest son and heir
To a proud king ruling there,
Dwelling at a peerless palace on a splendor-haunted strand.

But one day it came to pass
That you loved a beggar lass
In this Northern land of storm and shadow far away,
In this land of gloom and grief,
Wailing wind and autumn leaf,
Where the queenly summers perish in October skies of gray;

In this land of want and woe,
In this land of sleet and snow,
Where the sad September glimmers through a haze of
    tears,
Where the birds are poor and plain,
And the blossoms all are slain,
Where the dark December conquers all the kingdoms of
    the years.

And the beggar maiden thrush
All her silvery songs would hush
If she heard your footsteps coming to her secret nest;
For your love the lass returned,
And her fervent bosom burned,
And her gentle heart would flutter with a sweet and sad
    unrest.

But they tore you two apart,
Prisoned you with aching heart
Far away beyond the trackless oceans of the South,
Leaving her to pine alone,
With the winter winds to moan,
And your kisses fell no longer on her eager, upturned
    mouth.

But you prayed and pleaded so,
In your loneliness and woe,
That they let you come to see her as the springtime came,
And you lingered by her side,
Through the golden summer tide,
Till the mournful autumn shattered all her palaces of
    flame.

And you come to see her still
When the springtime bowers thrill,
When the gorgeous summer blossoms on the hill-tops blaze,
When the tiger-lily blows,
And the trumpet-flower glows,
And the golden August harvest glimmers in a mellow maze.

From the South you flutter forth
To the grim and gloomy North,
And you bring the fiery splendors of the tropic noons,
Bringing dreams of plumy palms,
Bringing dreams of slumbering calms,
Where the everlasting summer in delicious languor swoons.

But when autumn showers come,
And the blossoms all are numb,
You must leave the little maiden, whom you love, alone;
When the winds of winter blow,
And the fields are filled with snow,
She must wander, broken-hearted, as the bitter tempests
        moan.

Oriole, swift oriole,
So it was with mine own soul
When the One Love came to greet me with his flags of fire;
All was piercing, burning bliss,
Life was like a clinging kiss,
And my breast was palpitating with a sweet and strange
        desire.

Love has brought me days of dole;
Love my peace and quiet stole
When he came with fierce embraces from the fervent
        South,
When he came from fabled lands,
And he pressed my trembling hands,
And I felt the honeyed kisses from his passion-pulsing
        mouth.

[190]

Oriole, swift oriole,
Like a black and smouldering coal,
Is my heart, that once was burning with a golden glow,
And the fields of lambent light
Now are hid in solemn night,
And my summer's tropic splendors shrouded in December
 snow.

THE WOOD THRUSH

Bird of the brown wing and the dotted breast,
  Who dwells in deep woods, cool and dark and green;
In dewy, dim retreats he rears his nest,
  By all save barefoot truants left unseen.

In Spring and Summer, at the dusk and dawn,
  He floods the forest with his liquid trill;
At burning noon, in solitude withdrawn,
  The hours doze on while all his songs are still.

Like rival troubadours, from every spray,
  To all his notes his brethren make reply;
They speed the splendid sunrise on his way,
  And chant a requiem when the light must die.

When morning, like a tulip flecked with fire,
  In scarlet and in orange breaks in bloom,
Bird answers bird, and in one heavenly choir
  They hail him from their forest-temple's gloom:

"O day of joy, haste thy nimble feet!
  All earth is happy, like a sweet love-story.
Come on, come on, where Youth and Pleasure meet,
  To crown thee as thou risest in thy glory!"

When sunset lingers over Western hills
   In ashen purple, like an exiled king,
Bird answers bird in melancholy trills,—
   Ah me, that song the wild wood-thrushes sing!

"O perfect day, how soon thy joys shall end!
   Thou wilt return, O never, never, never;
Far, O how far, thy weary feet must wend;
   O day of joy, farewell, farewell, forever!"

THE REDBIRD

I

Redbird, Redbird, brave and brilliant, flitting on thy
    wings of flame,
Tell me, Redbird, shrill and startling, whence thy blood-
    red plumage came?

Like a scarlet-crested poppy, blazing in the sultry noon,
Like the frail, enchanted crescent of the crimson setting
    moon;

Like a spray of fiery tulips, lit by hearts of golden light,
Like a ruby star arising in the shadows of the night;

Like the burning blush of sunrise, driving all the dusk
    away,
Like the sunset's splash of splendor from the bleeding
    heart of day;

Flaming through the dogwood blossoms, creamy-clustered
    locust trees,
Swinging on the grape-vine's tendrils, flying with the boom-
    ing bees;

Mingling with the scarlet trumpets, where the verdant
creepers twine,
Flushing like a falling goblet, spilling out its sparkling
wine;

Blushing through the cypress branches, through the green
swamps, cool and still,
Waking all the emerald shadows with thy sharp and sudden trill;

Redbird, Redbird, brave and brilliant, flitting on thy wings
of flame,
Tell me, Redbird, shrill and startling, whence thy blood-red
plumage came?

II

I was once an Indian maiden, in the dream-years, long
ago,
When the red man in these forests first beheld his pale-
browed foe.

Then a young knight with his comrades marched within
our fatherland;
Never had our simple people seen so bright and brave a
band;

And their leader trod before them, with a gay and gallant
air,
With his blue eyes, dark and dreamy, with his clustered
golden hair;

With his sweet mouth like a wild rose, and his cheeks in
boyish bloom,
With his white brow overshadowed by his helmet's snowy
plume.

All my people bade him welcome, though their hearts
were filled with hate,
And they gave their hands in friendship, but in secret
planned his fate.

Yet I often met the stranger, and he kindly spake to me
In the strange and broken accents of his home beyond the
sea;

And I often wandered with him, through the forest, field
and dell,
And his sweet and subtle whispers bound me in a blissful
spell.

I would tell him mystic legends of our tribe in vanished
days,
Names of birds and trees and insects, blossoms budding in
our ways;

Habits of the crawling serpent, cunning of the crafty
fox,
Of the hare and hawk and squirrel, and the eagle in the
rocks.

He would tell me of his people in the realms beyond the
sea,
Of their kingdoms and their cities, like a wonderland to
me.

So my soul was made his captive, and I longed to follow
him,
As a slave beside her master, over lake and mountain-rim.

Once I stole among our chieftains, slipping like a stealthy
spy,
And I heard the painted warriors swearing that my knight
must die.

Then with bare feet in the midnight, through the dank and
    chilling dew,
Crawling, cringing, creeping, running, stole the silent vil-
    lage through:

Then I found my lover sleeping in his quiet tent, near by,
And revealed to him the secret, that he might not stay and
    die;
Then I pressed his bounding bosom to my palpitating
    breast,
Felt his fond farewell embraces, nevermore to be caressed;

Then I blest him and I kissed him, to our village took
    my flight,
And I lost my love forever, on that anguish-haunted
    night.

And he fled from out our forests, baffled all the Indians'
    hate,
But he left me with my people, left me there to meet my
    fate.

For the warriors knew me guilty, led me to a lonely woods,
And they stabbed my burning bosom, till I perished, dyed
    in blood.

But my lover, false and fickle, never dreamed or cared for
    me,
Wooed and won a beauteous maiden in his home beyond
    the sea.

So my ghost is flitting ever, like an autumn leaflet red,
When the summer suns have faded, and the summer
    blooms have fled.

So I seek to hide my sorrow, as I flit from tree to tree,
As the cynic hides his anguish with a hollow-hearted glee.

So a woman's love, once given, nevermore shall pass away;
But the jewel, by her lover, soon is trampled in the clay.

THE BLACKBIRDS

As the blackbirds flit through the tossing trees,
And the brown leaves float on the mad March breeze;
As the blackbirds carol and call and call,
And the dead leaves flutter and fall and fall;
My heart is elate with the silver songs,
And casts care aside like the dead-leaf throngs;
Hope burgeons again, and my soul takes wing
As the blackbirds soar and the blackbirds sing.

Like a sable cloud in the cold blue sky,
A-battle with winds, see the blackbirds fly!
And the gaunt old trees are all young again
As the vital sap tingles through vivified vein.
As the dead leaves flit, so my dead fears fall,
And life leaps again while the blackbirds call;
As the March comes back, I'm a-thrill once more,
And my heart beats high as the blackbirds soar.

THE SAVANNAH

We ride through forests ever cool and green,
Where giant live-oaks join their boughs above,
All knit together by a thousand vines,
The trumpet flower, with its blazing blooms,
Whose martial music flashes into flame,
The brier, bramble, and the poison oak,
Like scaly serpents thrusting forth their fangs,

While spiders, like the Sirens long ago,
Spread silken snares bedecked with dazzling dew
To tangle in the feet of foolish flies;—
Through treacherous fens, by knotted cypress knees,
Above the black mould, ever dank and cold,

Burst through by lushy clumps of whitened sprouts,
Where lies concealed the deadly rattlesnake;—
By greenly-mantled ponds, made beautiful
With multitudes of water lilies white.

And then a blue lake shimmers in the sun
Or quivers in the gloomy cypress shades;
A gorgeous wild duck floats upon the waves
With plumage polished like a coat of mail;
The snakes are twisted on the rotten limbs
Of dead trees that have fallen in the lake.
On yonder logs, the turtles in a line
Are drying broad backs in the burning sun;
The blue jay, like a noisy trooper, calls,
The redbird flutters like a flower of flame;
The gaunt gar, like a Turkish scimitar,
Leaps from the lake, and circling, sinks from sight.

THE OLD MANSION

I see a ghostly ruin of the past,
And tread its cedar-bordered avenues.
Around its porticoes the pillars tall
Stands like a row of trusty sentinels
Guarding the glories of a perished race
Amid its desolation and decay;
A few tall roses and magnolias stand
Around a fountain choked with water-weeds.

See the great rooms, whose mirrored walls are crushed
And marble mantels now are overthrown.
My footsteps falling in the haunted halls,
Seems waking from the dead and dusty years
The far-off echoes of a hunter's horn
Blown by the master of a thousand slaves.

Amid the shadows of this archway old
I see a beauteous, high-born lady stand,
And hear the rustle of her silken gown;
Amid the broken mirrors on the walls
The softest brown eyes ever seen on earth
Shine on me from their dewy, dusky depths
With starry splendors of a tropic night.
My whisper, stealing through the ruined rooms,
Brings back the laughter of the yester-years,
And all the revels of a nuptial night,
Until the dead bride from her mossy tomb
Comes treading by me in her robes of white;
Amid the cobwebs on the acient stair
I see the shimmer of her snowy veil,
The withered orange blossoms on her brow,
And then, her sweet face swiftly vanishing
Amid the glimmer of her golden hair.

THE DUNGHILL AND THE MOON

Said the Moon one night to the dunghill, "I am better
      by far than you,
For I am the queen of the heavens, while you are the scum
      and the spew;
I am throned on a throne of silver, I am wearing a starry
      crown,
While you reek and you rot and fester in the slums of the
      dirty town.

"I am type of all that is splendid, and I stand for all that
      is pure,
While you are the source of the cesspool, and the fount of
      the stinking sewer;
I am type of all that is noble, and I stand for all that is
      high,
While you are the imp of uncleanness, the beast that is
      sore to the eye.

"I am sung in songs of poets, I am hailed as empress
     sublime,
While you are the jest of the vulgar, and the theme of the
     blackguard rhyme;
I am hailed by the lips of lovers, as I sail in my silver boat,
While you, the obscene, the disgusting, make the laugh
     for the ruffian's throat.

"I am Joy, I am Love and Beauty, I am Glory, Silver and
     Gold,
While you are the stench and the offal, and you the decay
     and the mould;
I am lady beloved of mortals, I am favorite daughter of
     God,
While you are the shame of creation, and the bastard
     spawn of the Sod."

But the dunghill answered the scoffer, "It is true that your
     throne is high,
It is true that your state is splendid, and true I am foul to
     the eye;
It is true you are gowned in glory, it is true I am poor
     and low,
It is true you are queen of heaven, with beauty I never
     shall know.

"But deny as you will, my sister, we are sprung from the
     self-same womb,
And deny as you will, my sister, we must go to the self-
     same tomb;
You may call it a lie, my sister, yet we come of the self-
     same clod;
You may call it a lie, my sister, yet we serve but the self-
     same God.

"It is true, while I pass to-morrow, you are good for a million years,
But your day of death is appointed, though you laugh and
scoff at your fears;
In vain are your crown and your sceptre, and in vain are
your kingdoms vast;
Like myself, you merely are mortal, and must come to
your end at last.

"But, indeed, if your crown is splendid, your heart is but
sterile and chill,
Your valleys are treeless and barren, your mountains are
lifeless and still;
You are stony and bleak and forsaken, not a bird seeks
your blasted heath;
Though your crags and your cliffs may glitter, they are
only the ribs of Death.

"But I who am butt for your laughter, and I who am stock
for your scorn,
Am the cradle of bud and blossom; from my bosom all
sweets are born.
In the dunghill slumbers the harvest, all the gold of the
garnered wheat;
In the dunghill sleeps all the plenty, all the rich and poor
man's meat.

"I am food for the mellow apple, for the fig and the peach
and plum,
I furnish the comb and the honey for the bee in his hollow
gum;
I have given the lilac perfume, I have given the red to the
rose,
The morning-glory out of me blossoms, and the dandelion
glows.

"I am help to the hand of the sower, I am faithful to hands
  that reap,
My herbage gives milk to the cattle, and my grass gives
  fat to the sheep;
I look on the fields that are fruitless, and lo! they are rich,
  they are good,
And the barley and corn are rising where the sedges and
  nettles stood.

"I thrill through the veins of the vineyards, through clusters of purple and red,
And they swell with their luscious nectar, and they swoon
  as their sweets are shed;
I am snow-white bread for the peasant, I am cakes for the
  queen and king,
Though spurned by the slave and the monarch as a vile
  and an unclean Thing.

"Though I fester in foul corruption, I am pure in the lily's
  leaves;
Though I rise from the rankest of poison, I am sire of golden
  sheaves;
Though Death and Decay may attend me, I shall find Res-
  urrection still;
Though the lowest of all God's creatures, I am true to his
  royal Will."

THE FALLEN GODS.

British Museum

The careless crowds in hurry pass them by,
 The fallen gods who reigned in years of yore;
Ah, who would think that gods like these could die,
 Or see their glories fade forevermore?

Here Juno dreams with slowly crumbling charms,
   And Hermes trips on slender shattered feet;
Here Venus mutely lifts her broken arms,
   Her smile, though half erased, still strangely sweet.

Here Iris bends with bosom cleft in twain,
   And Proserpina wears a shivered crown;
Here Jove, dethroned, longs for his old-time reign,
   Though cankering crust has gnawed away his frown.

Here Isis still is hid behind her veils,
   Osiris still is wrapped in quiet sleep;
Dumb like the other gods, they tell no tales,
   Still jealous of the secret that they keep.

Half-men, half-bulls, with giant eagle plumes,
   Long-bearded gods of old Assyria stand,
Colossal shapes dragged from their desert tombs,
   To please the idlers in this impious land.

Through broken teeth this South-sea idol grins,
   This Hindoo god looks down with hideous scowls;
Here gods of Congo squat on battered shins,
   With heads of dogs and beaks and claws of fowls.

O, gods, for you have men and women bled,
   For you mankind has slaved ten thousand years,
For you were slaughtered mountains of the dead,
   For you we shed an ocean of our tears.

O, gods, to you we wildly called for aid,
   To you, poor creatures fashioned out of mud;
No answer! Not a moment's heed you paid,
   Although we gave you rivers of our blood.

From you have men beseeched for wealth and fame,
   For glory Kings have made your altars red;
What folly! From afar you watched the game,
   Then laughing, smote your fawning flatterers dead.

From you have maidens begged their lovers' lives
  Then seen their lovers brought from battle slain;
From lips of fathers, mothers, husbands, wives,
  A million million prayers have wailed in vain.

Whoever begged your blessings found you dumb,
  Whoever craved one glance has found you blind;
O, men may call you, but you never come,
  And men may seek you, but shall never find.

But now your reign is ended.   Nevermore
  Will incense rise to greet you at the dawn,
And never, never on the sea or shore
  Shall you regain the glory that is gone.

The children laugh to see Mars' shattered limbs,
  The booby tries to spell Apollo's name;
O fallen gods, who now will chant your hymns,
  And who will fight to save you from your shame?

And yet, O fallen gods, yours is the doom
  Which living gods must suffer soon or late;
Our fables soon shall follow to your tomb,
  And every god we worship share your fate.

The gods are but our children, not our sires;
  We carve them, pet them, thrust them on the shelves;
In them we breathe our own dreams and desires,
  And only make an image of ourselves.

The man who loves his brother, who is free
  From malice, who will stoop to nothing foul,
Needs not to gloze the gods with flattery,
  And never needs to tremble when they scowl.

ORCHIDS

Like blossoms changed to butterflies
   With wings of purple, yellow, brown,
Or pheasant plumes with ebon eyes
   And soft and clouded silken down.

Serpents in garnet, gold and green,
   With graceful neck and glossy crest,
Or humming birds of brilliant sheen,
   With glowing throat and dotted breast.

Swart, rich-robed princesses, that hide
   In tangled Afric jungle shades;
Fawn-footed Indian maids that bide
   By wild Brazilian forest glades.

With flowers such as these, of old
   The witch enwreathed her golden head;
They grew in Circe's haunted wold,
   Or oped in dreamlands of the dead.

THE MOON-FLOWER

I see the splendor of thy blooms of white,
   Spotless and stainless as a cherub's plume,
Adorning solemn shadows of the night,
   As though to waste thy glory on the gloom.

Not like the gorgeous blossoms of the morn,
   In princely purple or in royal red,
Amid the glories of the sunrise born,
   To wither when their lover, Dawn, lies dead;

Nor like thy radiant sisters of the noon,
   With burning bosoms blushing in the sun,
Whose fierce embraces make them sway and swoon,
   Until they perish as the day is done;

For they have felt their fervent love returned,
   And all the ardor of a clasp and kiss,
Have palpitated and have thrilled and burned
   In sweet delirium of the lover's bliss;

While thou, pale virgin, pinest all alone,
   A shrouded star, in ghostly robes of white;
No lover's kiss thy pearl-pure face hath known
   To make thee pant with passionate delight.

No brown bee ever comes to taste thy lips,
   No bird will ever sing his songs to thee,
No sunbeam steals to touch thy tingling tips,
   Thy maiden charms no bridal day shall see.

And yet, O peerless, pearly, pure moon flower,
   Thy sweet mouth trembles with a strange perfume,
And thou dost make a heaven of thy bower
   Though no true lover comes to cheer thy doom.

And so thy tale of love is never told,
   Thy secret dieth with the morning light,
Though virgin bosoms throb, we call thee cold,
   And see thee die in barrenness and blight.

And so True Love amid the darkness blooms,
   In silence, desolation—all alone,
With snow-white splendor lost in mournful glooms,
   And lives and dies unheeded or unknown.

L'AMANTE DU DIABLE

"Woman wailing for her Demon Lover."
—*Coleridge.*

All around me in the darkness, monstrous mountain ridges stand,
Guarding all the haunted pathways to this dim enchanted land.

In the west I see the tatters of the dull and drooping clouds,
Where the faded sunset glories slumber in their gloomy shrouds;

And I see the moon's frail crescent near a dewy, diamond star,
Shining from the gates celestial, where the saints and seraphs are;

But an awful tempest gathers in the perished twilight's path
As a shaggy lion rises, trembling with terrific wrath;

And the lightnings flash and quiver like the scorpion lashes' stings
Drawing blood from cheeks of demons, flying with their routed kings;

While the thunder bolts gigantic far across the cliffs are hurled,
Crashing like prodigious planets on a wrecked and ruined world;

And the winds, aroused and startled, moaning in their frantic flight,
Fill my soul with strange forebodings on this horror-haunted night.

Once two brothers, deadly foemen, met upon this wrinkled
    wold,
And within each other's bosoms drove their daggers keen
    and cold;

And a pair of guilty lovers, hiding in this place of woe,
At the stake were burned to ashes in the ages long ago;

And a traitor seeking refuge when this ancient land was
    young,
By a throng of furious yeomen on this withered tree was
    hung.

Here I come to meet thee, Satan, ruined king whom I
    adore,
Thou, my prince, my lord, my master, and mine idol
    evermore!

Now I see thee come to meet me, and I rush within thine
    arms,
While my bosom bounds with passion for thy wild and
    wondrous charms.

I, the seraph, blest and beauteous, robed in radiant starry
    light,
With my golden locks encircled with the lilies pearly
    white;

I, that soar on swan-like pinions, blossom-bosomed, flower-
    fair,
I, with eyes like lucid dewdrops, twinkling in the azure
    air;

I have come to meet thee, Satan, with thy wings of ashen
    gray,
Seared with sins and seared with sorrows that shall never
    pass away!

With thine eyes so grand and gloomy, raven tresses flecked
with frost,
And thy mien so melancholy, hapless Emperor of the Lost!

With thy step so proud and princely, as it seems to spurn
the sod,
With thy high brow, scarred and blasted by the cruel bolts
of God!

I have left the vine-clad vistas and the palms of paradise,
Where the song-birds sing forever under diamond-tinted
skies,

Where the silken, saffron roses swoon with odors rich as
wine,
And the sprays of jasmine blossoms through the myrtle
branches twine,

Where the crystal fountains bubble under woods forever
green,
And the fields are gemmed with glories like a gorgeous
Eastern queen,—

Left them all to meet thee, Satan,—left my throne and
crown and lyre,
Flying through the myriad systems, past the whirling stars
of fire!

Satan, grander than the mountains, with their gloomy
giant forms!
Satan, grander than the heavens, with their wild, majestic
storms!

Satan, grander than the ocean, with its vast and solemn
waves!
Satan, grander than the desert, with its withered waste of
graves!

Like a fierce volcano rising with its regal crimson crest,
Like a weird and wondrous comet, terrifying every breast!

Let me heal thy wounded visage where the jagged light-
　　nings fell,
Kiss thy worn feet, burned and blackened by the flaming
　　dust of hell!

I have angel wooers, Satan, who can never win my love,
For my heart was hurled to Hades when they hurled thee
　　from above;

And those angel lovers, Satan, all are most sublimely fair,
With their gray eyes, soft and saintly, with their waving
　　golden hair,

With their princely eagle pinions, sandals flecked with
　　sparkling gems,
And their broad, majestic foreheads, wreathed with starry
　　diadems,

With their voices sweet and solemn, like the poet kings
　　of old,
As they stand before the Master with their wondrous
　　harps of gold.

And they sing me songs of passion, melting from their lips
　　divine,
And around my clustered ringlets purple lotus blossoms
　　twine.

But I turn from angel faces, come to cheer thee in thy
　　doom,
Kiss the wan, wild star thou wearest in thy forehead's
　　mournful gloom.

So I steal from heights of heaven and the realms of death-
　　less day,
Meet thee in benighted deserts in this lone world far away;

Or I wander till I find thee, flying on from zone to zone,
And I throw mine arms around thee on thine ever-burning
　　throne.

A DEFIANICE

You leave me alone, and you wend your way
With a face as bright as a springtime day,
And you seem to think, as our pathways part,
That my name is erased from your careless heart.
You say to yourself: "I shall soon forget
We have ever loved, or have ever met,
Though his fervent words may have thrilled me so
In the beautiful years of long ago."

But you can not forget how you blushed one day,
When I held your hand as we went our way,
And you can not forget how I kissed your lips
And you tingled with joy to your finger-tips.
You cannot forget how the bluebirds sang
Till the meadows and fields and wildwoods rang,
And we laughed with delight in a dream divine,
When you knew I was yours and that you were mine.

And you can not forget you loved me then,
Ere I went sad ways through the world of men;
How happy we were in the dear dead years
Ere the dawn-light died in a flood of tears.
O no! You will sigh for the sweet slain past,
Its heroic hopes, too brilliant to last,
When life with her frowns has sullied her smiles
And sundered us twain by a thousand miles.

Wherever you go, through the whole wide earth,
Through gloamings of grief, through mornings of mirth,
Wherever you go, wherever you bide,
You shall miss one face, close by your side.
Whenever you tread under skies of spring,
Whenever you hear the autumn winds sing,
You will sigh for the lover of years of yore,
Who left with your youth, to return no more.

Unless you can say that your soul is dead,
The past forgotten, and memory fled—
Unless you can say, in sincerest truth,
You are glad to have lost the glory of youth;
Unless you can feel in your innermost heart
You rejoice when you see life's summer depart—
O then, not till then, may your lips declare
You love me no more, and you do not care.

LIFE

I saw a throng of prisoners in a cell,
Who, one and all, were doomed to die next day.
Some laughed and shouted in a reckless way,
Some raved and cursed and swore like demons fell,
Some sobbed and bade their friends a last farewell,
Some shuddered in a dream of dull dismay,
Some ate, some drank, or sat with cards at play,
Some seemed to hearken to a funeral bell.

Mine eyes with pity for them filled with tears;
But they are living just as you and I.
The prison is this world of fitful fears,
The prisoners but our doomed humanity;
Our day is set within a few short years,
And laugh, or weep, or curse, like them we die.

IDYL OF SPRING

Thrushes up there in branches of blossom
    Twitter and trill to swaying of trees;
Rose's red heart and lily-bell's bosom
    Tingle with buzzing and boom of bees.

Over the way, where in billows of bloom
   Creamy and pink as a cloud of pearls,
Apple and peach in loveliness loom,
   Linda goes laughing, my girl of girls.

Linda, my lass of but sixteen years,
   Glides with grace of a floating flower,
Stranger to sorrow, untaught in tears,
   Fairest of fays in the bud-scattered bower.

Standing alone in her frock of white,
   Sprinkled with snows of the plum-tree blooms,
Stainless and sweet, she is crowned with light,
   Seeming a seraph with folded plumes.

Pigeons of gray and purple and green,
   Burnished with copper and blue and brown,
Flutter beside the feet of my queen,
   Swirling and sweeping to touch her gown.

Treading there, too, is a peacock proud,
   Gaudy with gems like a Hindoo King,
Spreading his train like a rainbow cloud,
   Switching the grass with his lowered wing.

Moments flit fast, and my Linda goes
   Out of my sight, and she takes away
Out of my spring the red of the rose,
   Mirth of my morn, delight of my day.

May-apples budding beneath her feet
   Chalices lift of whitest of wax,
Seeming to show that her footsteps fleet
   Left them behind to trace out her tracks.

Morning may glow like a pearly shell,
   Purple and pink and iris and blue,
Dangling with dews the sweet-scented dell,
   Linda, my lass, yet I yearn for you.

ONE SUMMER

The thorns upon this world of ours
Sometimes bud forth in gentle flowers;
Where night has made our earth forlorn
Will rise at last a radiant morn;
On this short journey to the tomb
Some thrilling voice will break the gloom;
But Youth and Love, when once passed by,
Leave all our dearest hopes to die;
Their piercing joy and blissful pain
Once felt, are never felt again.

A sojourn at a farm in June,
When fields were fresh and woods in tune,
When bare existence was a joy
To me, a fond and foolish boy!
Ah yes, my dearest dream was done,
At setting of that summer sun.

Ah, little modest country maid,
Doomed with the summer day to fade,
Too fragile and too fair to last,
Lost flower of the happy past!
I see you still beside me here,
Just as you looked that bygone year.
Your sweet face smiles within my reach
Amid pink blossoms of the peach,
Or wreathed with wild grapes from the wood,
Your cheeks stained with their purple blood,
Or rising like a pure, pale flower
Amid a scarlet poppy bower.

I see you still with eyes of blue,
The darkest pansy's deepest hue;
Your brown hair gently wavers down
And glimmers like a copper crown.

A basket on your arm you bear,
An awkward little bonnet wear;
Fresh as the dewy wildwoods green,
My little sweetheart, and my queen!

Her goodness warms misfortune's dearth
And makes a heaven out of earth;
Singing she cooks the scanty meal,
Or chatting, turns the creaking wheel.
With hoe and huge straw hat, she leads
Destructive war against the weeds,
Till I, a dapper city clerk,
Begin to help her with her work,
And sometimes try to milk her cows,
Or with her drive them out to browse.

She tells me names of birds and trees,
And habits of the honeybees.
She shows me where blackberries grow,
And where the pink wild roses blow.
She sits with me in mossy nooks
Of sylvan shades and bubbling brooks.
And then we see the red-bird shy,
A blazing blossom, flutter by,
And proudly shake his crimson plumes
And chirp amid the verdant glooms;
The brown thrush, of a humbler crest,
With calm eyes watches from her nest.
We roam beside the deep green pools
In which the bullfrog blithely rules
And leaps among the daffodillies,
Blue flags and snowy water lilies.

With her I watch the evening star
Begin to tremble from afar,
The moon arising in the night
And robing all the world in white;

Then, when the mock-bird, sweet and wild,—
The forest's untamed poet-child,—
Begins to twitter trills of bliss,
I snare my sweetheart with a kiss!

But Autumn comes with footsteps chilly,
And slays the blue-bell and the lily;
The purple and the golden asters wave
Above the pansy's lonely grave.
I leave her, and I turn once more,
To see her waiting at her door.
And then another look,—the last,
When dying day is nearly past;
Her hands are curved above her eyes
That watch me like two jealous spies;
The setting sunbeams light her hair,
Then leave her standing lonely there;
She lingers still, until the night
Shuts her forever from my sight.

Amid the dust and roar and heat
That choke the city's crowded street,
I see her looking to the town
Across the autumn fields of brown,
Towards a higher, happier life,
Than waits the future farmer's wife,
While heartless fortune holds her down,
And mates her with a common clown.

Ah, precious little country girl,
Who beamed forlorn, an ocean pearl,
A sweet, low-waving wildwood rose,
Frail poem in a world of prose!

Again I ponder all alone,
While snowflakes fall and bleak winds moan,
And hear the tread of restless feet
Along the city's dingy street,

And yearn to see her face again
To ease my weary heart of pain,—
Returning from the Long Ago
Beyond her silent shroud of snow.

A STORM IN SUMMER

The August sun blazed with a blasting heat
And down on yellow corn-fields fiercely beat;
The sky was burning with an ashen blue
And glaring with the hot beams darting through;
The hazy dust was rising everywhere
And floated slowly on the stifling air.
All day the katydid chirped sharp and shrill
And green grasshoppers answered from the hill;
Deep in the lushy grass the cricket purred,
While in the trees all day the locust whirred;
All day the dry-flies from the leafy limbs
Ground forth their sawing, nasal-twanging hymns.

Sometimes we watched the reapers in the field
In a long line their flashing sickles wield.
We hunted for the quail's nest through the wheat
And found it hidden, quiet, snug and neat;—
A nest of grass, filled full of snowy spheres,
Strewn like the grains upon the ripened ears.
Pure as the pearls that gleam in Indian seas,
Or milk-white buds upon the locust trees.

But when noon came, the breeze began to blow
Delicious coolness through the feverish glow;
And then from out the west dull clouds arose
And skimmed along, too restless for repose.
More clouds began to follow, till they grew
Darker and broader, while the strong winds blew.

Soon deep-toned thunder echoed from the clouds,
And sword-like flashes drove the mists in crowds.
Ah, how delicious to the eager eye
Where those cool shadows, swiftly drawing nigh!
It seemed unto the anxious farmer's mind,
That loftiest music rode upon the wind.
It seemed as if the God of manly sport
With horns and hounds had come to hold his court,
Returned through faded earth to rove at will
And caper gladly o'er the yellowing hill;
To shout and laugh amid reviving flowers,
And drive his baying hounds through forest bowers.

The clouds grew blacker, till they loomed like night,
And then the blasts came roaring in their might;
The ancient elms were swayed from side to side,
For like a demon did the tempest ride.
The oaks groaned and their giant limbs were crushed;
The rafters creaked as by the roofs he rushed.

And now, upon the mountain's distant side,
A shroud-like sheet of rain was seen to glide;
Then soon the valleys at its feet were crossed,
And nearer, nearer by, the fields were lost:
Next, the hard gust came with a mighty stride,—
The driving rain was scattered far and wide!
Yes, here it was at last in all its strength,
And fast was filling all the country's length;
It came as in an overwhelming flood,
And drenched the meadow, the field and wood.

All through the storm we nestled on the hay
That, piled in huge heaps, through the barn-rooms lay;
The tempest flooded all the roof without,
And great gusts shook the rafters with a shout.
Far up above, the mud-flies worked away,
Building their cells of well-cemented clay;

The little wren within her nook peeped out,
And squeaking mice would slyly skip about;
The lithe, slim swallow fluttered on her nest,
Her chattering fledgelings robbing her of rest.

At last the rain ceased, and the clouds flew by,
Showing the dark blue of the dewy sky;
Upon the outskirts of the dying storm
The glorious rainbow reared his regal form;
But soon the winds tore down the fragile arch,
As frosty footsteps through the roses march.

BY THE SUMMER SEA

Far in the distance meet the sky and sea,
    And melt together in an azure haze,
As dim and dreamy as eternity,
    With vast void spaces lost in mellow maze.

The white-winged ships are flitting far away,
    The white-winged gulls are circling there on high;
O snowy wings, I long to leave this clay,
    And follow, follow you through sea and sky!

Warm breezes from the far-off tropics blow,
    The sunlight shimmers on the brilliant beach,
Until the Eve, with blushes all aglow,
    Is mellow as a pink and yellow peach.

I watch the billows with their emerald glooms,
    Forever restless, rushing on and on,
The breakers beating like an eagle's plumes—
    Wild beings, hunting peace forever gone!

Here, wading with their pink and pearly feet,
    The beautiful barefooted children play;
Their faces, like their joys, are fresh and sweet—
    Blonde childhood in a blonde midsummer day!

Their life is laughter, and their love is bliss,
    Free from regret for perished years of yore,
Their world is one great blossom, youth a kiss,
    Ere storms shall thunder, "Fled forevermore!"

I watch them, pensive, till the day is done,
    And melancholy twilight follows noon,
Till, like a blood-red tulip, sinks the sun,
    And like a snow-white lily comes the moon.

A NIGHT IN JUNE

Lucy, my sweet, as we went last night
Down the garden walks in the moon's white light;
As a startled thrush from the peach trees flew,
And you plucked a rose that was decked with dew;
As the mock-bird sang to the evening star
And the sheep-bells clinked in the folds afar,
The words that you spoke were sweeter in spell
Than moonbeams or dews or bird-song or bell.

Lucy, my own, as the roses blushed,
As the cannas flamed and the dahlias flushed;
As the lily arose in her snowy gown,
You trembled, my lass, with your eyes cast down.
Peonies in pink and purple and white
Were watching your face in the silvery light;
They listened and smiled and nodded, my sweet,
As though they had heard your timid heart beat.

[219]

Lucy, my queen, as the dewdrops fell,
And the whippoorwill called in the tangled dell;
As the honeysuckles twined and the honeysuckles trailed,
And from golden blooms their odors exhaled;
Like a king who comes to his rightful throne,
I clasped you and kissed you, my sweet, my own;
Then the roses turned in amaze untold
To think that a lover could be so bold.

Lucy, my bride, in that ardent kiss
We were born again, to a life of bliss;
Yet glory and gladness were blended with gloom,
And thistle and thorn with the bridal bloom;
For we breathed not vows to last for a day,
But Passion that never should pass away;
Our hearts, lives and souls with our hands we gave
From gardens of youth to gates of the grave.

Lucy, my life, when the morning came
With its golden spears and its banners of flame,
In purple and pearl and orange and red,
Its dews were not light as my joyous tread.
For after that morning had passed away,
And after my locks are sprinkled with gray,
When lovers unborn by my grave tread alone,
No night like that night shall ever be known.

MISSISSIPPI IN JUNE

The blithe breezes croon through forests of June,
    And the swallows skim on through the sky;
Then the goldfinch comes and the wild bee hums,
    While the martins go sailing on high.
The indigo bird in the hedge is heard
    As he seeks for his sweetheart and sings,
And the tanagers flush and the redbirds blush
    Like a flurry of tulips with wings.

The cotton-field heaves with its glossy green leaves,
 With its blossoms of crimson and cream,
While the corn's sharp spears with their juicy ears
 And their tassels of silk are astream.
The cantaloupe swells, and the cantaloupe smells
 Like a gold-carven casket of musk;
On the watermelon vine is a flagon of wine
 In the rosy-red heart of the husk.

The blackberries lush hang ripe on the bush
 Like a gypsy girl's ebon-hued eyes,
While the strawberry bed is sprinkled with red
 For the barefooted truant's surprise.
The apricot glows like a yellow rose,
 And the apple a globule of gold,
While the damson's dark blue and the cherry's red hue
 Stain the beak of the woodpecker bold.

With pansies a-glow, peonies a-blow,
 Cometh June in her maidenhood sweet,
And I see her glide where the crape myrtles bide
 With their petals as pink as her feet.
The magnolia bloom, like an ostrich plume,
 Is a-waving to welcome the queen,
And the iris rears through its serried spears
 Like a banner through bayonets keen.

JULY NOONTIDE

In Oriental Sultan, July comes
 In all the brilliance of barbaric state,
While bumble bees and locusts beat their drums,
 And shrill grasshoppers at his call await.

And like Sultanas listening for his tread,
 In gorgeous harems, splendid salvias flame;
His marigolds, in yellow and in red,
 Put Sheba and Semiramis to shame.

There, rank on rank, the bright geraniums burn,
  With pungent, sultry, suffocating breath,
And hardy buff and orange zinnias yearn
  To crown the Master with a gaudy wreath.

Petunias, garnet-hued and white and pied,
  From dewy trumpets to the Caliph drink;
Verbenas, closely clustered at their side,
  Weave him rich rugs in purple and in pink.

Above the rest, slim oleanders rise
  Like rosy-footed dancers, full of grace,
And passion flowers with their peacock eyes
  Climb on the wall, enrobed in azure lace.

The humming-bird, a corsair, flashes by,
  His ruby throat glows like a winged blush;
The cockscomb, a muezzin there on high,
  Uplifts his turban, made of crimson plush.

July strews watermelons by yon fence
  More luscious than mellifluous nectar old,
Muskmelons with their fragrant frankincense,
  More tempting than Hesperian fruit of gold.

Dewberries burst with black fermenting juice,
  While over-ripe raspberries fast decay,
And, like freebooters in a field aloose,
  The hornets suck their sugary sweets away.

We long to leave this surfeit of perfume,
  This glare of color and this blaze of heat,
And tread by pools in leafy woodland gloom
  Through dewy grasses, with our cool bare feet.

There we should see marsh lilies pure and white,
  And feathery ferns o'erhanging silver springs,
Brooks bubbling through the mint, the grove's green night,
  And pale daturas, wan as mothy wings.

The broad-leaved pawpaws with their green young fruit,
    Blue velvet ageratums by the streams,
Tall cottonwoods and live oaks dark and mute,
    Would be our comrades, as we dozed in dreams.

So, when with passion, human hearts may burn,
    And anger chokes the soul with dust and heat,
To Contemplation's greenwoods we may turn,
    And see her lilies in their cool retreat.

DROUGHT

The pale white skies hang in an ashen haze,
    The far-off hills are veiled in faded blue;
Dust-clouds obscure the rambling country ways,
    Half hiding teams and wagons straggling through.

Hour after hour the heat grows more intense;
    An angry wasp drums on the window pane;
A panting peacock on the old rail fence
    Peeps at the skies as though he prayed for rain.

An old ox dozes in a weary dream;
    Long lines of sheep in patient silence pass;
Two horses tread a muddy half-dried stream,
    Dust-powdered cattle browse on withered grass.

The passion-vine is withered at the gate,
    A sickly rose is falling leaf by leaf;
Sunburned and thirsty, faded asters wait
    For death to bind them in his yellow sheaf.

The splitted husk flips out its floating down,
    The bursting pod shells out its rattling seeds.
The pasture is a desert burned to brown,
    The garden is a withered waste of weeds.

O let dark clouds like ocean billows roll,
    Let mellow thunders throb like muffled drums!
Let lightnings rouse the west wind's sleeping soul,
    To rush with shouting as the rainstorm comes!

And yet this sickly, sweltering August day
    Marks but the place we all must travel soon;
This is the end of all the mirth of May,
    And this the ending of the joys of June!

When all the zest of youth is on the wane,
    We sigh for storm-clouds of the bygone years;
The heart cries out in one long prayer for rain
    To fall on parching lids in dewy tears.

Above my desert bosom, as of yore,
    Once more let lightnings glitter, thunders roll!
Drown dusty memories; let there be no more
    Drought in the heart, or famine in the soul!

SEPTEMBER IN TENNESSEE

The sad September comes with asters in her auburn hair,
Her lovely face transfigured with a gentle touch of care,
With pale blue morning-glories, paler than her pale blue
    eyes,
And pearly hillsides hazes, dimmer than her dreamy skies.

She comes with cataracts of amber honeysuckles sweet,
With golden-rods that powder all her garments and her
    feet,
With humming-birds for heralds, all bedecked in starry
    scales,
With glow of jeweled armor, burnished throats and twink-
    ling tails.

[224]

Amid her forest depths, like white limbed giants in the
    land,
The clean athletic sycamores in naked grandeur stand;
And now the sweetgum overflows with aromatic drops,
While pungent sassafras perfumes the bramble-tangled
    copse.

Pecans on bending branches hang their wealth of clustered
    nuts,
And chinquepins and hazels ripen by the negro huts;
The brown buckeyes are swelling, purple wild grapes swing-
    ing low,
And sumach berries by the fence like blood-red torches
    glow.

But now the year has lost the gladness of her girlhood
    time,
And prose of homely autumn follows spring and summer
    rhyme;
Deserted by the song-birds, hang her melancholy bowers,
And like a cobweb curtain her deathly-pale moon-flowers.

The lonesome cat-tails quiver by the marsh's dreary wave,
And nightshade sprays are rising by the proud peony's
    grave.
Beneath the summer blossoms that have withered into
    brown,
Our bygone summer blisses in the dust are trampled down.

A smothered Desdemona, here the lily hangs her head,
The iron-weed, a huge Othello, scowling by her bed;
And, like a ghostly Romeo, calls a lonesome whip-poor-will
To some forgotten Juliet in her grave on yonder hill.

OCTOBER IN TENNESSEE

Far, far away, beyond a hazy height,
  The turquoise skies are hung in dreamy sleep;
Below, the fields of cotton, fleecy-white,
  Are spreading like a mighty flock of sheep.

Now, like Aladdin of the days of old,
  October robes the weeds in purple gowns;
He sprinkles all the sterile fields with gold,
  And all the rustic trees wear royal crowns.

The straggling fences all are interlaced
  With pink and azure morning-glory blooms,
The starry asters glorify the waste,
  While grasses stand on guard with pikes and plumes.

Yet still amid the splendor of decay
  The chill winds call for blossoms that are dead,
The cricket chirps for sunshine passed away,
  And lovely Summer songsters that have fled.

And lonesome in a haunt of withered vines,
  Amid the flutter of her withered leaves,
Pale Summer for her perished Kingdom pines,
  And all the glories of her golden sheaves.

In vain October wooes her to remain
  Within the palace of his scarlet bowers,
Entreats her to forget her heart-break pain,
  And weep no more above her faded flowers.

At last November, like a Conqueror, comes
  To storm the golden city of his foe;
We hear his rude winds, like the roll of drums,
  Bringing their desolation and their woe.

The sunset, like a vast vermilion flood,
   Splashes its giant glowing waves on high,
The forest flames with foliage red as blood,
   A conflagration sweeping to the sky.

Then all the treasures of that brilliant state
   Are gathered in a mighty funeral pyre;
October, like a King resigned to fate,
   Dies in his forests, with their sunset fire.

(Song 4)

SUNSET IN TENNESSEE (5)

In Tennessee, the ancient mountains stand,
   Guarding the green fields to the far, far west,
The Mississippi folds her further strand,
   And all her hills and plains and valleys rest.

In Tennessee, the sunset lingers long,
   Till shades of twilight gather near and far,
And now is heard the home-bound negroes' song,
   The mock-bird's trill beneath the evening star.

In Tennessee, the friends I used to know
   Gather in scenes I loved in bygone days,
By hearthstones where I lingered long ago,
   Before I trod these far-off Northern ways.

I wonder if those old-time boyhood friends
   Will sometimes wish to see my face once more,
Or if they miss me when the daylight ends,
   And long to greet me as in years of yore.

In Tennessee, there is a lass I know,
   Who trod beside me under skies of May,
Whose coming steps would set my heart aglow,
   Whose smile would make me happy all the day.

I wonder if she ever feels regret
   For happy moments that she spent with me,
And longs to see, when suns of Autumn set,
   Her old-time lover, there in Tennesee.

AUTUMN IN THE SOUTH

This livelong day I listen to the fall
   Of hickory nuts and acorns to the ground,
The croak of rain-crows and the bluejay's call,
   The woodman's axe that hews with muffled sound.

And like a spendthrift in a threadbare coat
   That still retains a dash of crimson hue,
An old woodpecker chatters forth a note
   About the better Summer days he knew.

Across the road a ruined cabin stands,
   With ragweeds and with thistles at its door,
While withered cypress vines hang tattered strands
   About its falling roof and rotting floor.

In yonder forest nook no sound is heard
   Save when the walnuts patter on the earth,
Or when by winds the hectic leaves are stirred
   To dance like witches in their maniac mirth.

Down in the orchard hang the golden pears,
   Half honeycombed by yellow-hammer beaks;
Near by, a dwarfed and twisted apple bears
   Its fruit, brown-red as Amazonian cheeks.

The lonesome landscape seems as if it yearned
   Like our own aching hearts, when first we knew
The one love of our life was not returned,
   Or first we found an old-time friend untrue.

At last the night comes, and the broad white moon
　Is welcomed by the owl with frenzied glee;
The fat opossum, like a satyr, soon
　Blinks at its light from yon persimmon tree.

The raccoon starts to hear long-dreaded sounds,
　Amid his scattered spoils of ripened corn—
The cry of negroes and the yelp of hounds,
　The wild, rude pealing of a hunter's horn.

At last a gray mist covers all the land
　Until we seem to wander in a cloud,
Far, far away upon some elfin strand
　Where Sorrow drapes us in a mildewed shroud.

No voice is heard in field or forest nigh
　To break the desolation of the spell,
Save one sad mocking-bird in boughs near by,
　Who sings like Tasso in his madman's cell;

While one magnolia blossom, ghostly white,
　Like high-born Leonora, lingering there,
Haughty and splendid in the lonesome night,
　Is pale with passion in her dumb despair.

AN AUTUMN MORNING

A rich October morning, calm and still,
When saddened skies hang in a dreamy haze.
The red and yellow leaves dance in the light,
Arraying every hill in regal robes.
The flocks of squirrels gather ripening nuts,
The luscious wild grapes in blue clusters cling,
And bright woodpeckers whisk amid the leaves.
The dry broom-sedge grows over wasted fields,
Fringing red gullies and rough banks of clay;
Along the highway and meadows brown
The golden-rods and asters are ablaze.

Here stands a planter's house amid his farms
Of snowy cotton and of golden corn,
Specked here and there by low-roofed negro huts,
Whose dusky denizens in fleecy fields
Sing with a sweet mysterious melody
The songs of Salem in this western world
With all the fervor of its ancient bards.
Far, far above, amid the dreamy skies
The buzzard glides on still and stately wings,
While birds of passage, in a blending line
Fly from the far north to the southern seas.

A MISSISSIPPI SWAMP

Here in this sultry Summer afternoon
   The white light through the shade seems gloomy green;
Here lies, all motionless, the long lagoon,
   Through twilight where no sun is ever seen.

What lonesomeness, what weight of solitude!
   As solemn as those far primeval days
When earth was teeming with a giant brood,
   Still unprofaned by man's intrusive gaze.

Huge turtles bask by yonder sluggish lake,
   A hoarse bull-frog is croaking on the bank,
And like a jeweled necklace swings a snake
   From dead limbs where a fallen cypress sank.

Here like a shipmast rooted in the soil,
   A sycamore defies the future gales;
Gigantic grape-vines, twisting coil on coil,
   Have weaved his cordage and his mighty sails.

A scarlet splash of color, here and there
   The trumpet-blossom's flag is all aflame;
Beside this stream, the cardinal flowers glare
   Like eyes of tigers none can ever tame.

Here a magnolia with resplendent buds
  Seems a green billow strewing peerless pearls,
Or bearing flocks of swans on emerald floods,
  A-flutter in a maze of snowy swirls.

The sluggish waters, green with curdled scum,
  Are glorified by lilied robes of white—
Lilies so pure, so lovely, that they come
  Like myriad moons in some enchanted night.

The purple bunting that is glinting by
  Seems like a pansy that can soar and sing;
The scarlet tanager that flutters nigh
  Seems like a poppy warbling on the wing.

The redbird, like a crimson shooting star,
  Burns on the vision with a blaze intense;
And, like two jeweled daggers, from afar
  Two humming birds pierce through the shadows dense.

The yellow-hammer for a moment glints,
  A golden-breasted, dotted Autumn leaf;
The oriole, in black and orange tints,
  Glows through the greenwood like a flaming sheaf.

 The hermit-thrush, that forest Hamlet, sings,
  Asking the old, old questions, ever new,
Yet still unanswered by created things,
  And hid forever out of mortal view.

TO A FRIEND

Tormented sorely by the chastening rod,
I muttered to myself: "There is no God!"
But, faithful friend, I found your soul so true,
That God revealed Himself in giving you.

[231]

"I LOVE THY FAULTS"

I love thy faults. If angels said to me,
  "We give thee power to change her at thy will,"
My heart, forever loyal unto thee,
  Would leave thee as thou art, my darling, still.

If, like a sculptor in the days of old,
  My hands might mould a form and face divine,
Mine eyes would turn from all their beauty cold,
  And see no sweet face in the world but thine.

If I should tread through blest abodes above,
  And win the love of angels wondrous fair,
My soul would fear their chill perfection, love,
  And then return, thy lowly lot to share.

If thou hast faults, my creed shall make them right;
  I love thee only, and I ever will.
If thou art lowly, yet thy hut is bright—
  If heaven disown thee, I shall claim thee still.

MARY OF JONESBURG

O beautiful Mary of Jonesburg town,
With your dusty locks and your eyes of brown,
You come like a breath of the country air
From the cotton- and corn-fields over there,
In the good old hills of West Tennessee;
So blithesome and bright, so fresh and so free,
As the queen of bells I vote you a crown,
O beautiful Mary of Jonesburg town.

Mary of Jonesburg, I can see there still
The Methodist church on the old green hill;
Then the wood where the redbird rears his crest,
And the fence where the bluebird builds his nest.

I see the school-house in the field of sedge,
And the old saw-mill on the village's edge
Where the Democrats come from the country down
To carry the box of your Jonesburg town.

Mary of Jonesburg, though your frock be plain,
You never know need of a sweeping train.
Your laughter, as light as a cat-bird's call;
Your sighing, as soft as a peach-bloom's fall;
Your cheeks, as ruddy as apples in June,
Have thrilled my old heart-strings back into tune.
No duchess so fair in her silken gown
As beautiful Mary of Jonesburg town.

Mary of Jonesburg, here in New York town
I long for your smile and your eyes of brown.
Though free-silver rules in the Jonesburg fold,
Your heart, I am sure, is a heart of gold.
Though I see Wall Street, or on Broadway tread,
I find your enchantments have turned my head,
And my heart steals back, to be there cast down
At the feet of Mary of Jonesburg town.

THE FIRST TRANSGRESSION

Eve, sweet tempter, lovely sinner, God hath cursed the
    deed which thou hast done,
Paradise is lost forever, and the stricken world's woes
    have begun.

Over Eden's eastern mountains flame the purple glories
    of the morn,
Welcomed by the waking warblers and the dewy blossoms
    newly born.

But I see the leaflets trembling, and I hear the quivering
    breezes sigh,
Feeling that for thy transgression thou and I and all the
    world must die.

Yet a spirit whispers to me that to save the world 'tis not
    too late,
If I turn my heart against thee, sin not, and desert thee
    to thy fate.

Then the fleeting years would scatter pallid autumn lilies
    on thy tomb,
I, thy consort, live forever, radiant with inmortal youth-
    ful bloom.

Then mayhaps the great Creator would another woman
    mould for me;
I might twine her locks with roses, give her kisses that I
    once gave thee.

But I could not, wondrous being! for thy smiles and wist-
    ful, pleading tears
Still would follow, hunt and haunt me through the maze
    of never-dying years.

Twilight shades would find me ever lying by the bride I
    could not save,
And the piping birds at morning still would find me weep-
    ing at thy grave.

Earth would be a barren kingdom when, without my queen,
    to rest I stole,
Life eternal, bitter anguish, if I lost the idol of my soul.

Thou hast conquered, sweet enchantress! I forsake the
    fields of Paradise
For thy bosom's realm of rapture and the blissful glory of
    thine eyes.

[234]

It is done! I see the tiger, maddened, eyes ablaze, come
    creeping hither!
It is done! The birds cease singing, and our glorious gar-
    den bowers wither!

So my sons shall ruin empires, cast away their honor,
    treasures, fame,
Sink to hell and turn from heaven, when a woman bids
    them share her shame.

GERALDINE GRAY

Geraldine Gray, by your ruined home
The negroes build huts and the gypsies roam;
The cattle browse there by its quiet streams,
And the truant treads with his school-boy dreams;
In its gnarled old elms the woodpeckers call,
And its rotting plums and apricots fall;
The lilies decay in its shattered urns,
And overgrown weeds choke the fountain's ferns.

Geraldine Gray, on your lonesome grave
The brambles entwine and the grasses wave;
The roses that grew by your headstone low
Have withered and died in the long ago,
While the marble wreath and the marble cross
Are cankered and green and mottled with moss.
Birds sing overhead, but they do not care
For the beautiful being who slumbers there.

Geraldine Gray, in the years of yore
You have loved me much, but ambition more;
You sought to restore the fortune and fame
Of your falling house and your old-time name;

You sought after wealth, but I had no gold
To bring back the pride, the pleasures of old.
You watched your old home in its slow decay;
For its sake you were false, O Geraldine Gray.

Geraldine Gray, when you broke your vow,
I whispered to you, "How I hate you now!
I will tread far lands, I will gather gold,
I will harden my heart, be crafty and cold;
I will sweat and starve, I will stint and save,
All dangers will dare, all buffets will brave.
I will then return, and will laugh to see
How you long, too late, to return to me!"

Geraldine Gray, through sun after sun
I digged and I toiled till the fight was won;
And so from afar in that stranger land
I brought all the gold a prince could command.
Then I came to look in your face once more,
In triumph, revenge, for the wrongs of yore;
But at length, as I reached your ruined hall.
I staggered aghast, and I knew it all.

Geraldine Gray, at whatever cost,
You had vowed to win, but at last you lost.
You plotted, you schemed, every art you tried;
Defeated, heart-broken, despairing, you died.
And then, as the mist crept over the lea,
As the moon, like a ghost, rose over the sea,
As the chill dank dews in your churchyard lay,
I knew I still loved you, Geraldine Gray.

WILL YOU LOVE ME STILL?

Dear heart, I can not spare thee from my side,
   I look to thee when wrecked and tempest-tost,
O thou still faithful when my hopes have died,
   Friend of the fallen, lover of the lost.

Though Sin hath bound me, wilt thou break the snare?
   Though glooms may gather, wilt thou bide with me?
And though Dejection lures me to his lair,
   Wilt thou, O true love, come to set me free?

Like hapless Norma in her dark despair,
   Seeking to slay her gold-haired girls and boys,
My soul had raised its deadly dagger there,
   To pierce the bosom of its old-time joys.

But thou like David with his soothing strains,
   Coming to calm the stormy soul of Saul,
Canst quell the tempest of my poignant pains,
   Till rainbow gladness arches over all.

When foemen gather I will feel no fear,
   Though sorely tempted and though sorely tried,
If thou wilt whisper, "Courage, courage, dear!
   Remember, true heart, I am by thy side!"

Ah, thou shalt ease me of my weight of woe,
   My one true hope when other hopes are dead;
Ah, thou shalt be my Northern Star aglow,
   The one true friend when other friends have fled.

Come quickly, like a brave Joan of Arc,
   My shattered banners in the breeze to fling,
To bear a torch of courage through the dark,
   And win the lost crown for your ruined King.

THE MORNING-GLORY

Morning-glory, morning-glory,
Fragile as a fairy story,
Robed in gowns of purple and of white and red,
Diademed with dew,
There are none so fair as you,
Empress of the world of blossoms ere the youth of day is
      dead.

Lovely handmaid of the morning,
Lowly earthly scenes adorning,
An enchrantress who is peerless and is proud,
Decked in brilliant blooms,
Like the silks of Tyrian looms,
Or the oriental splendors of a spangled sunrise cloud.

But amid the noonday splendor
Fade away your bosoms tender,
As the dewdrops vanish from your feverish face;
So you pant and pine,
Ere the dazzling day's decline,
Losing all your glow of color and your gladsomeness and
      grace.

So I ponder and remember
In a green and gold September,
I have seen a maiden fair and frail as you;
But she drooped and died,
As you perish in your pride,
For the blithest and the brightest vanish with the morning
      dew.

Morning-glory, morning-glory,
From her tombstone old and hoary,
Do your dying blossoms go to meet her there?

There in marvelous morn,
Plucking roses with no thorn,
In the empire of the angels, does she heed my heart's
    despair?

So I bless you now, and kiss you,
Tell her, "Darling, how I miss you!
If in heaven you are treading, sweet, to-day,
Does your bosom thrill
When you hear I love you still,
And are you still faithful, sweetheart, to your lover far
    away?"

BRIDAL BALLAD

Two roses nestling in one blissful bower,
Two dewdrops in the bosom of a flower,
Two sweet birds singing songs of deep delight,
Two stars that meet in glittering fields of night,
Two roseate clouds that mingle far above,—
Such is the union of the souls that love!

With pearly treasures gathered from the sea,
Or starry gems from desert Araby,—
With golden heaps from India's wondrous caves,
Brought to their master by a thousand slaves,
The owner turns from that for which he strove,
And feels but poor without some one to love.

May all your sorrows be but April showers
To deck your pathway in a wealth of flowers;
And never may your cheeks with pining pale;
May noons and nights flit like a fairy tale;
May youth, all glorious with his old-time fire,
Lead ever through your land of Heart's Desire!

THE BACHELOR

Old friend, you ask me why, on this November night,
When every home is filled with life and love and light,
I sit there lonely in this desolated room,
Beside this dying fire, and in this gathering gloom?

Yes, it is glorious on this gay Thanksgiving Night,
To look into those homes, so happy and so bright,
And sweet to see the loving eyes, the faces fair,
To hear the pattering feet of little children there.

Yes, it is true, I often long to steal away
From out the shadows of these dismal walls of gray;
But as I light my pipe, its smoke-wreaths pinions take,
And gazing in that smoke, a thousand dreams awake.

So I am not alone, although you smile at me,
And in this dingy place no friendly face you see;
For in the darkness beckon airy spirit hands,
And wandering with them I am borne to wondrous lands.

And now I see a nook with overhanging bowers,
Bedecked in sunshine and a wealth of summer flowers;
I hear the bubbling brook, I hear the lowing herds,
I hear the singing of a thousand blissful birds.

And in the leafy lanes I see a little face,
Upon whose cheek no sin or sorrow shows a trace;
Fresh as a blossom jeweled with the dews of morn,
Pure as a young dove in the leafy branches born.

Her eyes are darker than the purple pansies there,
Her laughter lighter than the bird-songs in the air;
Her cheeks are softer than the peach tree's clustering bloom,
Her lips are sweeter than the lilac's frail perfume.

And there we tread in joy, with violet skies above,
With humming bees, and birds that carol lays of love.
Her golden hair has snared me in a maze of bliss;
Earth fades and heaven descends around us as we kiss.

Another vision comes: I see her lying still,
With snowy blossoms in her waxen fingers chill.
Her sweet pale little face, that never knew a cloud,
Is mantled round with silken foldings of the shroud.

Another vision still: I see a new-made grave,
Above whose clouds November's wild winds madly rave,
With snowflakes falling at the wave of wizard wands,
While leafless branches moan and wring their withered
    hands.

But all those phantoms vanish now, and so I'm here,—
A dull old bachelor, all grizzled, gray and sere;
And that is why I sit and smoke my pipe alone,
Or watch the dying embers on my dim hearth-stone.

For when the curling whiffs of feathery smoke arise,
From out their shadowy depths, I see her love-lit eyes;
And when I watch the embers in the ashes there,
I see the gleaming of her wondrous golden hair.

And though for home and wife and childrens' laugh I yearn,
With her my heart was buried, never to return;
And though on earth I still see many a lovely face,
No angel from the skies could take that lost one's place.

"SCORN NOT THE HEART"

Scorn not the heart which may be proffered thee,
For burning love may change to burning hate.
When Summer pineth in her queenly state,
The wan, wild Autumn in her path shall be,
Blighting her blossoms as her footsteps flee;
When Day's white wings fade through her golden gate,
The shadows gather in the gloaming late,
And shroud her splendors in the solemn sea;

When through the tropic forest's noonday warm
The waking blasts invade the gorgeous bowers,
Their glories perish in the furious storm;
While selfish Life holds revel through the hours,
He starts at last to see Death's awful form
Creep, cold and cruel, through the fading flowers.

EDITH ADAIR

Edith Adair, as I went to-day
Down the long green lane, through the wildwoods gay,
By the hawthorn hedge, with its buds of white,
And the old oak tree on the breezy height;
As I walked through fields where the blackberries grow,
And the pink peach blooms from the orchards blow,
When songs of the thrush were loud in the air,
I remembered you ever, Edith Adair.

Edith Adair, I remember still
The long green lane and the oak on the hill;
I remember the songs and skies of Spring,
And the pink peach blooms, the birds on the wing;
I remember the thrushes in boughs above,
Who listened like you, to my words of love;
I remember the flush of your face so fair
When you said that you loved me, Edith Adair.

Edith Adair, that was long ago,
Ere youth and ere love lost their gladsome glow;
You said you were true, but turned at last,
And left me to brood on the perished past.
The hawthorn hedge is as lovely as then,
The thrush sings as sweet in the dewy glen,
The sky is as blue, the flowers as fair,
But you have forsaken me, Edith Adair.

Edith Adair, as you pass me by
With a haughty brow and averted eye,
You scorn the poor lover of long ago
Who plods the rough road with his footsteps slow
As you ride away in your silken gown,
As the diamonds flash in your tresses brown,
You taunt me with gold and with jewels rare—
The price of your perfidy, Edith Adair.

Edith Adair, you can not forget
The peach trees' blooms on the day that we met;
How, when under Springtime skies of blue,
You promised your lover to still be true;
You can not forget that under the moon,
With the buds and blooms and the mock-bird's tune,
I gathered you close in my strong arms' snare,
And I kissed you, and kissed you, Edith Adair.

Edith Adair, though my soul may pine,
While your hand is his, your heart is yet mine;
Though you hide your thoughts with a woman's skill,
I know—yes, I know—that you love me still!
Though you laugh and laugh in pretended glee,
I know that your heart turns ever to me;
You remember all, you sigh with despair;
For you can not forget me, Edith Adair!

TO ONE I SHALL SEE NO MORE

Come, let me look once more close in your eyes,
    Come let me feel the beating of your heart;
Our time has ended; we must break the ties;
    God knows I love you, but we two must part.

Nay, do not ask me why I turn away,
    And why these words at parting seem so cold;
Nay, precious, do not sigh and beg me stay;—
    Our dream must be a story left untold.

Ah, ere you came, the dead leaves hid my soul,
    My heart was buried in a shroud of snow;
Then, like the Spring across the waste you stole,
    And made the birds sing and the blossoms blow.

How sweet you were, O precious, when you came
    To let me know my soul had found its mate;
My autumn skies were flushed with vernal flame—
    And then I saw the warning face of Fate!

Come, clasp me once before I turn to go,
    Heed not these tear-drops as I kiss your feet;
How sweet my dreams were, you shall never know,
    How blissful, blissful, yet how fleet, how fleet!

Nay, do not blame me, it is best—is best!
    Forget me, though you take away my heart;
There! see, I laugh, and turn it to a jest—
    God knows I love you, but we two must part.

"TO ONE WHO SHALL BE NAMELESS"

Do you sometimes think, as you pass me by,
That I follow your steps with a stifled sigh?
Do you sometimes think as you fade from view,
That my heart is broken for the loss of you?

Will you think of me when the autumn blight
Shall sully my soul in the long years' flight,
When over my life, with its weight of woes,
Shall flutter the flakes of the winter snows?

Will you think of me in the fading light,
Will you think of me in the solemn night,
When the songs of spring and summer blooms
Are still and asleep in their lonely tombs?

Will you think of me when my hopes have fled,
Will you think of me when my heart is dead,
Will you think of me when my locks are gray,
And the light of my life has passed away?

Will you think of me when the azure skies
Are shrouded in gray, like my eager eyes,
When the wailing winds the blossoms blow through,
Like the hapless rhymes that I write to you?

Will you think of me when your wedding bell
Shall fall on my ear like a funeral knell,
When from me to another your steps depart,
And leave me alone with my aching heart?

Will you think of me on your wedding night,
While treading the aisle in your veil of white,
When the music swells and the soft lights shine,
And the bridal blooms in your tresses twine?

Will you think of me when you come at last
To regret your choice in the bitter past,
And know that I loved you far more than he,
When a great gulf severs your soul from me?

Then come back to me, my darling, my sweet,
With your gladsome face and your footsteps fleet,
With your springtime joys and your summer state,
Before we can say, "Too late, too late!"

SOUTHERN LOVE SONG

Lucy, my lass, when the jasmine blows,
And the dogwood decks in his blossomy snows;
When the daffodil's flag in the breeze unfurls,
And the cherry is flecked with a frost of pearls;
When the redbird soars and the buebird sings,
And the buff meadowlark through the broomsedge wings;
When the tanager flits like a flame above,
I think of you ever, my lassie, my love.

Lucy, my lass, in the summer's heat,
When the sun-rays flash in the golden wheat;
When I hear the call of the far-off quail;
When I see the swirl of the scythe and flail;
When the cricket chirps in the long lush grass,
And the zinnia glows like a shield of brass;
When the blue haze hangs on the dreamy hill,
My Lucy, my lassie, I am faithful still.

Lucy, my lass, when the asters shine,
And the muscadine hangs on its glossy vine;
When the golden-rod sets all the fields afire,
And the sad wind sighs like a lover's lyre;
When the sumach robes in velvet of red,
And the purple and gold of the woods are shed;
When the south-winged cranes fleck the evening sky,
My lassie, my Lucy, I wish you were nigh.

Lucy, my lass, when the snowflakes come,
And the blooms are dead and the birds are dumb;
When forest and fields are sullied with blight,
And the chill clouds spread in the winter night;
When the youth and joy of the year have sped,
And its royal hopes and its dreams have fled,
You come unto me like a darling dove,
And I welcome you gladly, Lucy, my love.

THE LORE OF LOVE

I

When do I love thee?   When the brooklets run
Through dandelion meadows of the June;
When horns of huntsmen greet the harvest moon,
And mellow autumn's vintaging is done;
When Spring's triumphant marches have begun,
When Winter winds through haggard branches croon;
At solemn midnight and at silvery noon,
At blush of morning and at set of sun.

Thy youthful splendor unto me is dear,
But I shall love thee still when youth flits by;
I love thee when thine eyes know not a tear,
And love thee when Disaster hovers nigh;
My soul shall crave thee when the Dark draws near,
And still be loyal through eternity.

II

How do I love thee?   As the slender lyre
Thrills with emotion when the breezes blow;
As roses love the morning's golden glow,
As dewy stars the dusky night desire;
As eagles to the heaven of heavens aspire,
As dove dreams fondly, breast to breast below;
As arctic pines love everlasting snow,
As tropic palms love everlasting fire.

I love thee as the victor loves his wreath,
The peasant loves his cottage, free from strife;
I love thee as Mortality loves breath,
The shepherd boy his harp and flute and fife;
As disappointed Hope loves welcome Death,
As human souls love Everlasting Life.

III

Why do I love thee?   Ask the artist there
Why does he love fair faces that he paints;
Ask of the poet why his spirit faints
Before his heroines of the golden hair;
Ask of the singer, why his sweet despair,
His glorious gladness, his melodious plaints;
Ask the young priest, before his haloed saints,
To lay the secret of his worship bare.

I love thee; for I long to soar from sod,
And tread in glory of celestial grace;
To live beyond the time my grave is trod,
Proving a crown-prince of immortal race;
To emulate beatitudes of God,
To reach His kingdom, and behold His face.

HE WHO HATH LOVED

He who hath loved hath borne a vassal's chain,
And worn the royal purple of a king;
Hath shrunk beneath the icy winter's sting.
Then reveled in the golden summer's reign;
He hath within the dust and ashes lain,
Then soared o'er mountains on an eagle's wing;
A hut hath slept in, worn with wandering,
And hath been lord of castle-towers in Spain.

He who hath loved hath starved in beggar's cell,
Then in Aladdin's jeweled chariot driven;
He hath with passion roamed a demon fell,
And had an angel's raiment to him given;
His restless soul hath burned with flames of hell,
And winged through ever-blooming fields of heaven.

THE SWAN OF THE SLUMS

Alone in the depths of the grimy town
I hasten along as the sun goes down;
Strange jargons I hear, strange faces I meet
In the motley crowds of the swarming street.
By the loathsome dives, by the dismal dens,
Where the castaways throng in their festering fens,
Where the reeking slums like a cancer spread,
I am sick of heart and dizzy of head.

Hovels on hovels in the byways scowl,
Blister on blister through the alleys foul!
Here the peddler yells and the fakir shrieks,
And the footpad lurks, the shoplifter sneaks.
Here the burglar scowls and the ruffian skulks
In the cellars and stairs of the rotting hulks;
Here the knife-grinder goes with his bells a-ring,
And the wounded thief with his arm in a sling.

Here the venders stand with their butter and eggs,
And their pungent cheese and their mackerel kegs;
Here are cheap junk stores, here are baker shops,
Where the beggar, half-starved, turns a-gazing, and stops,
Here alone at last, in the reeking slums,
As the daylight dies and the darkness comes,
A girl I behold, who is wondrous fair,
With her white-rose face and bright brown hair.

O maiden so pure, so lovely, so white,
As you stand alone in the coming night,
How came you, my child, in your peerless grace,
To the shame and sin of this putrid place?
Around you, the dark is a dismal pall,
But in heart and soul it is darkest of all;
O damsel so fair, by what demon spell
Have you sunk so low, in these dens to dwell?

In another life, and in perished hours,
A lady, you reigned in your castle towers;
Love brought you his bliss and pierced you with pain
As a princess there in the courts of Spain.
You have made kings bleed, made the kingdoms quake,
While the heroes fought and fell for your sake;
In another life, like a strange romance,
You have lived and died as the queen of France.

But you rose from your dusty tomb,
And this, lovely child, is your dreadful doom;
And you come like a dream on your delicate feet
To tread through the mud of this loathsome street.
So, marvelous maid, you are here from afar,
A lily, a dove, a swan, and a star;
And the maiden moon in the sky looks down
On the maiden moon in the grimy town.

MARTYRDOM

The martyr need not perish by the gallows, at the stake,
  or cross-tree high;
For often it is nobler and is braver for his creed to live
  than die.

"WHEN THOU ART NEAR"

When thou art near, when thou art near!
Life seems so sweet beside thee, dear.
I seem to touch an angel's wing,
I feel her arms around me cling;
Within my heart a lily blooms
And glimmers through the mournful glooms;
Peace, like a white dove, nestles there,
And soothes my deep and dumb despair,
                    When thou art near.

But when, O Love, thou art not near,
I shudder with a nameless fear;
I sit my lonely hearth beside,
Where Anguish and Despair abide;
I ponder in the solemn gloom,
And tremble at some coming doom,
I feel Temptation stealing nigh,
While Sin and Sorrow hover by,

     And thou not near!

When thou art near, when thou art near!
Return and save, O save me, dear!
Thou knowest I am weak indeed,
And how thy helping hand I need.
See how the shadows gather near,
And beckon thee to leave me, dear!
O come to me, refuse me not!
Then I may bless my hapless lot

    When thou art near,
     When thou art near!

TEMPTED

Wilt thou feel no pang of pity as I turn with tears to thee?
Ah, desist, thou darling Tempter, loose thy grasp and set
  me free!

In thine eyes I see the fury and the frenzy of desire,
Till my pulses thrill my bosom and my heart and soul with
  fire.

So I dare not spurn or scorn thee, so I dare not turn to
  fly,
And my feverish soul is longing in thine eager arms to die.

[251]

As the sparrow sees the serpent coiling close around her
    nest
Till the spell-bound mother flutters faintly on his jeweled
    crest:

As the terror-stricken traveler in the desert's devious ways
Sees a tiger crouch before him with his cruel eyes ablaze:

As the fated youth sits gazing at the goblet's purple rim
And behold his wreck and ruin rising in the future dim:

As the numb, enchanted dreamer sees the nightmare draw-
    ing near
When his lips are dumb with horror and his feet are chained
    with fear:

So I see thee, sweetest Tempter, snare me in thy fearful
    charms,
While I dare not shrink or struggle, but must sink within
    thine arms.

Ah, what joy, what bliss enchanting, soon to droop with
    blast and blight!
Ah, what brilliant blooms of morning, soon to perish in
    the night!

Now Remorse is faintly calling, dimly calling in mine ears,
Far away from days of childhood, far away through realms
    of tears!

As the horn of Roland sounded, far across the mounts and
    vales,
While his comrades, leagues beyond him, faintly heard its
    piteous wails;

As his myriad foemen slew him when no comrade's aid
    was nigh,
So Remorse, at bay, surrounded, soon must fall to dust,
    and die.

Now I see far in the future gathering hosts of deadly woes,
See my springtime blossoms perish in the chill white
winter snows;

See my old friends all forsake me, see them laugh to hear
my name,
See my mother's awful anguish, see my father curse my
shame;

See me sinking lower, lower, sinking, sinking lower down,
In the night-time, homeless, friendless, wandering through
the wicked town.

And I see thee, cruel Tempter, laughing at my loving
trust;
See thee turn the traitor, Tempter, see thee hurl me in the
dust.

But thy fearful fascination chains me in thine eager arms,
And I strive in vain to rouse me from thy fell and fateful
charms.

So I turn from all the glories of the blest abodes above,
That my soul may share the blisses of thy baleful, blasting
love.

So I turn from home and hearthstone, father, mother,
comrades, all,
So I cease to struggle, Tempter, and I waver, and I fall.

THE RESURRECTION

I have watched and I have waithed through the flight of
months and years,
I have watched and I have waited through a world of
doubts and fears.

Loving you through vernal vistas, when the Easter lilies
rose,
Loving you when chill December scattered swirls of fluttering snows;

Loving you when stately Summers reaped their wealth of
golden sheaves,
Loving you when mournful Autumns wove their crowns of
withered leaves;

Loving you amid the shadows of the melancholy night,
Loving you amid the carols of the birds at morning light.

But I lost you, and I heeded not their glory or their gloom,
For my loyal heart was buried in the shadow of the tomb;

And it crumbled in its charnel where the bolts of iron
rust,
Prisoned under walls of granite in the ashes and the dust;

Far away in haunted deserts, over solemn seas forlorn,
Far beyond the mystic mountains, never lit by light of
morn:

In a realm of mournful midnight, where no friendly feet
may tread,
Shrouded with the silent sleepers, in the dwellings of the
dead.

But I heard you calling, darling, through the bitterness and
blight,
Through the death and desolation, through the dark December night.

And the charnel bolts were broken, and a Seraph set me
free,
As the angel came at midnight to His tomb beyond the
sea.

Once again I feel the fervor of the swoonful springtime
 flowers,
Once again I feel the brilliance of the summer's blissful
 bowers.

Once again the brooklets bubble, and I see the happy
 herds:
Once again I hear the trilling of a thousand blithesome
 birds.

Like a dream of song and story, morning flames in skies
 above,
And my steps are strewn with lilies from the fairy-land of
 love.

And my hands shall scatter roses, arch her path with garlands green,
For my loyal heart is longing for the coming of the Queen.

She is coming, and shall never leave her love to tread
 alone;
Coming back to reign forever, to her scepter and her
 throne!

She is coming, she is coming! all is grand and all is glorious;
She is coming, she is coming, and my heart is now victorious!

So her sweet face smiling softly, shall be banished from
 me never,
And the night of desolation fadeth from my heart forever.

THE WITCH OF THE WINEGLASS

Robed like an empress of almighty Rome,
 I see a sweet seducer in her lair,
With creamy bosoms, light as flakes of foam,
 And yellow roses in her yellow hair.

A flush of fervor decks the queen of sin
  With all an autumn sunset's gorgeous dyes,
And Passion, like a panther, glares within
  The emerald-golden splendor of her eyes.

Around her palace door, the glossy vines
  Are bending with mellifluous grapes of gold,
The marble steps are splashed with purple wines,
  Like blood-stained altars of the days of old.

A poppy seems to blossom in her lips,
  Bearing the poison of enchanted sleep,
A leopard's velvet seem her finger-tips,
  To stroke her victim ere she makes her leap.

She comes to greet me with a glass of wine,
  Mellow and sparkling, flecked with feathery foam,
And murmurs, "Drink, and thou shalt be divine;
  Come, make this bosom and this heart thy home!"

She comes to meet me on a summer day,
  With blue and orange banners waved on high,
With blue and orange blossoms on her way,
  A blue and orange morning in the sky.

I kiss her on her fervent mouth of flame,
  And swear to love and serve her evermore,
To perish with her, deaf to voice of blame,
  As countless sons of men have done before.

But years glide by, and I am growing old,
  My footsteps totter through the fields of gray,
My soul is weary, and my heart is cold,
  And all my hopes of heaven have passed away.

Her marble palace, shattered in the dust,
  Is draped with brown sprays of her withered vines.
Her golden diadem is dim with rust,
  Amid her ruined columns she repines.

Her songs are now but lamentations loud,
  As Desolation follows in her track,
Her festal robes are now a funeral shroud,
  And all her brilliant banners now are black.

Her golden locks are sprinkled now with snows,
  Her blanishments of beauty all are dead;
My heart, like hers, is but a withered rose,
  My soul, like hers, a summer that has fled.

LITTLE SWEETHEART

Little sweetheart, years have passed
Since I walked beside you last,
Gazing in your eyes of blue,
As you promised to be true.

Love and Hope and Joy lie dead,
And my happy dreams have fled
Since I saw your face so fair,
Through its haze of golden hair.

All is lonesome, all is still
Where I used to hear your trill;
Youth has lost its morning glow
Since I left you long ago.

Little sweetheart, life seems cold
As my heart and soul grow old,
And my faith is less and less
As I miss your old caress.

Slowly, slowly earth grows sere
As I wait and listen here
Vainly for the cadence sweet
Of your dear bare little feet.

Honor, power, wealth and fame
I have sought to deck my name,
But they all have proved untrue,
And I call in vain to you.

Little sweetheart, come to me,
As of old, so fresh and free,
In your little dress of white,
In your ribbons gay and bright!

Does your true heart ever yearn
For your lover to return?
Shall I once more hear the beat
Of your dear bare little feet?

Little sweetheart, let me know
If you love me still below—
Tell me, sweetheart, as I pass
Through your silent churchyard's grass.

MORNING AND EVENING

In vanished years it seemed an easy task
    To win the hearts of others on our way;
To gain affection only meant to ask,
    To love meant only to be young and gay.

But like a rich convolvulus in bloom
    Amid the summer, under morning skies,
Young Love before the noontide meets his doom,
    And in his splendor and his glory dies.

Or like an oriole from tropic lands
    That blazes by us on a brilliant wing,
He flies afar to unknown foreign strands
    When Autumn gales their withered foliage fling.

Like blackened torches in abandoned vaults
    Are all the arts and wiles we used of yore;
For those who love us learn to find our faults,
    And having found them, never love us more.

So then, mine own, I cling more close to you,
    Though gray threads sprinkle through your locks of
        brown,
Your eyes no longer dewy, bright and blue,
    Your cheeks no longer like a peach's down.

And you are like a faithful mocking-bird
    Amid the gloam of life's fast-fading light,
Whose strange and sweet love-lyrics still are heard
    In brown boughs of the dim October night,

Or like a holly in the Christmas snows,
    Still green when Summer verdure all is shed,
Or like an autumn violet that blows
    Beneath brown leaves, when other blooms are dead.

When we were young and gay, and you were fair,
    We thought that love with youth would all be o'er,
But as I kiss your face, grown rough with care,
    We find, dear heart, we never loved before.

ZOLA

He comes in triumph to his native land,
    A Conqueror by the power of the pen.
Whose voice was stronger than the steel-gloved hand,
    Winning a battle with the minds of men.

Like Jacob, he was called upon by God
    To throw aside the errors of his past,
To purge his weakness, struggle from the sod,
    And fight through faults, triumphant at the last.

And though fanatics still revile his name,
  Though not one palm is strewn upon his way,
Though bigot lips dispute his hard-won fame,
  He is a monarch on this glorious day!

For roses twine to deck a weakling's head,
  Incenses burn to idols made of mud,
The palms are strewn to ease a despot's tread,
  And laurel wreaths are made for men of blood.

To make him great, no souls were sacrificed,
  No widow wept, no orphan's cheek grew pale,
For he has suffered in the cause of Christ,
  And he has sought and found the Holy Grail.

Now, Paris, pressing back her vague alarms,
  Uplifts her casque, and lays aside her lance;
Rejoicing, there extend the eager arms
  Of her, his lovely, once-disdainful France!

Though Gentile, Israel's Ruler summoned him
  To right a persecuted people's wrongs,
And he shall live when distant ages dim
  In Israel's stories and in Israel's songs.

Thy faults are overshadowed by thy fame,
  O warrior who hast lifted Gideon's sword,
O Champion of the Chosen People's name,
  O Captain in the legions of the Lord!
1899.

PONCE DE LEON

I

At midnight Ponce de Leon stood alone
Beneath the gray sails of his sea-worn ship,
His fierce eyes faded by the flight of years,
His broad brow withered by a thousand toils.
Around him spread the boundless southern seas,
Above him hung the mystic southern skies;
Seas never sailed by ships of men before,
The phantom gateway to a phantom world,
Unfolding marvels in their magic isles
Held close in secret since the world began;
Skies that have never seen their realms revealed,
Though watched and gazed upon six thousand years,
With starry isles that saw the birth of Time,
Whose godlike glories none shall ever know.

The mighty yellow moon began to rise,
Beyond the gaunt palms of a rocky isle,
In all the golden glory of the south,
Undimmed through ruins of the myriad years,
Revealing secrets of this new-found world,
Herself a secret never to be told.

And Ponce de Leon lingered still alone,
For none among his sailors knew his plans,
And none could understand his vague, vain dreams;
And though his feet were treading in their midst,
His soul was sailing in a ship alone,
Upon an ocean in another world.
And then he spoke in whispers to himself:
"I see the moon rise as in years of yore
She rose above the Andalusian skies,
And silvered castle turrets on the heights,
And haunted grottoes far away in Spain,

A wondrous blossom fading night by night,
And yet renewed in splendor evermore.
"But those who watched her with me when a boy,
Have passed forever from the sight of men,
And left me gray and lone and desolate,
A relic of a generation dead.
A thousand leagues of ocean sweep and swirl
Between me and their graves in distant Spain;
The same old moonlight trembling on their tombs
Far, far away in scenes of perished years,
Across the waves of ocean dark and wide
Now trembles on me, treading earth alone,
Surrounded by the youthful and the gay,
Dissevered from old faces that I knew,
A living spectre of the vanished years.

"In days long perished, with this loyal sword,
I smote the Moors on many a battlefield,
Or fought the savage in this new-found world;
But now it quakes and quivers in my hand,
And now its keen edge cankers into rust.
The younger soldiers watch me with a smile,
And whisper that my time has passed away.
Then, all the grand old friends that once I knew,
With whom I braved the perils of the deep,
When bold Columbus sailed the trackless seas,
Have left me, passing to another world
Whose seas forever shall be unexplored.

"Once, in those dear days, ere my raven hair
Was flecked with frost of melancholy years,
When my young heart seemed full of summer warmth,
And all the fragrance of the flowery fields;
When sunny skies hung in a mellow maze
And all the world was wreathed in garlands green;
When pearly peach-blooms in the orchards blew,
And tuneful thrushes wove their happy nests,

I wandered with a maiden whom I loved,
The fairest and the sweetest of the earth.
Ah, well I now remember when she said
'I love you,' how the tell-tale linnets trilled;
And when I kissed her loving little lips,
The dewy daisies kissed her little feet.

"But then we parted by the dear old gate,
Beside the roadway leading to the town;
And as I clasped her ere I went away,
We vowed to love each other evermore.
But leagues of desert, mountain, wold and wave
Came in between us, as an awful storm
Dissevers two ships far away at sea;
And yet we loved each other all the more,
Longing to press each other's lips again,
To gaze once more within each other's eyes,
To speak once more the old, old words of love.
But year by year sped swiftly, and at last
We both grew gray beneath their wizard wings.
So when at last we two had met again,
Both shrank back, startled, at the fearful change.

"Ah, poor old woman!   All thy golden locks,
Had grizzled long before to gray, while age
Plucked, one by one, the roses from thy face,
And dimmed with winter's tearful twilight gloom
The summer splendor of thy dear blue eyes.
My boyhood bloom had vanished from my face,
And left an old man, poor and desolate.
"Alas! I dare not tell the hateful tale
Of disappointment and of chill despair;
Of how I shunned her as she turned from me;
How all the leagues of ocean and of earth
Had bound us closer with a chain of love,
And yet the years had stolen in between,
And like a throng of traitors, slow but sure,
Had separated us forevermore.

[263]

"Since we have parted, I have roamed the world
To find the Fount of Youth, whose crystal waves
Shall make us young again; but evermore
My dreams and visions all are doomed to die.
The crafty red men, wishing to be free
From pillage of my soldiers, ever tell
Of this, the mystic fountain of my dreams,
As being just beyond their native lands.
Yet as I journeyed onward, hoping still,
They ever point me further to the north;
And so I seek forevermore in vain.
But I shall never cease to journey on,
Until I find Immortal Youth, or Death."

II

All worn and weary with his weight of cares,
He sank in troubled slumber on the deck.
He dreamed he wandered through a desert waste
Of red sands, parching underneath red suns,
Where withered rocks were never decked with dews,
Nor shriveled skies refreshed with cooling clouds,
But flamed forever with a feverish fire,
Like aching eyes too sore with grief for tears;
Where bubbling fountains, blossoms, birds and trees
Had not existed since the world began.

His feet were bleeding on the cruel flints,
His tongue was throbbing with a maddening thirst.
At last he sank upon the sands to die:
Then, ere he closed his eyes, far, far away,
Where the red sun was rising in the east
Like a great giant rousing in his wrath,
He saw the snowy peaks and plumy palms
Of an oasis green as emerald.

Then all his hopes revived like fading flowers
That open to the patter of the rain;
He roused himself and journeyed on again,
Until he reached that peerless paradise.
So, when his aching limbs reposed at last
On dewy mosses by its silvery springs,
He laughed and shouted with a frenzied joy,
Till reason came again to soothe his soul,
And then he gazed around in wonderment.

Magnolias waved their glossy boughs of green,
With great white blossoms bursting into bloom,
Like moonlight on the bosom of a swan;
The golden jasmines swung their chalices,
And scattered such sweet odors on the air,
That blithesome breezes swooned and reeled with joy,
And kissed them dying in delicious love;
The frail wild roses trembled on their stems,
Like modest maidens robed in spotless silk;
The redbird flamed amid the verdant boughs,
A royal ruby in an emerald throne;
The bluebird, like a feathered violet,
Whose fragile fragrance vanished in a song,
Played with the humming-birds, whose jeweled wings
Would sparkle like a dazzling shower of gems;
The mock-bird sang with all his fervent soul,
As though the ghost of some great bard of old
Had come to live in bosom of a bird,
With tongue of silver and a heart of gold.
And there, amid the blossom-tangled vines,
The trembling leaflets and the trilling birds,
A crystal fountain, like a storm of snow
Leaped in its sparkling splendor far on high,
In clouds of plumy vapor, frosty spray,
And dazzling dewdrops, with their diamond hues.

Beside it stood a maiden, bright as morn,
A crystal goblet brimming in her hands
With bubbling radiance, like a crown of gems,
Or like a spotless, palpitating star.
A gauzy garment fluttered round her limbs,
Too frail to hide her lustrous loveliness;
And there she stood, so pure, diaphanous,
The sunlight through her crystal splendor shone,
And one might see the pearly lily bells
Shine through the wine-like beauty of her breast,
And feathery ferns through light, tansparent arms,
While humming-birds were tangled and ensnared
Amid the mazes of her golden hair,
And frailest water lilies bended not
Beneath the tripping of her rosy feet.

She motioned him, the gray-haired mariner,
To drink the sparkling goblet that she gave
Out of the fountain of undying youth;
But ere his lips could quaff the cooling stream,
He woke to find it vanished from his sight,
To find his anxious comrades gathered round,
Awaked and startled by his dreamful sighs;
To see, with weary eyes, the same old world,
And the old story of its tears and toils.

III

Resplendent morning, flushed and passionate,
With eyes a-sparkle and with cheeks aflame,
Sinks in the white arms of the panting day;
And like a young bride on her nuptial night,
When first her lover sees her virgin breast,
Averts her eyes beneath his burning gaze,
Then leaps with fervor on his blazing heart,
Consumed within the white heat of his love,
Its swoonful blisses and delirious joys.

[266]

Along the sandy coast of Florida
The proud palmettoes lift their serried spears,
The giant grapevines twist their snaky arms
In monstrous coils around the live-oak limbs;
The verdant creepers cling to rotten trunks,
With crimson-clustered blossoms thrusting forth,
Like bloody fingers of a murderer's hand.
The wondrous wildwoods with their emerald shades
Are like the forests under ocean waves.
The jasmine blooms like mellow amber clings,
The dogwood blossoms hang like lustrous pearls,
And redbuds glimmer like a coral grove;
The dead trees lift like masts of sunken ships,
And humming-birds flit through the verdant gloom,
Like jeweled fishes flashing golden fins.

The red flamingoes throng the sandy coast,
Like splashes of a bloody sunset sky;
The snow-white pelican, the awkward crane,
Thread with the spoon-bill in the shallow bay;
While far above, a secret evermore,
The ancient sacred ibis floats along.

All day they sail along the yellow coast;
All day they look upon the wondrous woods;
All day they watch the red flamingoes flame,
And see the ibis circling through the skies.
But still they see no face of living man,
No cheerful cottage and no curling smoke,
As though the land were Adam's paradise
Where nevermore his banished sons should tread.

And now the evening, like a Bacchanal,
In all the splendor of her streaming hair,
In all the flush of madness jubilant,
Arrayed in purple and in cloth of gold,
Lifts in the skies her chalice crystalline
  And splashes all the clouds with rosy wines,

Tingling and trembling with voluptuous thrills,
Amid her throngs of frenzied revelers,
Till all the spectral shadows of the night,
Like stealthy foemen at some ancient feast,
Creep in with daggers of the flashing stars
And slay them in the blossom of their bliss.

Again the moonrise in the mystic night,
Again the glimmer of the silent stars,
Again the secrets never to be told,
Again the lonely vigil in the gloom!

Once more the gray-haired sailor stands alone,
Beneath the gray sails of his sea-worn ship;
Once more he dreams of scenes in perished years,
Of faces in the tomb of long ago.
He wanders through the fields that once he trod,
In blithesome boyhood, far away in Spain;
He sees the village just beneath the hill,
He sees the vineyards and the cottages,
He sees the peasants toiling in the fields.
The birds are singing as in days of old,
The bees are booming in the clover blooms
Just as they boomed around him when a boy.
He hears the children laughing in the lanes,
And almost thinks he hears them call his name,
Or beg him join them in their happy play.
He sees the foolish lovers wooing still
Beneath the peach-blooms, while the mild-eyed dove
Peeps at them as she hovers in her nest.
He sees the old spring with its little brook
In which he waded when a bare-foot boy;
Here stands the old stile where he met her first;
Here runs the lane where first he told his love,
The ancient oak that saw him press her hand,
And saw him steal his first kiss from her lips,—
Then the old gate that saw their fond farewell.

But all the dear young faces that he knew,
Are sleeping yonder on the lonesome hill;
All,—all but one! his heart can not forget
Yon poor old woman tottering up the road,
With slouching headgear and with wooden shoes,
Bent almost double o'er a knotty stick,
Bearing a basket with a few scant herbs,
Gathered together for her meager meal.
Too well his heart remembers, long ago,
This poor old crone was young and beautiful,
Though now all grizzled, gaunt and full of pains,
A ruined relic, scorned by all the world,
That only loves the young and gay and fair;
Forgotten by them all save one old man
In this lone world, a thousand leagues away!

He knew that soon for her the end would come,
Thus toiling feebly as the days went by.
"My God, my God!" he faltered through his tears,
"Grant me the power to find the magic fount,
That I may save her, make her young again,
Ere all my toils may be too late, too late!"

IV

Day after day they sailed along the coast,
Until they reached a river, deep and broad.
Day after day they sailed its green expanse,
Seeking with sorrow for the Fount of Youth.

Day after day comes laughing in the east,
Day after day lies bleeding in the west;
Day after day, hope blossoms in their hearts,
Day after day, their hopes are doomed to die.

But the great river narrowed in their course,
Or spread its waters into shallow bays,
Until at last they reached a tangled pass,
Where the good ship could sail no further south.
The broad lush lily pads, with myriad blooms,
Like snares of Sirens meshing peerless pearls,
Threw mazy network all around the prow:
The cypress and the live-oak threw their limbs
Like giant arms to bar them on their way;
The grapevines and the creepers joined above
And like a cobweb tangled in the mast;
The scaly alligators on the logs
Were strewn across the islands and the bays
Like hideous dragons of the days of old,
Guarding the gold fruit of Hesperides.

The heron, standing stiffly, looking wise,
With one foot resting in the water-cress,
Seemed mocking at him with a lazy leer;
The gay kingfisher, garbed in gaudy robes,
Seemed smiling at him and his foolish quest;
The crane flew by him on her spectral wings
Like a white ghost of dead and buried years;
The radiant redbird paused amid his flight,
To see the stranger in this western world.
Lost in the mazes of his deep despair,
The gray-haired sailor heeded none of them,
Save a sweet mock-bird in magnolia boughs,
Whose soft song soothed his bleeding heart like balm.

Then with a faltering voice he gave command
To turn the vessel northward in return,
Though like a bird hemmed in an iron cage
His soul, still beating at its prison bars,
And raging at its fetters and its chains,
Was longing to pursue its visions still.

That night he pondered long unto himself,
Upon the sphinx-like riddle, Life and Death.
"Alas!" he murmured, "ages glide away,
And desolation conquers all at last.
Like mists of morning, nations disappear,
Like leaves of autumn, kingdoms quiver by.
As Egypt perished with her hoary kings,
As gray Assyria saw her columns fall,
So all our empires, with their myriad souls,
Shall be the same old idle story still;
And countless kingdoms that shall follow them,
Like them shall vanish in the same old tomb.
Age follows age, till earth is shriveled up,
For all the universe is but a grave.

"Why live, if youth shall ever end in age?
If death shall ever triumph over life?
What mean our petty triumphs and our toils
If all are offerings at the shrine of death?
Could I but find the blessed fount of youth,
I would be greater than the kings of earth,
Than all immortal poets of the past,
Than all the prophets and the priests of God.
But nevermore my hopes shall come to pass;
So all the world shall perish with my dream."

And then in troubled sleep he treads again
His boyhood pathways, far away in Spain;
Once more he wanders by the mossy brook,
Once more he sees the castle on the height;
Once more he treads the orchards, all a-bloom
With crimson clover and with pearly peach;
Once more he sees the village, old and quaint,
Through whose dull streets he trod so long ago,
Before he yearned to roam around the world,
And seek his fortune in the courts and camps.
Once more he sees the house where he was born,
And then, alas! the graveyard on the hill.

But soon he sees, with looks of deep dismay,
A throng of peasants plodding up the hill,
Poor, simple creatures, dressed in coarsest garb,
With threadbare doublets and with wooden shoes.
Before them walks an ancient barefoot friar,
With eyes downcast upon a crucifix;
Then four stout yoemen follow close behind,
And bear a box-like coffin, rough and rude,
Wherein he sees a woman's furrowed face;
Her withered hands are folded on her breast,
Her wrinkled eyelids now forever closed.

But no one weeps above her pallid corpse
And no one sighs to see her pass away
Save this old man, far in a western world,
Whose heart is buried in her humble grave.

The days dragged on, and Ponce de Leon strove
With patient hands to conquer Florida;
To build a city and to till the fields,
And make a goodly province for his king.

His feet were worn, yet he had found no rest;
His hands were feeble, yet had toiled in vain;
His eyes were dim, yet he had never seen
The mystic marvels of the magic fount.
All hope had vanished from his withered heart,
Yet still he lived, as in a weary dream;
But life, which long had kept awake his woes,
Was soon to bring him to the bitter end,
To tread the hideous border-land of death,
Where dark despair eclipses every star.

One cloudless day, when pensive evening pined
Above the tangled forests of the west,
After a bloody battle bravely won
Against the crafty Indians of the land,—

Won in a manner worthy of the man
Who plucked the crimson flower of his fame
Not on a carpet, but a bloody field,—
He wandered from the outskirts of his camp,
And sat beside the margin of a pool.
A little pool it was, fed by a brook,
That twisted like a serpent through the grass,
Half choked with reeds and rushes and with mint.

The lakelet was so clear that one might see
Its sandy bottom, fathoms five below,
And watch the writhing fishes wave their fins,
With shining scales, and twirling, twisting tails,
And gaping jaws and huge and glassy eyes,
Like grotesque phantoms in a haunted land.
The swallows dipped amid the dewy spray,
The heron stood amid the water weeds
And watched the gray coot diving in the depths.
The bluejay in a scaly sycamore
Cried as she saw a black snake slide below;
The staid woodpecker, crowned with crimson plumes,
Climbed slowly up an oak-tree's aged trunk.
The brown thrush fluttered to her cosy nest,
Where, like a roguish gypsy maiden's eyes,
The round blackberries, gemmed with diamond dew,
Seemed peeping at her as she sank to rest.
An oriole, arrayed in royal robes,
Shown with the mingled glory and the gloom
Of orange sunrise and of sable night.

Long sat he there, and dreamed of other days,
Till sombre twilight trod the forest depths,
Draped all the splendor of the sunset skies,
And robed the woods in funeral garb of gray.
But with the death of that eventful day,
The gray-haired sailor was to meet his doom;
For in the shades a stealthy foeman crept,
Nearer and nearer, with a sharpened spear.

Then all at once the Indian leaped in view,
And pierced him through his armor with the spear;
The old man struck the savage to the ground,
And slew him with his ever-trusty sword.

He called his comrades, in the camp near by,
Who bore him in a litter to the ship,
But sought in vain to cure his mortal wound.
Scarce could he speak; yet gathered strength at last,
To bid them turn to Cuba, on the morn.

So they obeyed him, trimmed the ready sails,
To bear him southward, there to see him die.
But ere he left, there came a zealous priest
To breathe the gospel in his deafened ears,
And point its pathway to his fading eyes;
He held the crucifix where one might see
The writhing Christ nailed to the cruel tree.

"O Ponce de Leon," spake he solemnly,
"Long hast thou searched to find the fount of youth,
But seen thy searches evermore in vain:
And thou hast found that, drink where'er thou wilt,
Thy thirst returns and thou must drink again;
Yet, as thou searchest, still thou growest old,
And as thou seekest thou shalt surely die.
But, hapless man, the fountain shall be found,
And I shall show it to thy fading eyes:
For if thou drinkest of the well of Christ,
Thy thirst shall pass away forevermore,
And drinking of that well, thy youth returns,
And thou shalt dwell in palmy Paradise,
Forever happy and forever young."

But Ponce de Leon beckoned him away,
And turned his dim eyes from the crucifix.
"Oh, thou hast been deceived," the priest replied,
"But God will keep His promises to thee."

Still Ponce de Leon beckoned him away,
And still refused to see the crucifix.
"Unhappy man," the priest replied again,
"Like mildew on thy hopes and happiness,
Descends the curse of infidelity,
Which holds the scepter in the shades below,
Where demons laugh to see one flee from God.
Come back, come back!   It is not yet too late
To reach the portals of thy Father's home,
Where saints and seraphs with their starry crowns,
Bask in the sunlight of the smile of God,
And wait to welcome thee on thy return
With sounds triumphant like the swelling sea.
Look up to Heaven! seest thou no signal there,
No smile of seraph, and no helping hand?
Seest thou no torch to guide thee in the gloom?
Seest thou no golden city, far away?
Behold the Lamb of God, and thou shalt live!
Cry out to Christ, and He shall comfort thee!"

The dying warrior turned his haggard face,
First tried to speak, then feebly shook his head,
As if to say "No! I shall hope no more:
All, all are fables; I will not believe:
For you deceive me as the rest have done."
The priest fled horrified, and left him there,
To die the death of those who turn from God.

The sails were spread, the harbor soon was cleared,
The vessel glided far away to sea.
The old priest watched it, through his blinding tears,
Till the dim sails had faded from the skies;
A ship of death, that bore one to his tomb,
A ship of death, doomed by the curse of God!

Still beams the moon on Andalusian hills,
As in the dead years of the long ago
When Ponce de Leon and the maid he loved

[275]

In blissful silence heard each other's hearts
Beating together with a bounding bliss,
And told each other with their eager eyes
The sweet old story that shall ever live
When kings and queens have crumbled in the clay,
And all the empires of the earth are dust.

The moonbeams falter on her grassy grave,
Upon a lone hill, far away in Spain,
While he is sleeping in his sepulchre
Beyond the oceans of the western world.
The foolish lovers, in their thoughtless bliss,
Still woo each other as they tread the fields
Where those two lovers, centuries ago,
First told their passion to each other's eyes.

Still shines the sun in skies of Florida,
With all the glory of the yester-years,
When Ponce de Leon trod her wondrous woods,
To find the fountain of immortal youth.
Another people rules her palmy plains,
Another nation, with another tongue:
Yet never has the marvel of the fount
Arisen before the eyes of mortal man.

Like him, we long to see its crystal waves,
When old age, like November, chills the skies,
And all our dead hopes, like her withered leaves,
Are falling at the coming of the night.
Like him, we long to see our youth again
Bring back the withered roses of the past,

The mirth of May, and joys of jeweled June,
When April buds are all forever dead,
And suns of Summer have forever set.
Like him, we see our toils are all in vain:
Like him we see that we are growing gray:
We seek forever, and we never find,
And as we seek it, we shall surely die.

NARCISSUS

I

The morning flamed above the Doric hills
In all the joyous glory of her youth,
As though her roses would be red forever,
And deck the whole world in unfading bloom.
Her sparkling eyes dimmed all the night's wan stars,
Her red cheeks tinged the clouds with crimson fire,
While silvery arrows from her lands of light
Dispersed the shadows from the verdant woods.
The lithe stag started from his grassy couch,
And shook the dewdrops from his branching horns;
The falcon spread his light wings to the winds
And darted upward like a sharpened spear.
The herdsman led his oxen to the brook,
Whose wavelets wondered at the great round eyes:
Then merry laughter from the roguish fauns
Resounded keenly through the leafy dells;
But louder than them all, some piping sprite
Made liquid music with the warbling birds.

But soon Narcissus left his flowery couch,
Narcissus, ever young and beautiful!
And there amid resplendent beams of morn,
Amid the blossoms, odorous, soft and sweet,
And wildly graceful spirits of the woods,
Narcissus shone the wonder of them all.
No red deer's skin, no tawny lion's hide,
No woven fabric round his shoulders hung,
For young Narcissus roamed in beauty nude;
His soft round limbs, fair as a lily's buds,
Were never hidden in a useless garb.
The flush of boyhood still adorned his face,
A childish beauty budding into youth;
He scampered nimbly like a half-grown god,
With shrill songs varying to a deepening bass.

Sweet little dimples flitted round his mouth,
His curving arms were lovely as a babe's,
His little feet like frail and tinted shells,
With tiny peeping toes like purest pearls.
His roguish eyes bent downward timidly,
As though ashamed to see his nakedness;
His golden ringlets hung upon his breast,
Too short to hide his sweet, enchanting charms.

The nymphs beheld him in his boyish grace,
Enraptured by his rounded, naked limbs,
Drinking his beauty like some wondrous wine,
That makes the blood break into flowers of flame,
Their bosoms madly throbbing, eyes afire,
Breathe wildly panting in an eager love,
So that they longed to clasp him in their arms
Forever in delirious blissful swoons.
And often would they follow him all day,
Untiring, through the distant woods and fields.
They'd stroll beside him and call him pet names,
Clasp his soft cheeks and stroke his curly hair.
Oft would they leap upon him from the ferns,
And kiss his sweet lips time and time again,

Or madly beg him for one word of love,
Or one embrace to give them in return.
The pretty boy, half angered, like a child,
Would pout, then laugh, half relishing their love.

But often, wearied of their close pursuit,
He longed to wander lone and unharassed.
In vain! for everywhere the roguish spies
Would watch his path and haunt his flying feet.
Through meadows, fields, and forests deep and dark,
Still grottoes, lonely dells, high mountain-tops,
By winding rivers, lily-covered lakes,
He sought in vain for rest in solitude.

Among the nymphs who thus would follow him,
Poor Echo vexed him more than all the rest;
And while his cunning thwarted other eyes,
This maiden always wandered at his side.
Full oft when gathering violets in the woods,
And thinking him unseen, he'd quickly start
To feel a burning kiss upon his lips,
And see her lithe form swiftly vanishing;
Full oft, beneath some hoary oak's green boughs,
His tired head resting on a bank of moss,
While sleep was weaving meshes round his eyes,
Would hear wild words of deep, despairing love,
Sad, soulful sighs, with fond reproaches breathed,
And waking, there behold two great dark eyes
Bent o'er him, and a passion-heaving breast
His pillow, that had first been mossy earth.

Again, while wandering through the caverned hills,
Amid the shades would Echo glide along,
And clasp his hands within her fingers wan,
Or, while the hot tears trickled down her cheeks,
Would sob and murmur of his cruelty.

A curse had long been laid on Echo's head
By jealous Hera, heartless in her hate.
For Echo often had assisted Zeus
In hiding amorous sins from Hera's eye,
Till, being seized at last, confessed her guilt,
And felt the fury of the queen of heaven.

Perfidious Zeus refused the nymph to shield;
So she was banished from the gods' abode,
To wander lonely through the waste of Earth,
Where rove swift-fated mortals to the grave,
And Autumn blights the glory of the year;
To pine amid the solemn wilderness,
And long for high Olympus, lost forever.

And Echo was not bright or beautiful,
But plainest, darkest of the woodland nymphs.
Her form had faded to a flitting shade,
Her voice had wasted to a mournful cry.
Her eyes were large, dark as a cavern's gloom,
Her tresses like the dusty clouds of night;
Her face was like a specter, and her sighs
Like bitter moaning of the winter winds.
Each word that reached her would her tongue repeat,
For so the high gods cursed her for her sins.
She loved the shades, the solemn solitudes,
The lonely grottoes and steep mountain sides.
So while she haunted close Narcissus' path,
She dared not show her visage openly,
But stole behind him ever stealthily,
And vanished when he turned to speak reproach,
Or, when he sat, would hide in thickets near,
And gaze upon him from the sullen shades.

Sometimes Narcissus, out of cruel spite,
Would wound her heart with stinging jealousy
When smiling on some other rival nymph,
Who madly kissed or fondly folded him.
Her dark eyes glittered with a blasting woe
To see him laughing on a swelling breast,
Some nymph, with round arms close embracing him,
And drinking in his lovely boyish charms.
But oft Narcissus scorned the charms of all,
And on this morning shunned each maiden's face.

II

The first who met him as he tripped along
Was one who hunted there with Artemis,
A stately maid with waving ebon hair,
With cheeks as crimson as a poppy's bloom,
With dark and wondrous splendor-streaming eyes,
And queenly brow of softest olive hue.

She seemed like dusky twilight, gemmed with stars,
And sprinkled by the bleeding heart of day.
Her pure, white feet, with golden sandals decked,
Were stainless and as soft as Eros' wings;
Her green cloak, waving in the morning wind,
Betrayed a rounded bosom like a swan.
Upon her back a bow and quiver hung,
Within her hand a scintillating spear.

"Is this Narcissus?" said she, with a smile;
"I've seen you in these hills but once before;
Yet one so beautiful no eye forgets,
And so my memory can not be at fault.
But hark, my pretty boy, a face like yours
Will often carry with it deep despair;
The nymphs whose love you scorn are plotting now
To have revenge upon you.   This I know.
For on Olympus only yester-eve
I saw a throng of them with Nemesis,
The stern-browed spirit, feared of gods and men,
Whose only joy is marring lives like yours.
I heard them murmur at your cruelty,
Then beg dark Nemesis to curse you, boy,
And she, I think, assented.   Watch them well,
For much I fear some evil day will come."

"Was Echo there?   'Tis like her spiteful way;
I always hated her, and always will."
"You wrong her, foolish boy; she was not there,
She long ago was driven from on high.
I can not tell you more, for hark, oh, hark!
The deep-mouthed hounds are baying through the woods,
In hot pursuit of some affrighted stag.
Ye gods!   My heart leaps in exulting joy,
And all my veins are tingling for the chase.
Farewell!   I follow swiftly to the hunt."

"What thanks, fair goddess, shall I offer thee?—
But yet, alas! I have no gift of worth."

"A gift, thou foolish boy?   Give me a kiss;
For kisses from a young man's amorous mouth
Will buy from woman more than gems and gold.
Another kiss!   Another!   Clasp again!

"Just one more kiss, Narcissus, then I go!
My mistress would reproach me for this act,
But for its joy I'd bear her frown forever.
Beware, O youth.   Echo thou needst not fear;
She loves thee as the banished god loves heaven,
But would not harm thee to regain her throne."

Narcissus stood, stunned with a curdling fear.
The smile died on his quivering, ashen lips,
His heart grew numb, his youthful blood grew cold.
"Why should they wish to harm me?" muttered he;
"Am I not free to spurn them if I wish?
Shall I be blamed because I love them not?
Shall I be blamed because they pine for me?"

Soon turned he on his heels, and musing, went
Along the brook, then sat beneath an elm.
He paused a while, then, growing restless, turned
And lay upon his back, while his fair locks
Were pillowed on a bank of feathery ferns.
But then the sun, ascending high in heaven,
Sent through the parted boughs a tiny beam
That fell upon his eyes and made him wince,
So that he leaped up, restless and annoyed.
Soon sitting down again, he dipt his feet
Within the crystal waters just below,—
Those beauteous feet, more soft and sweet and white
Than all the spotless water-lilies there.

The wavelets kissed their delicate blue veins,
And fondled them, and babbled petting sounds,
While silvery minnows, growing bold at last,
Began to nibble at the tiny toes,
Which tingled till they blushed like rose-buds pink,
When he, to rout the minnows, shook his foot,
Splashing the water into foaming spray,
And sent them scampering up the brook in fright,
To peep back at him through the water-cress,
And wonder at his roguish, ringing laugh.

He gazed upon his image in the brook,
And marveled at his own enchanting charms;
His cheeks, like ruby wines, blue eyes, bright hair,
The rounded, flower-like beauty of his form.
He blushed to see his utter nakedness,
And that which mortals seek to hide from sight,
But felt a boyish pride and secret joy
To feel and see his manhood drawing near.
He knew no maiden could resist his beauty,
And in his heart exulted at the thought.
"I'll scorn them all," he said unto himself,
"And drive them mad to get one stingy smile.
I'll rule them, chained before me by their love,
And they shall long in vain to kiss my feet."

Then turning round, he saw Leona there,
With jealous passion burning in her eyes;
For much she craved the sweetness of his charms,
Yet hating him because his heart was cold.

"Leona!" faltered he; "art spying still?
I am a-weary of thy hateful eyes."
"Narcissus!" cried she, quickly, "I am mad,—
Mad with fierce love and flaming jealousy.
Beware! Beware! lest thou shouldst force thy slave
To bring destruction on thy hapless head."

Selected Poems

"Leona, I defy thy silly threats.
I am the son of water-god and nymph:
Free I was born, and free will ever be.
I am immortal; what have I to fear?
For Zeus himself can never take my life,
And thou art but a weak and wandering sprite."

"I know, Narcissus, thou canst never die,
But, selfish creature, I may curse thee still;
I may call down such anguish and despair
That life itself would be an agony.
Be mine, Narcissus, hearken to my prayer!
Be mine, or I will curse thee and myself!"

"Begone! Begone!" he cried, impatiently,
And turned his eyes in anger from her face,
Looking towards the woods beyond the brook.
A deadly silence seemed to shroud the place,
And all the forest huddled close with fear.
He turned again; Leona's face had fled,
But oh, the spectre there before his eyes!
For just a pace beyond him stood a Shape
Whose awful presence curdled all his blood.
It was a woman with a sweeping robe
That shrouded her in ghastly spectral folds.
In her right hand she held a scorpion whip,
And in her left a leafy branch of ash.
Her face was livid, pale and pinched and wan,
With burning eyes beneath her haggard brows,
Like fiery embers in volcanic cones.
He could not move, as though his limbs were stone,
His brow was damp with cold and clammy dews.
She gazed upon him sternly; then she said,
"Thyself shalt bring a curse upon thyself.
He who loves not another, loves himself,
And he shall long in vain to soothe his soul;

[284]

True love drinks life-blood from another heart,
But selfish love doth gnaw upon his own.
Farewell! thy choice is made, and thou shalt find
In loving self thou graspest at a shade."

III

She glided from him like a ghost of night,
And glimmered faintly through the branching boughs
Till lost to sight amid the forest gloom.

Narcissus shivered, for the breeze had chilled,
And trembling birds for fear had ceased to sing.
The nymphs, aroused, had fled before her face.
The startled, shuddering trees with horror moaned,
Like huddled cattle, when, on tainted air,
With horns erect, eyes starting, mad with fear,
And lowing, groaning deep and piteously,
From altar stones they smell their comrade's blood.

Again he turned and gazed upon the brook,
And saw himself reflected in its waves.
Again he saw his sweet lips, glowing cheeks,
His azure eyes, his rippling golden hair,
His rounded, dimpled arms, his dainty feet,
And all the naked wonders of his form.
Then what a world of wistful agony
Seized on his soul while gazing in the brook!
Oh, how he loved that shadow of himself!
Oh, how he longed to clasp it in his arms,
Oh, how he longed to kiss its rich, red mouth!
What eager yearning swayed his bounding heart,
What flaming passion fired his leaping blood!

Such deep desire, such maddening thrills of love,—
A heaven of bliss, but just beyond his reach!
His pulses, throbbing wildly to his head,
Swooned through him like a fierce, voluptuous dream.

He sought to kiss his own lips in despair,
His own breast struggled vainly to embrace.
And then the deep eyes of the shadow there
Seemed begging him to share their languorous sweets.
Its mouth seemed longing to be pressed to his,
Its arms inviting to their swoonful realm.

Pierced with his pain, he could resist no more,
But leaped to clasp the shadow to his heart.
In vain, in vain!   A splash, a chilly thrill,
And then the shadow fled before his eyes!
He struggled with the icy, mantling waves,
Clung to the grassy bank, and climbed to shore,
But cold and shivering with the trickling drops.
Again he looked upon the cruel brook
That now had cursed him with his own fair face,
And once again he saw the shadow sweet
Gaze fondly at him from the mirror there.
No lover ever longed to clasp his love
With half such fervor as Narcissus did.
But yet, alas! that passion could be fed
On rounded beauties of the loved one's breast,
And lulled to sleep by blissful blandishments.
All others who have loved, with amorous play
Have felt at last their passion satisfied,
Have drank the bubbling cup of Cupid's joy,
And cooled the raging fever of desire.
But his love was a fire with naught to quench,
A sleepless craving that had naught to lull;
He hungered for a fruit he could not taste,
He thirsted for a cup he could not quaff.

The lover who hath not his love returned
Hath yet the sympathy of every heart,
Hath others, placed like him, to share his grief,
And feels ennobled by his sad, sweet pain.

The guilty lovers, scorned by all the world,
Still find a happier world within themselves.
But oh, the horror of unnatural love,
Beyond the sympathy of every soul!
With no one sharing in that agony,
His hectic cheeks a-flush with baffled shame!

And then, again, he felt such agony
He leaped once more amid the chilly waves.
Ah, still in vain!   A splash, an icy thrill,
And once again the Shape eluded him!
Then deep despair fell on him like a shroud,
And like a child lost in the night, he sobbed.

The twilight, like a priestess, crowned with stars,
Draped Day's fair ringlets in the veil of night,
Stabbed his white bosom, lit his funeral pyre,
And with her victim died in crimson flames.
The swallow glided to his eave to sleep;
The wild dove fluttered to her peaceful nest;
The shepherd drove his thirsty flocks to drink,
Then led them, bleating, to their nightly fold;
The new moon, like a harvest sickle, shone
Through golden grains and flowers in fields of heaven;
The gentle shadows gathered in the woods,
And laid kind hands on Nature's dreaming soul.
But still Narcissus lay beside the brook,
Longing to perish with the hapless day,
Whose curse had pierced him with an agony
Which never could be soothed by balms of night.

IV

The weary days lagged on like crippled churls,
And sweet Narcissus withered in despair.
His blue eyes faded with their sleepless cares,
Like desert skies with parching fervor wan.

His crimson lips were mutely quivering
Like flaming dead leaves in the autumn winds.
His dimpled cheeks were pinched, and blanched and thin,
Like great white roses fading day by day.
His graceful step came to a weary halt
Like stiffened lameness of the wounded doe.
Hour after hour he gazed upon the brook,
And the big tears dropped in its azure waves.
But still he lived while ever loathing life,
And begging heaven to be allowed to die.
He gazed in anguish at the ghostly face
Which in despair looked up from depths below,
With mournful eyes, and outstretched bony hands
That beckoned to him like an aspen's leaves.

One day when lying on a bank of moss
He heard a rustle,—Echo's stealthy step.
"Narcissus!" said she sweetly in his ear.
He turned toward her, bursting into tears.
No longer did he try to flee her face,
But longed to blend his bitter grief with hers.
"Narcissus," said she, "I shall share thy woe.
My hapless heart shall ever throb with thine.
Long have I watched thee, feared to come to thee,
But thou, I know, wilt never drive me hence.
Thy hopeless love consumes thine own sad heart,
And mine upon that heart is cast away;
Our souls are bound together by a bond
Of mutual, never-changing misery."
He wept, then laid his head upon her breast,
And soon with sobbing lulled himself to sleep.

What bounding, leaping throbs of wild delight,
What dreamy, balmy, soothing spells of bliss,
Filled all her soul while clasping him to heart!
She softly smoothed his thin, disheveled locks,
And tenderly she stroked his pallid cheeks.

She would have given the treasures of the sea
For one strong pressure on that dreaming face,
And all the gold of all the tribes of earth
For one close clasping of those lovely arms,
And all the glories of the starry skies
For one warm kiss from that delicious mouth—
But she dared not, for fear of waking him!
Ah, hapless hearts, that beat together now,
Yet parted by a universe of tears!
Ah, hapless souls, each craving for the same,
And each forever doomed to pine in vain!
Ah, would that Fate had bound you both together
Like bride and bridegroom on their nuptial night!

Soon through the woods was heard the bay of hounds,
And then the huntress nimph of Artemis
Came tripping down the pathway to the brook,
The hounds still yelping as she moved along.
Her naked breasts were heaving joyously
Like water-lilies on the rocking waves,
While silvery laughter fluttered on her lips.
Her shoulders bore the skin of spotted pard,
Torn warm and bleeding from the victim's back.
She opened her lips to cry out in delight,
And speak to Echo of the morning's sport;
But Echo beckoned her to tread tiptoe,
And speak in whispers, that he might not wake,
"Is this Narcissus?" asked the huntress maid;
"Oh, what a fearful, wasting change is here!
Once I beheld him like a milk-white fawn,
But stricken now, and sinking down to die;
Once I beheld him like a lotus flower,
The peerless, swelling blossom wonderful,
Then budding in unearthly loveliness,
Now lying withered in the sultry dust.

"Once I beheld him like the round, full moon,
In naked beauty rising on the night,
With mellow, golden glory in its orb,
O'er lovers true in odorous gardens sweet,
But now, as gaunt and haggard as its wane,
When hanging shattered, after night is dead,
Above the bare boughs of a blasted wood,
He sinks to perish in the Western wilds."

Poor Echo could not answer for her tears.
The huntress gazed in silence at the hounds
Laving their gray flanks in the crystal stream,
Lapping sweet waters with their jagged jaws,
And shaking dewdrops from their hanging ears.

Then said the huntress, starting, "I forgot,
In speaking of Narcissus' great despair,
To tell of that which surely brings thee joy.
Thou dost remember that, on yester-eve,
Down through the Western scarlet skies of flame
A spotless swan came fluttering to thy feet,
A cruel arrow rankling in his breast.
Then thou, with kind hands, didst remove the dart,
So that the swan arose and soared away.
Know thou that swan belonged to Artemis,
And she is grateful to thee, hapless girl.
She bids me tell thee beg one boon of her,
Speak the one wish that lieth next thy heart,
And thou shalt see at once thy dream come true."

Echo at first by this was so amazed
She scarce made answer to the kindly nymph,
But overjoyed, at last shed floods of tears,
Gave heartfelt thanks, and cried out in delight,
"Oh, I shall now to heavenly scenes return.
Long have I wandered through these earthly wilds,
And yearned again to see my happy home.

How often when November filled the skies
With dead leaves flying from the haggard trees,—
How often when the winter winds on high
Bore flocks of cranes toward the Southern seas,—
How often when the mortals passed me by
In funeral trains, with some enshrouded form,—
How often, in those days, I craved for thee,
Olympus blest, free from decay and death!
I long to see thy banquet-halls again,
And take the ruby wine from Hebe's hands.
I long to see dear Iris laugh once more,
And spend sweet converse on the days gone by,
To gaze on youthful Eros' face, and drink
Immortal glory from his wondrous eyes!"
But Fate would hearken not to Echo's prayer,
Creating other woes to smite her soul.
For then Narcissus murmured in his dreams,
"Oh, would that I could die! but I can not;
Immortal life the gods can not destroy.
Oh, would that heaven, in pity on my grief,
Might change me to some painless, dreamless flower!"

Echo seemed stricken with a deadly wound,
And then grew still and rigid as a stone.
A moment like a century slowly passed,
And then she said, "Will kindly Artemis
Grant more than one wish unto hapless me?
May I return to heaven, and save him too?"

"Alas!" the nymph cried; "it can never be;
For jealous Hera hates thee, hapless maid.
My mistress scarce could gain consent from Zeus,
Who hath betrayed thee to his furious queen,
To let thee have fulfillment of one wish,
And much great Hera murmured when she knew
That this one favor was bestowed on thee.

[291]

Thou mayest choose to help Narcissus there,
But if thou dost Olympus thou shalt lose.
The curse upon Narcissus must remain
As long as life is left within his breast,
And as he is immortal, he must change
His present shape, and live another life.
He must be buried as the mortals are,
And from his grave a blossom will ascend
To take the life of him now in your arms.
But that would be a special boon of heaven,
And the great gods would do no more for thee."

"Oh, no," cried Echo, "do not change his form!
How can I bear to see my precious love
Changed to the lifeless beauty of a plant?
Oh, spare him, spare him! pity, pity me!
For this would sink me ever in despair!"

"But," said the other, "if he changes not,
His soul must writhe in never-ending pain."
"Ah!" Echo cried, "shall I be doomed forever
On cheerless Earth to roam in banishment,
And nevermore behold Olympus blest?
And must I, hapless maiden, doom my love
To sink forever in the dismal grave?
What countless ages shall I wander here,
To see earth wither in myriad years,
Behold her cities ruined, desolate,
And generations pass away and die!
To think that I must tread those endless years,
Amid these deserts of decay and death,
Without my love, the idol of my soul,
And live, still live, alone, alone, alone!"
"Still," said the huntress, "he must either change,
Or live a life of endless agony."

"I love him," cried poor Echo, through her tears.—
"Let it be so: his good shall be my prayer!
I choose not to return to heaven with thee,
But beg thy mistress to relieve his woes!"
The huntress glided from her through the woods,
But heard behind the piteous sounds of sobs;
Turned, and beheld doomed Echo clasp her love
As some fond mother hugs her dying child,
Speak words of burning love within his ears,
Then kiss her darling's face a thousand times;
And as the nymph towards Olympus soared,
She heard, blurred by the distance, many moans,
Till misty clouds obscured her view of earth,
And rushing winds stilled all its dreamy hum.

V

And now the morning, like a gorgeous rose
Bursts into blossom in a field of fire.
Once more Aurora, in eternal youth,
With pearly feet trips to her chariot throne;
Once more her white steeds, shaking silvery manes,
Leap forth, caparisoned in blue and gold;
Once more her handmaids wreathe the clouds with flowers,
From crystal goblets sprinkle ruby wines;
Once more the pale moon in their veils of light
Is shrouded like a dead bride for the tomb;
Once more her sweet kiss thrills the dewy stars,
Till all those orbs celestial faint with love,
Then melt their glories on her milk-white breast,
And perish in the splendor of her hair.

But as the light fell on Narcissus' brow
Its rosy flame tinged livid hues of death.
The dryads swung amid the leafy boughs,
The water-nymphs arose above the waves,

The sylphs flew round like jeweled butterflies,
And zephyrs hummed like golden-winged bees.
But Echo heeded not those beauteous forms,
And saw naught save her darling dying there.

His head lay pillowed on her tender breast
Beneath the shadow of a hoary oak.
His breath was coming slower, slower still,
His eyes were ever growing dim and dark.
He had been told how Artemis had given
This one boon to her desolated heart.
Oft had he thanked her for remembering him,
But never knew what sacrifice she made.
Alas! how often doth unselfish love
See all its tears unnoticed or forgot!

"One boon I beg," sobbed Echo, timidly;
"Wilt thou kiss me, my love, before thou diest?"
He put his thin white arms around her neck.
And faintly smiled upon her pallid face;
He held his fevered, quivering lips to hers,
And fell back fainting in her trembling arms;
Then, sinking slowly, bowed his golden head,
And with one lingering, piteous moan, he died.
A curdling cry pierced through the startled air,
And woeful Echo held a leaden corpse.

The pensive Evening trod the Western hills,
Her saffron mantle glowing in the skies
Like yellow foliage of the autumn woods.
Through silent dells and lonely mountain groves
Her dusky shades, like mourners, crept along.
Then all the shepherds of the neighboring vales,
And all the lovely mortal damsels there,
Came gathering round to look upon his face,
Soon to be hid beneath the chilly clods.

[294]

And maiden hands brought many a fragrant flower
To scatter on his sad, untimely grave,—
White, azure, pink and purple hyacinths,
With valley-lilies, frail and delicate,
And crocus-blossoms, pansies rich and dark,
Soft buttercups and creamy daffodils,
The modest white and purple violets,
New-opened daisies, with their hearts of gold,
Sweet cowslips, and primroses gemmed with dew.
But he was lovelier than those beauteous buds,
And sweeter than their faintly odorous breath.
His pearly eyelids, closed forevermore,
Now hid the azure of his dreaming eyes;
His pallid cheeks lay slumbering calm and still;
The tiny dimples slept around his mouth;

His soft white hands were folded on his heart,
Like two sweet doves dead in one little nest;
Pure water-lilies wreathed his golden hair,
And rich musk-roses bloomed above his breast.

They buried him in chill and cheerless earth,
To be the prey of death's corrupting hand,
And every clod that fell upon him there
Dropped like a mountain upon Echo's heart.

Months passed away, and then a pallid plant
Arose and blossomed on his lonely grave.
And even now it bears Narcissus' name.

Then Echo glided from the sight of men,
And wandered through the trackless wilderness,
Through lonely valleys, mountains high and still,
Forever weeping, calling out his name.
She pined away, grew pale and paler still,
Then flitted like the shadow of a curse,
Until at last her voice alone was left
To answer vaguely every idle sound.

Great nations perish, but she can not die;
Vast empires crumble, but she lingers still.
The gray gods in Olympus' lofty halls
From jeweled goblets quaff their nectar still;
She, unforgiven, never can return,
Her name forgotten by them long ago.
And so she wanders ever, suffering still
Undying anguish and undying love.

TO DR. J. J. WHEAT

There is a wondrous power in earthly song,
    Whose eagle spirit soars to Paradise,
Too free and happy for this world of wrong,
    Too glorious for our cloud-encircled skies.
The liquid bird-notes at the dawn of day,
    The wanton winds that kiss the budding flowers,
Breathe echoes of an Eden far away,
    And sing the beauties of its fadeless bowers.
Our yearning hearts leap forth with them to soar,
    And by their airy wings are borne on high;
We break the chains of clay which once we wore,
    And feel too happy for a tear or sigh.

But eloquence like thine can sway the mind
    More strongly than the trumpet's loftiest peal,
More deeply than the moaning midnight wind,
    More sweetly than the witching wavelet's spell.
The organ's grand triumphant harmony
    Moves not the soul more than thy swelling voice;
The master-singer's notes that mount on high
    Have not more power to make man's heart rejoice.
And like Arion singing to the sea,
    Till gathering dolphins shone like rainbow clouds,
I marvel as thou bringest forth for me
    Sweet dreams and visions out of tombs and shrouds.

When listening to thee, Fancy breaks her bars,
    And follows in thy free, unbounded flight;
She wends her way beyond the farthest stars,
    And bathes her pinions in eternal light.
We wander with thee by blue Galilee,
    Where every wavelet sings a sacred song;
The vine-clad rocks of Nazareth we see,
    Where Jesus, weak and foot-sore, passed along.
We see poor Mary shedding bitter tears,
    Which wash forever all her sins away,
And then the woman at the well, who hears
    Of that unfailing fount which springs in endless day.

A FEBRUARY SUNSET

Beside this frozen marsh the sedges sigh,
    While keen-edged winds like sabres cut their way;
A water-fowl is floating there on high,
    Seeking some far-off home at close of day.

The ghostly hills are shrouded white in snow,
    Brown boughs, a-shiver nakedly, are numb;
A wandering black-robed friar, limps a crow,
    To find on hardened clods a stingy crumb.

Here weeds and brambles, thickly interlaced,
    Hangs frail embroidery of hoary frost;
Here tiny tracks of hares are lightly traced;
    A crying snow-bird seeks the mate he lost.

A herd of cows goes stumbling up the hill,
    Sunk to their knees in drifts like billowed foam;
Waving a stick and whistling sharp and shrill,
    A red-cheeked farmer-boy directs them home.

Near by, the haggard wild-rose bushes spread,
  Like bristling porcupines of prong and thorn;
A lonesome leaf, where other leaves have fled,
  Is all a-shiver, faded and forlorn.

A cottage rises in the fields of white,
  Its smoke is curling tremulous and thin;
Its windows glow like jaspers through the night,
  Rich with the warmth of blissful love within.

There like a dewdrop in a scarlet flower
  A star is twinkling in the ruddy sky,
And sprinkling snow-fields in a silver shower,
  The new moon's horn of plenty hangs on high.

The sunset splendor makes the twilight glow
  In purple and in orange clouds of fire,
As conquering Alexander long ago
  Gave to the torch imperial towers of Tyre.

The world seems woeful, all its laughter lost,
  The golden dreams of June forever dead,
No bird, no bud, it seems could brave this frost,
  No May-time resurrect the foliage fled.

And yet the landscape seems expecting Spring,
  The harsh north wind seems chanting prophecy,
As though a dead man felt an angel's wing,
  And smiled to know his soul could never die.

OUT OF THE FOLD

One is astray from the Shepherd's fold,
One is astray on the mountains cold,
Treading alone through the fading light,
Treading alone through the coming night.

And the shepherd calls in his sweet, wild way
Through the dreary dusk of the dying day,
Through the falling dews and the misty gloam,
For the one poor sheep that has strayed from home.

Weary and worn, with a piteous cry,
Weary and worn, he is sinking to die,
While the gaunt, gray wolves through the deserts dark,
Follow him fast with their fearful bark.

Will the Shepherd bear on his bosom warm
The wounded sheep from hurt and from harm?
Shall the poor lost lamb be left to his fate?
Shall the Shepherd come too late, too late?

So runneth the story so sweet and so old
Of the sheep astray in the mountains cold,
Treading alone at dusk to his doom,
While the Shepherd calls through the gathering gloom.

So I am treading in piteous plight
Through the grief and gloom, through the coming night,
Treading the streets of the wicked town,
Treading the streets when the sun goes down.

Bearing a breast all burdened with woes
Through the biting winds and the bitter snows,
Suppressing a sob and choking a cry,
Hopeless of rest, yet fearing to die.

I have scoffed and scorned to smother my fears,
I have laughed aloud at thy streaming tears,
I have sung gay songs and quaffed of the wine
To forget thy face with its love divine.

Where the red light glares like an eye of fire,
In a gaudy room and in gay attire,
In the poisoned air, like a dragon's breath,
I stand at the stairs of the halls of death.

But behold, at my door the Shepherd stands,
And beckons to me with his bleeding hands,
And I see his feet all weary and worn,
His wounded breast and his crown of thorn!

Merciful Christ, with the princely grace,
Merciful Christ, with the sad, sweet face,
Merciful Christ, with the mournful eyes,
Remember me when the daylight dies!

Merciful Christ, thou hast followed afar
Under midnight moon, under evening star,
Treading with tears through forest and flood,
And tracing thy path with the stains of blood.

Merciful Christ, thou hast sought me here,
Through the mountains cold and the deserts drear;
Merciful Christ, am I left to my fate?
Merciful Christ, hast thou come too late?

I have heard thy voice as I passed along
Through the reveller's shout and the siren's song,
Through laughter, through fall of the dancing feet,
And the wicked jests of the crowded street;

But I perish alone in shame and in sin
Though I long to arise and welcome thee in.
Merciful Christ, I cry unto thee,
Merciful Christ, have pity on me!

But the revellers riot, and the lewd songs swell,
And they numb my soul like a funeral knell;
In the noisy night, with its glitter and glare,
I wring my hands in my dark despair.

And I turn to thee in my dumb dismay,
As the demons cry like the wolves for prey;
Merciful Christ, shall thy feet depart
And leave me alone with my broken heart?

O Shepherd, come with thy footsteps fleet,
With my falling tears I shall wash thy feet,
And thy love shall lave my stains of despair,
As I wipe them dry with my streaming hair.

"JESUS WEPT"

My Master bides not at the rich man's palace on this day,
Where mirth and music, wine and feasting speed the
      hours away;
His weary, way-worn feet have brought him to this humble
      door,
And there the Prince of Heaven sits weeping with the
      friendless poor.

O blessed Lord, friend of the friendless, happy should
      they be,
Their burning grief and anguish sharing side by side with
      thee!
For in this doubting age we can but moan and beg thy
      grace,
But can not see thy loving tears nor know thy gentle
      face.

Though in that rich man's palace swells the sound of
      revelry,
To-morrow in that palace shall the wail of anguish be;
Though in this poor man's hovel stalks the horrid spectre
      Death,
Soon shall he vanish at the great King's life-inspiring
      breath.

Oh, wondrous sight, a Monarch sitting in that peasant cot,
Oh, wondrous sight, the Lord of angels in this lowly lot;
Oh, wondrous sight, here treads the ruler of the suns and
      stars,
Oh, wondrous sight, our God is weeping at Earth's prison
      bars!

I wonder if his moanings did not change to music sweet,
I wonder if the blossoms did not spring to kiss his feet,
I wonder if the watching angels gathered up those tears
And made them starry clusters, shining through the end-
less years.

For they were purer than the dews on lilies newly blown,
More brilliant than an empress' jeweled diadem they
shone;
More radiant than the treasures that the ocean caves
adorn,
More glorious than the Oriental splendors of the morn.

Those blessed, blessed tear-drops, falling on our dreary
dearth,
Have wooed a golden harvest from the withered breast of
earth,
Have melted, too, a myriad million selfish hearts of stone,
And blotted out uncounted sins in earth's vast records
shown.

And though a thousand demons seek to give thy cause a
thrust,
Those burning tears have worn their cruel daggers into
rust,
And though a hundred empires at thee hurl their gathered
powers,
Those holy tear-drops, like a flood, sweep down their
haughty towers.

And though a host of bigots burning with a furious zeal
Have sought to aid their false creeds with the chain and
stake and wheel,
Those tears have quenched their fires, torn down their
walls and iron bars,
Thy cause triumphant over steel and torch and wrecks
and wars.

Oh, blessed tears, with rainbow colors yearning earth
      illume,
Oh, blessed tears, with lotus flowers make blissful heaven
      bloom!
Rain on the sons of men, on every soul that ever fell,
And like a mighty ocean quench the flaming gates of hell!

BURIAL OF AN OLD SLAVE

Around me, brambles tangle on the graves,
   And ivy sprays are creeping on the stones;
Beside one shattered urn a foxglove waves,
    While awe-struck thrushes chirp in undertones.

Outside, a field of broomsedge, waste and bare,
   And thickets of the red and yellow plum,
And nearer, on the purple thistles there,
    Goldfinches in a brilliant cluster come.

Here tombstones hanging sideways to the earth
   By winds and rains are dappled into gray;
Brown lichens have erased the dates of birth
    And years in which the sleepers passed away.

Grim sentinel, still facing to the west,
   The old slave-master's granite headstone looms;
His young wife and her baby lie at rest
    Where yon wild rose sheds pink and pearly blooms.

Almost effaced, you read a young girl's name;
   Just sixteen when she died!   Here passed away
The first-born son, who like a triumph came;
    In whose dead hands Hope crumbled into clay.

Down there are buried all the family slaves,
  Relics of ways and customs obsolete;
A few headboards of wood slant on their graves,
  As, year by year, weeds grow and weathers beat.

Up yonder lane a strange procession comes,
  And sounds of weird, sweet singing strike the ears;
Then a shrill fife, and then the beat of drums,
  A chant that seems the ghost of bygone years.

Ah, many lives have passed since neighbors came,
  Bringing a sleeper to this home to bide;
But this gray negro, last of all the name,
  Has sought again his old-time master's side.

Nearer they come, a wagon for a bier;
  The rails are lowered at the roadside fence;
The team pulls through—two mules in well-worn gear—
  Welcome, old friend, to your last residence!

What songs are these, so mellow, wild and sweet,
  Of Salem and its glories far away,
Where Change and Death glide not on stealthy feet,
  Nor leaves in dim October skies decay?

What child-like faith, that sings of princely palms,
  Of fountains gushing through the fields of green!
What child-like faith, that sings of blissful calms,
  And splendors that no sage has ever seen!

Strange, a poor negro in this far-off place,
  Trusting a Friend, sinks in his coffin low,
Believes that Friend, forgetting not his face,
  Will find him where these weeds and brambles grow.

Rose-breasted grosbeak, lighting on yon limb
  And singing as no bird hath sung before,
Is it a note of triumph trilled for him,
  The dead slave, free and happy evermore?

RENAN'S LIFE OF JESUS

Wonderful story of sad, sad years,
Wonderful story of toils and tears,
Annals of anguish, of grief and gloom,
Breaking at last into brilliant bloom.

Over and over again I tread
Vistas where Jesus has begged His bread,
Soothing and healing, with words of love
Whiter than wings of a snow-white dove.

Beautiful words that silence our strife,
Beautiful words of light and of life,
Beautiful words no doom can destroy,
Beautiful words bringing dreams of joy;

Beautiful words that shall right all wrongs,
Beautiful words like the angel's songs,
Beautiful words that have calmed my fears,
Beautiful words that have dried my tears.

Sweeter than breath of the springtime flowers,
Softer than swirls of the autumn showers,
Splendor of song and splendor of story,
Decking his brows with garlands of glory!

Lighter than touch of an angel's fingers,
Clearer than notes of the stateliest singers,
Pathos of winds in the pine-trees sighing,
Sobs of a harp in the distance dying!

Dreaming of Thee, I ponder alone,
Longing for Thee, I sob and I moan,
Doubting and fearing, forever I grieve,
Crying to Thee, "O make me believe!"

Selected Poems

After Your feet have trod to each door,
After You bless the rich and the poor,
After You smile on hut and on hall,
Come unto me, the vilest of all.

When the daylight dies in twilight cold,
And the watchers come my hands to fold,
When my poor dim eyes no pathway see,
O Prince of Heaven, will you think of me?

THE HYMNS OF CHARLES WESLEY

What simple strains are these, to live so long,
    To move so many in so many lands,
When self-appointed arbiters of song
    Are all effaced like scribblings in the sands.

In dens of London, choked with sin and shame,
    The beggar and the burglar stop to hear;
And in the night, beneath the street-lamp's flame,
    The ruined woman feels a burning tear.

In mines of Cornwall, underneath the sea,
    The grimy laborer hears their martial tread,
Their fervent call from coming wrath to flee,
    Above the ocean thunders overhead.

Amid Missouri forests, dark and lone,
    And by the Mississippi's turbid waves,
In nameless churchyards, bramble-overgrown,
    Their converts fill a thousand graves.

Among the rude huts of the pioneers,
    Those hymns awoke the wilderness at dark,
Above the cries of wild beasts, fraught with fears,
    The panther's growling and the gray wolf's bark.

So I remember, when a barefoot boy,
   I thrilled to hear thy wondrous trumpet-call
To Zion, and its days of deathless joy,
   Its crystal river and its jasper wall.

And, led by thee, I saw its clustered palms,
   Its shining summits with their diamond skies,
A Beulah-land, with everlasting calms,
   And lilies wet with dews of Paradise.

And thou didst sing the Savior's loving care,
   Seeking his lost sheep through the fading light,
To snatch and save him from the lion's lair,
   Amid the deserts, in the coming night.

These hymns have raised the peasant from the sod,
   Have made the rude half-savage nature sweet,
Have reared a score of Kingdoms unto God,
   And laid a million hearts at Jesus' feet.

EPITAPH FOR MYSELF

Stranger, that passeth my lone house of clay,
Pause for one moment in a gentle mood;
Think not your sigh of pity thrown away,
For I would say "God bless you," if I could.

Date Due		
P I I 1932		